Dannie Abse was born in 1923. He began writing when he was a sixth-form schoolboy in Cardiff. Soon afterwards he was to leave his native country to study medicine at Westminster Hospital, London. While still a student, a play of his was produced and his first book of poems published (*After Every Green Thing*, 1948). For many years he combined his work as a doctor in a London chest clinic with writing poetry and prose. Many volumes of his poems have been published, as well as memoirs and novels – most recently *Goodbye Twentieth Century* (Pimlico, 2001) and *The Strange Case of Dr Simmonds and Dr Glas* (Robson, 2002). Among his plays, which have been produced at such venues as the Young Vic and the Birmingham Rep., are *In the Cage* and *The Dogs of Pavlov*. He has also edited anthologies, including *Voices in the Gallery* (with Joan Abse) and *The Hutchinson Book of Post-War British Poetry*.

Dannie Abse is a Fellow of the Royal Society of Literature and past President of The Poetry Society. After his retirement from medical practice his poetry output increased from six poems a year to eight. His *New and Collected Poems* (Hutchinson) was published earlier this year.

Dannie Abse

The Two Roads Taken

A PROSE MISCELLANY

ENITHARMON PRESS

First published in 2003
by the Enitharmon Press
26B Caversham Road
London NW5 2DU

www.enitharmon.co.uk

Distributed in the UK by
Central Books
99 Wallis Road
London E9 5LN

Distributed in the USA and Canada
by Dufour Editions Inc.
PO Box 7, Chester Springs
PA 19425, USA

ISBN 1 900564 68 8

British Library Cataloguing-in-Publication Data.
A catalogue record for this book is available
from the British Library.

Enitharmon Press gratefully acknowledges the financial assistance of
Arts Council England.
This publication has been supported by the Arts Council of Wales.

Typeset in Bembo by Servis Filmsetting Ltd
and printed in England by
Antony Rowe Ltd

Contents

Introduction 7

1

Authorship and Medicine 11
A Skull in the Wardrobe 14
Following in the Footsteps of Dr Keats 26
The Charisma of Quacks 46
More than a Green Placebo 54
The Experiment 61

2

Ninian Park Blues 85
Pegasus and the Rocking Horse 99
I Accuse 114

3

Playing to the Gallery 121
The Dread of Sylvia Plath 125
Without Self-Importance 142
John Ormond, a Neglected Poet 153
Introductions:
D. H. Lawrence 160
Ezra Pound 165
Thom Gunn 171
Fleur Adcock 177
Poetry and Poverty Revisited 183
The Ass and the Green Thing 192

4

Abse's 1984 203
Replies to an Enquiry 221
Interview at Princeton University 229

Introduction

Robert Frost, in a celebrated poem, spoke of two roads that diverged in a yellow wood and how sorry he was that he could not travel both. He concluded his poem by remarking that he took the one less travelled by 'and that has made all the difference.'

I have called this collection of 'non-fiction' prose pieces *The Two Roads Taken* because I have travelled down one road that has led me to wear the white coat of a doctor and, more colourfully clad, I have trespassed down the other road familiar to Frost himself. Sometimes these 'two roads' have merged, as is evident from many of the moonlighting, fugitive articles, essays, interviews, lectures, gathered here from literary journals and anthologies of past decades.

Three of the pieces included in *The Two Roads Taken* were previously published in a similar miscellany of mine, *A Strong Dose of Myself* (1985) – a book long out of print. Acknowledgements are also owed to *The Anglo-Welsh Review*, *Aquarius*, *Daily Telegraph*, *The Hampstead and Highgate Express*, *The Jewish Quarterly*, *The Lancet*, *Modern Poets in Focus*, *The New Welsh Review*, *Perfect Pitch* (Headline), *Poetry Review* and *Sea-Legs*.

D.A.

1

Authorship and Medicine

In paintings of the Crucifixion before 1630 wounds are depicted on the right side of the body of Christ. Later painters generally moved the wound to the left side. Why? Surely it was because William Harvey had published his revolutionary *The Circulation of the Blood*.

Harvey had dissected 80 species of animal and had discovered that earlier medical doctrine was wrong, that the heart was on the left and the circulation of the blood circular. Harvey's discovery left its mark on the representation of the Crucifixion in art.

Inevitably, medical knowledge also penetrated literature. Yet, powerful as medical facts may be, the personal experience of them is even more sovereign. Therefore we would expect the dramatic clinical experiences of doctor-writers to colour their novels, their plays, their poetry.

This is not always the case. We could read, say, the poetry of John Keats or Robert Bridges without realising they were once, as doctors, buffeted by unforgettable, often brutal, medical experiences.

Other doctor-writers, though, have captured these real-life, bloody scenarios and transformed them. Even Somerset Maugham, who gave up medicine soon after qualifying, recognised how much he, as a writer, was indebted to his doctor experiences.

'Even now forty years have passed,' Maugham confessed, 'I can remember certain people so exactly that I could draw a picture of them. Phrases that I heard still linger in my ears. I saw how men died. I saw how they bore pain. I saw what hope looked like, fear and relief.'

Daily Telegraph (October 1993)

Many things are common to the practice of authorship and medicine, not least an inordinate interest in people and a keen, observing eye. Both professions, too, recognise the ubiquity of cause. Writers know they must eschew the arbitrary, that their plots, for instance, must have an inevitability about them, that their characters' actions should not be without causality. Similarly, medical students are taught that all symptoms have causes. I sometimes think that Chekhov's law – fire a gun in the last act only if it is loaded in the first – was one he learnt in medical school.

Doctors, as a profession, have a poor reputation as communicators. In the past, deliberate obfuscation seemed the order of the day when it came to conversing with patients – their prescriptions written in Latin, their handwriting notoriously difficult to read, bombast their best vocal language, their whole demeanour open to the joyous satire of a Molière, a Bernard Shaw or, most recently, our own lavatorial Alan Bennett.

Today, while trying not to be recondite, too many doctors fail to supply the patient with simple explanations. Besides, sometimes the truth is harder to tell than a lie. Yet, here is a conundrum. The one characteristic general enough to doctor-writers of note is their stylistic accessibility. 'Only connect.' And they do.

It would seem, in their case, that their medical education, their experience of regularly decoding mysterious signs and symptoms, and their physicians' sense of community, have made them impatient of those who, as Nietzsche puts it, 'muddy their own waters so as to appear more deep.'

Oliver St John Gogarty was being very much a subversive doctor-poet when he objected to Robert Browning's opacities: 'When I read his translation of Aeschylus,' he remarked, 'I find it very useful to have the Greek beside me so that I may find out what the English means.'

Certainly, twentieth-century doctor-poets such as William Carlos Williams in the USA, Miroslav Holub in Czechoslovakia, Gottfried Benn in Germany, Rutger Kopland in Holland, Edward Lowbury in England, are not among those difficult to read – unlike, say the German writer Paul Celan or the American, John Ashbery.

No, doctor-poets have clarified their own poetry for us without losing depth. Nor have they avoided portraying emotion any more than earlier doctor-writers such as Chekhov. After all, emotion articulated is something all doctors have listened to who are not deaf, and those doctor-writers who have contributed to the genuine pages of literature have, like William Harvey, dissected in order to bare the heart.

A Skull in the Wardrobe

Half the family are doctors. There is my eldest brother Wilfred, my father's brother Max, my mother's brother Joe. There are my two Ammanford cousins and also two other cousins from Cardiff, Michael and Jack. So when the family meets on those rare ceremonial occasions of celebration or lament, it is less a family gathering than a medical conference.

In 1937, when I, a small boy, said, 'I wouldn't mind being a vet' – the cat lay motionless on its cushion on the carpet, its electric eyes staring at nothing, and would not sip even a little of the warm milk I was offering it – my brother Wilfred said masterfully that I might as well become, like so many others in the family, a doctor. 'Sick people,' he maintained with the authority of one who had read *Twelve Great Philosophers*, 'are more important than sick animals.' I stared unhappily at the cat while my father, overhearing our conversation, teased, 'You think this duffer has enough intelligence to become a doctor?' My eldest brother replied without irony, 'All you need is average intelligence to become a doctor. He'll manage it. We ought to think seriously about putting his name down for the new Westminster Hospital medical school that they are planning.'

My mother used to say, 'Dannie never thinks of tomorrow.' She was wrong. I did and I do. But I rarely think of the day after tomorrow. That is why, perhaps, I have always resisted the idea of buying life insurance and that is certainly why, also, since the question of what-are-you-going-to-be-when-you-grow-up had been solved, I thought more of being a medical student than a doctor.

From *My Medical School*, ed. Dannie Abse (Robson, 1978)

Wilfred had just qualified. For years I had heard about medical student experiences and pranks. Had not Wilfred cured a baffling case of hysterical blindness through hypnosis? (Wilfred was going to be a psychiatrist.) And only eighteen months earlier Wilfred had been doing his midwifery and the telephone had sounded *after midnight*. That's how important it was to be a medical student.

True, on that occasion, Wilfred had to go to a house in Zinc Street to deliver a baby. The voice commanding him to do so had, apparently, been Welsh and urgent and hoarse. So my big brother, hero Wilfred, with his little black bag, climbed on to his bicycle and made for Splott. He did not know that Mr and Mrs Jones of Zinc Street had only just married, were still on their blissful honeymoon, and had no immediate plans to have a baby. He did not know that the hoarse, urgent, Welsh voice was that of another medical student conning him.

It was raining in the district of Roath, Cardiff, where we lived then and from where Wilfred set out, and it was raining in the district of Splott, Cardiff, when he arrived on his bicycle, flustered and damp, at a dark door in Zinc Street. Clutching his little black bag he banged at the front door till a light went on upstairs, then a light in the hall, and finally the door opened to a sleepy, burly, tall lock forward in pyjamas asking, 'Mmmm?'

'Where's your wife, Mr Jones?' asked Wilfred.

'Upstairs in bed,' replied the burly man, surprised.

And he was even more surprised when Wilfred said, 'Good,' as he pushed past him and ran up the stairs enthusiastically.

Yes, I thought, it may be fun to become a medical student, to mess around like that, and save every now and then one or two lives! I fancied myself walking down Queen Street with a stethoscope sticking, like a credential, out of my pocket.

Some years later, in 1941, during my last year in school when I was studying those pre-medical subjects, biology, chemistry and physics, I was to hear much more about the crises and practical jokes of 'med' students. Three of my friends – a year older than I – were already at the Welsh National School of Medicine. When I joined them at their students' union to play poker they were full of medical gossip: how Spud Taylor after a rectal examination on a woman had diagnosed, to the delight of the other students, an enlarged prostate; better still, how Tonker Davies had cut off a penis from one of the cadavers in the anatomy room, put it in his trouser pocket before going to a student dance and, eventually, when the last waltz was being played – 'Any umbrellas, any umbrellas, don't mind the rain' – Tonker had pulled it out of his trousers much to the consternation of his partner!

Such was the tenor of the conversations of these friends of mine, these first-year medical students. Their talk was frequently anecdotal in that way, bawdy or about sport. They were never philosophical while sober. As the record turned on the Medical Students' Union radiogram and Dinah Shore sang 'Body and Soul' or 'Smoke Gets in Your Eyes' or 'Sophisticated Lady', I never heard any of those poker players vulnerably say why he wanted to become a doctor or confess to aspirations of doing good in the world. They pondered on nothing more awesome than a Royal Flush. Or so it seemed. As for me, though I was beginning to write poetry (I was told it was 'just a phase'), I felt happy in the company of such friends. I certainly did not feel like the composer Berlioz who had written, 'Become a doctor! Study anatomy! dissect! witness horrible operations . . . Forsake the empyrean for the dreary realities of earth! the immortal angels of poetry and love and their inspired songs for filthy hospitals, dreadful medical students . . .'

No, I wanted to become one of those dreadful medical students myself. My regret was that I could not stay at home and study at the Welsh National School of Medicine. Finally, though, I did not so much leave home as home left me! For, during a February air raid (the night turned luminous green because of flares), it seemed some German pilot mistook Roath Park Lake for Cardiff Docks and bomb after bomb whistled down to cause explosions followed by lonely silences. The house next door disappeared and part of our house collapsed. Injured, I was taken to Bridgend Cottage Hospital where I was looked after by one of my Ammanford cousins. 'Look after this boy,' he kept winking at the nurses, 'he's valuable, he's going to become a doctor.'

⋆

Nineteen months later, in September – that month of cool suggestions and pleasant sunlight a shade too yellow – I arrived in wartime London, the train doors in Paddington station banging behind me like gunshot reports. My cases made my arms long for they contained not only predictable contents but my brother's weighty medical textbooks and the half-skeleton he had bequeathed me.

These I unpacked in a boarding-house room in Swiss Cottage. I put the femur, tibia, the armbones, the wired foot, the wired hand and the skull in the wardrobe and the textbooks – on the flyleaf of each was written, 'D. Wilfred Abse, *Nil Desperandum*' – on the mantelpiece. I was ready 'to go', ready to begin my studies at King's College in the Strand where Westminster Hospital students, along with those from Charing Cross Hospital, King's College Hospital and St George's Hospital, spent their pre-clinical years.

King's College in the Strand was cold, shabby, capacious and murky. It sounded of footsteps on linoleum and stone. Even when no one was about, the place sounded of ghosts in slippers. It smelt of stone and the nineteenth century. Because of air raids, most students, other than the medics, had been evacuated to provincial cities, so it was more obviously empty, stony, murky than ever. My first ordeal was to firewatch on the roof of King's one moonless night when the air-raid siren had sounded. The second ordeal, a daytime one, was to enter the anatomy dissecting room and to be assigned one half of a male body.

The formalin that preserves the cadavers pricks the eyes and has a reeking odour that seeps insidiously, pervasively, into one's clothes. And the cadavers themselves seemed so helpless and naked! Still I did not bolt as Berlioz had done in his day. 'Robert,' wrote Berlioz, 'asked me to accompany him to the Dissecting Room at the Hôpital de la Pitié. When I entered that fearful charnel-house, littered with fragments of limbs, and saw the ghastly faces and cloven heads, the bloody cesspools in which we stood, with its reeking atmosphere, the swarms of sparrows fighting for scrapings and rats in the corners gnawing bleeding vertebrae, such a feeling of horror possessed me that I leapt out of the window as though Death and all his hideous crew were at my heels.'

Revulsion does not endure. I remember how, a few weeks after the commencement of our anatomy course, I observed one student, who earlier had been particularly fastidious, drop his lit cigarette accidentally into the open cavity of a dead abdomen; then, unthinkingly, he picked his cigarette up, put it back in his mouth and went on dissecting with no sense of disquiet or disgust. The medical student soon forgets that the body he is dissecting was once alive. It becomes a model. Later I was to learn, during my clinical years, the live patient in the same way would often become a 'case'.

I did not enjoy anatomy; it was a chore to commit to memory the coloured plates of the anatomy book, to recall in detail, and as clearly as an eidetic image, the Rembrandt painting one had made for oneself by laying bare muscles, tendons, arteries and nerves of a body that gradually became smaller and smaller as it was dissected away. That I had to spend so many hours in the anatomy room, that students everywhere had to learn in minute detail the anatomy of the human body (and embryology) seemed ridiculous to me. By the time we qualified most of us would have forgotten all but the most important details. Now I know that this cloudy remembrance of the subject makes us no worse doctors, for the knowledge we acquired so obsessively, and at such pains, and that we lost with such felicity, is quite useless for the most part in the general practice of medicine. Even those who, as postgraduates, specialise in surgery, have to relearn the subject.

It amuses me, as I write this, to try and remember the vessels and nerves close to the ankle – I have worked in a chest clinic for years – but all I can recall is the mnemonic that helped me to pass a viva: Please Don't Vaseline Nellie's Hair. The *V*, I suppose, stood for one vein or another and *Nellie* for a nerve the name of which, at present, I cannot recall.

I preferred the physiology lectures. Professor MacDowell entertained us. 'We have three instincts,' he would say, 'three instincts, gentlemen. One could call them the three *F*s: fear, food and reproduction.' It seemed Professor MacDowell would sometimes be consulted by patients concerned about their hearts. But that year, for reasons of wartime economy, the lifts at King's were not working and the Professor's office was high, high up, close to the roof. Thus the heart patients had to climb all those endless stone steps.

'I don't have to examine them when they reach my door,' he said. 'If they make it that proves their hearts are sound; if not, then it's just a question of writing out the death certificate.'

In the early summer of 1944 I took my anatomy and physiology examinations. I passed them and so at last entered Westminster Hospital where I could wear a white coat with a stethoscope sticking out of its pocket. It was the time of the doodlebugs and suddenly there was I in the Casualty Department, hopelessly at a loss, while some stricken woman, lacerated to pieces by flying glass, was lifted from a stretcher in great pain and just kept on saying over and over, 'Oh God, oh dear, oh God, oh dear, oh dear, oh dear, oh God.'

I wonder how many medical students during the war had a sense of guilt. I had sometimes. My brother Wilfred was in the army in India, and my brother Leo in the RAF in Egypt. My cousin Sydney had been killed at Dunkirk. All my old friends, other than medical students, were in the services except those few who had already died '*pro patria*'. In some ways one's vague sense of guilt in being allowed to complete one's studies was mitigated by working unnecessarily long hours in Casualty, assisting the harassed doctors even if it was only by putting in stitches and bandaging, by tapping hydroceles, or giving gas and oxygen anaesthetics.

One afternoon, escaping from Casualty, I attended Psychiatric Outpatients. Wilfred in a letter had suggested, 'Make yourself known to Dr Ewing whom I know quite well.' But that afternoon another psychiatrist was taking Outpatients. He had a strong Viennese accent, a most reassuring thing in a psychiatrist, and he seemed pleased to see me. In fact he was enthusiastic. 'You can take Outpatients yourself,' he beamed. 'You've come just in time.' Startled, I explained that I had only been at Westminster Hospital three weeks or so and did not feel capable of taking on any Outpatients, never mind psychiatric ones. 'I haf to be somevere at three,' he said. 'It is good. And don't vorry, you know how to take a case history, yes? Zen take a case history and zen tell them to return next week ven I vill see them myself.' Even as I was objecting he was racing for the door shouting, 'Nurse! Nurse!'

So, wearing a white coat, I sat behind a desk like a real doctor and the nurse sent in the first patient for me to see. My very own first patient. I knew how to take a case history. Only a week earlier I had been taught that in Casualty. First you had to put down *Complaining of*, and then you asked the patient, 'What are you complaining of?' and the patient would say, 'I have a pain here in my left chest, doctor, that comes on after exercise.' And so you would write that down opposite *Complaining of*. It was quite simple really. Then there were other headings such as *Past History*, *Present History* and so on. Easy as winking. Except my first patient complained of his wife. 'She gets up in the middle of the night,' he told me, 'because she reckons she hears voices. Then she walks up and down, walks up and down for hours and hours. I can't stand it.' After listening to his grumbles, inspired I said, 'Now I want you to bring your wife here next week and then we'll sort things out.' To my horror he replied, 'But she's outside, doctor. She's come along with me.' It was evident that I had to see her so, swallowing, I nodded and said, 'Then I'll see her right away. Would you mind waiting outside?'

His wife baffled me. She complained of her husband. 'He says he hears voices and gets up in the middle of the night and walks up and down remorselessly for hours. I can't bear it,' she said.

I did not know which one was crazy, who was hallucinating, which one was telling the truth. On her case-history sheet I wrote 'complaining of her husband's strange insomnia' and on his case-history sheet I wrote 'complaining of his wife's strange insomnia'. And the following week I never came back when they came back and I avoided that Viennese doctor ever after. The great thing was they both had called me 'doctor'. Neither of them called me 'sonny'.

In the autumn I joined my first medical firm and attended ward rounds. A dozen white-coated students on the firm would accompany the white-coated consultant physician, his white-coated registrar, his white-coated house physician, into the ward where sister and nurses fussed next to the beds of those patients who were to be examined and demonstrated to us. The consultant would walk two inches above the parquet floors unaided while the rest of us laughed at his quips, fawned, nodded wonderfully at his aphorisms. 'One finger in the throat and one in the rectum makes a good diagnostician,' the consultant said, quoting Sir William Osler, and some of us remembered another saying of Osler's which was, 'Look wise, say nothing, and grunt.' I often had to grunt when cross-examined on ward rounds.

Occasionally I would identify too much with the patient. I remember frequently worrying as we withdrew to the corner of the ward to discuss Mr Brown's symptoms that he, over there, half supine in bed, staring at us, would overhear low voices muttering 'malignant' or 'progressive'. However kind, consultants were not invariably tactful.

Indeed, on one occasion, as we stood around the bed of a patient whose history had been related to us in detail, I was asked to hazard a diagnosis. 'A duodenal ulcer,' I suggested. The patient smiled at me benignly. The consultant shook his head. 'No, Mr Green hasn't a duodenal ulcer. He has a chronic gastritis. You need to have some intelligence to have a duodenal ulcer, don't you, Mr Green?' Mr Green laughed – perhaps it was the laughter of contained aggression, I don't know. But he laughed and the students laughed a second later, so did the house physician, and the registrar, and the consultant most of all. 'Yes,' said the consultant, patting Mr Green's shoulders as if he were a good boy. 'Ha ha ha. You're lucky. You're too stupid to have an ulcer.' As we walked towards the next patient I looked back. Mr Green's head lay on the pillow. His eyes were closed.

A few weeks later, one afternoon while the firm waited for that same consultant who for some reason that day had been delayed, his registrar decided to teach us a singularly important principle of medicine. He asked a nurse to fetch him a sample of urine. He then talked to us about diabetes mellitus. '*Diabetes*,' he said, 'is a Greek name; but the Romans noticed that bees liked the urine of diabetics so they added the word *mellitus* which means sweet as honey. Well, as you know, you may find sugar in the urine of a diabetic.' By now the nurse had returned with a sample of urine which the registrar promptly held up like a trophy. We stared at that straw-coloured fluid as if we had never seen such a thing before. The registrar then startled us. He dipped a finger boldly into the urine then licked that finger with the tip of his tongue. As if tasting wine he opened and closed his lips rapidly. Could he perhaps detect a faint taste of sugar? The sample was passed on to us for an opinion. We all dipped a finger into the fluid, all of us foolishly licked that finger. 'Now,' said the registrar grinning, 'you have learnt the first principle of diagnosis. I mean the power of observation.' We were baffled. We stood near the sluice room outside the ward and in the distance, some anonymous patient was explosively coughing. 'You see,' the registrar continued triumphantly, 'I dipped my *middle* finger into the urine but licked my *index* finger – not like you chaps.'

Apart from ward rounds, I also attended lectures. I do not know now, objectively, whether they were tedious and badly presented, or whether it was simply that I was a poor listener. But Dr Ernie Lloyd's introductory lecture I found memorable. I did not know then that he delivered this same lecture in the same way every year. Ernie could have been a stage Welshman. He looked more like Lloyd George than Lloyd George did, and certainly he was just as histrionic.

He began in his sing-song accent, 'Today I shall talk to you about the heart, the old heart. It beats, do you see, seventy, duw, eighty times a minute; minute in, minute out; hour in, hour out; week in, week out; month in, month out; year in, year out. The old heart.' And as his incantation continued he used his hands like a conductor as if we, his audience, were a silent orchestra. I hear his voice still: 'And the sound, oh the sound of a mitral murmur, it is like, oh aye, it is like . . . the wind; the wind rustlin' gently through the corn. [Long pause.] Po-etic, isn't it, boys?' At Outpatients, I learned many things from him – also 'facts' that later I was to discover were quite wrong – for instance, that pulmonary tuberculosis never affected the right middle lobe. Well, I also learnt that there never was a 'never' in medicine.

There were many other Welshmen besides Ernie Lloyd at Westminster, not least C. Price Thomas, a brilliant chest surgeon (who was to operate on King George VI) and who, having visited the USA before the Second World War, exchanged his Welsh accent for a strange Yankee one. Drawling, he would address each student as 'professor'. Touching his glasses he would ask some timid student, 'Why do you think that, professor?' Many of the students themselves were Welsh. On one notable occasion so many of the cricket XI were from Wales that when we went out to field our captain gave us his orders in Welsh. The opposing side called us Welshminster.

In 1945 I joined my first surgical firm. It was always a question of doing things for the first time: first time to take blood from a vein, first lumbar puncture, first major operation, first postmortem, first childbirth, first death of a patient one had attended in the ward. Only repetition can lead to confidence so all these first times were a strain. No wonder so many medical students are frivolous. They are seldom mature enough to cope with so much ineluctable human sadness and sickness. What can young men and women do but make jokes, laugh and respond by some form of activism – in one mood horseplay, in another by trying to comfort and give help to those in the sick wards they so timidly linger in?

The most radical surgeon at Westminster Hospital was Sir Stanford Cade. How many times did I, along with other students on the firm, hear him conclude a graphic description of a patient's disease with the decision, 'This is inoperable.' And then, after a pause, 'I will operate.' One student on the firm at that time was 'Charlie' Westbury who was to become Sir Stanford's most brilliant pupil. Today Charlie gives those same ward rounds at Westminster Hospital and he too has become a radical surgeon, one universally respected.

Recently I met Charlie again. He startled me. He said that he had read a poem of mine called 'The Case' and wished to take issue with the suggestion advanced in the poem – that doctors too often see patients not as rounded human beings but simply as cases. (My poem was about a physician who knew the electrocardiograph of a patient but not the patient's name.)

'You see,' Charlie continued, 'if I saw some of my patients as rounded human beings and not as cases, because of the distressful nature of the surgery I have to undertake – sometimes in severely ill, pathetic children – I wouldn't be able to function. Give me so many inches of anonymous skin under the lights in an operating theatre and then I can use my skill; but if I were in a street and someone was knocked down then I'd find it difficult to cope.'

So much then for the so-called extroverted, tough personality of surgeons. Charlie was sensitive as a student and he is sensitive now. All the same, I do not think he found his student days, with their blatant confrontations with suffering, such a testing time as I did. The medical student learns more than the art and practice of medicine. He learns something about himself – and this is so whether he studies at Westminster Hospital, the Welsh National School of Medicine or Timbuctoo.

For my part, I found myself more and more given to reactive though purposeful daydreaming. For instance, I would be in the postmortem room and as the pathologist was trying to teach us morbid truths about diseased tissues I would not hear what he said as I kept thinking how the mesenteric colours inside the exposed abdomen resembled those of a cathedral window; or at Outpatients or on a ward round I would find myself trying to write a poem in my head. Mr MacNab, on one ward round, woke me up, I remember. The rest of the firm were all staring at me. Evidently I had been asked a question. They waited. Mr MacNab waited. 'Your name is Abse,' he said sarcastically. 'This is Wednesday afternoon, this is the Westminster Hospital, Christmas is coming and it is 1946.'

In fact the consultants at Westminster were amazingly patient with me. Earlier, in June 1946, my first book of poems was accepted for publication by Hutchinson so perhaps they expected a budding poet to be somewhat disarrayed.

I was more than disarrayed. For the next eight months I hardly attended Westminster Hospital and in the summer of 1947 I returned to Cardiff where I pronounced to my brothers that I no longer wished to become a doctor, I wanted to become a writer. I had a book coming out, some of my stuff was being published in periodicals, I had also written a play. 'You can't give up medicine,' Leo said angrily. 'Father has made many sacrifices so that you can study in London.' Wilfred agreed and added forcefully, 'It will be better for you – I tell you as a psychiatrist – to finish something that you've begun. If you don't it will mark you for the rest of your life. Besides, if you knuckle down you could qualify in a year. Then you could do what you like. Become a freelance writer if that's what you want – *after you've qualified*.'

It took me over a year to qualify but I am glad that after a further six months' absence from medical school I eventually took their advice. When I did return to the wards again, continuously, seriously, I must have been intensely self-righteous and smug. For I had decided that one must act purely, selflessly! In order to do so, I argued, one must live like a patient recovering from a serious illness. One must always be grateful – for a grateful man is more likely to bear gifts to others. I would take the skull out of the wardrobe to help me in my meditations. I discovered, then, with exalted melancholy, that the skull ceased to be an anatomical artifact but truly a skull and reminder of my own destiny. It became a threat, a sacred object that could help me extend my consciousness. I wanted to achieve lucidity and to act only with awareness. For some months a number of patients at Westminster Hospital had to endure my over-enthusiastic acts of kindness.

Two years later, when I, a doctor, returned to Cardiff to take on a general practice locum for my Uncle Max, I was not only aware of my own inadequacies but also the inadequacies of my medical education. I no longer stared at the skull and indeed rarely thought of the skull beneath the flesh. Worse, I understood the truth and shame

> Of motives late revealed, and the awareness
> Of things ill done and done to others' harm
> Which once I took for exercise of virtue.
> Then fool's approval stings and honour stains.

But such introspection was time-consuming and, perhaps, self-indulgent. A voice on the phone was saying plaintively, 'Doctor, please, doctor.'

Following in the Footsteps of Dr Keats

I

In the Vth-Form chalky classroom of St Illtyd's College, Cardiff, an embarrassed boy stood next to the blackboard with a green-covered book in his hand: *The Golden Treasury of Longer Poems*. Mr Graber, the English master, had hauled the boy out in front of the class to read a poem by Keats. Half a century ago youngsters in Wales had to study samples of the major English romantic poets of the nineteenth century in order to matriculate. 'Go ahead, boy,' shouted Mr Graber. 'Read what's in front of your nose.' That boy, who looked remarkably like the portrait-photograph of myself when sixteen, read what was in front of his nose:

> St. Agnes' Eve – Ah, bitter chill it was!
> The owl, for all his feathers, was a-cold;
> The hare limp'd trembling through the frozen grass

'Louder, boy, louder. Stop mumbling,' interrupted Mr Graber.

I can't say that I liked Keats's 'The Eve of St. Agnes'. When Mr Graber finally asked me my opinion of the poem I said, without enthusiasm, ''s all right.' Mr Graber did not seem content with the sweet economy of my opinion. With heavy sarcasm he said, 'Abse here, thinks "The Eve of St. Agnes" to be all right and he said it in a tone that suggests that he did not think the poem was all right. On the other hand, an eminent critic and contemporary of John Keats, a certain Leigh Hunt, believed "The Eve of St. Agnes" to be a most delightful and complete specimen of John Keats's genius –

Lecture at the Cheltenham Festival of Literature

that the poem was, I quote, "glowing with the colours of romance". Now, would you like to revise your opinion, boy? If so, please do it at slightly greater length.'

'I suppose,' I conceded with youthful pomposity, 'Mr Leigh Hunt knew what he was talking about, sir. It's easy to admire the rhyming and picture-making, but the story, struth.'

Perhaps I – and the rest of the class – would have found more interest in the poem if Mr Graber had told us something about Keats the man: how the Apothecaries Act in England had been passed in 1815 to prevent unqualified medical practice and how, that same year, young John Keats had been accepted for training at Guy's Hospital in London. Mr Graber could have told us, too, that 'The Eve of St. Agnes' was a romantic celebration of an erotic fantasy probably inspired by Keats's imaginings of Fanny Brawne whom he had met a month or so earlier and whom he had become – to use schoolboy vocabulary – 'stuck' on. I wonder now how the class would have responded had Mr Graber read out one of Keats's later love-letters to Fanny? With embarrassed laughter? With sympathy? With curiosity? With an invincible superior dismissal as Matthew Arnold had once done?

> My dear Girl, [Keats wrote vulnerably]
>
> . . . I cannot exist without you. I am forgetful of every thing but seeing you again – my Life seems to stop there – I see no further. You have absorb'd me . . . I have been astonished that Men could die Martyrs for religion – I have shudder'd at it. I shudder no more – I could be martyr'd for my Religion – Love is my religion – I could die for that. I could die for you. My Creed is Love and you are its only tenet . . . I cannot breathe without you.
>
> Yours for ever,
>
> John Keats

But Mr Graber never even told us of the existence of Fanny Brawne.

It was not until I became a first-year medical student that I learnt something of Keats's life: the nature of the medicine he had studied at Guy's; how he had nursed his mother and young brother, Tom, when they were on their deathbeds, how he had contracted TB himself and had died of it when he was only twenty-five. I knew little enough of Keats's life, not having then read a proper biography, but I knew odd facts like that. More importantly, I had discovered poems of Keats which I liked much better than 'The Eve of St. Agnes', not least among them the famous 'Ode to a Nightingale'.

Pity, I thought then, pity that Keats had to focus, even in that poem, on such things as 'charmed magic casements' and 'fairy lands forlorn'. That kind of confectionery reminded me too much of 'The Eve of St. Agnes'; but how memorable the poem was and how vehement with authentic feeling. Surely Keats had been thinking of his young, diseased brother, Tom, when he wrote 'where youth grows pale and spectre-thin and dies'. And wasn't Keats, an angry young doctor, referring to TB and its relation to poverty in such a bitter, wonderfully bitter, line as 'No hungry generations tread thee down'? In London, then, one death in five was due to tuberculosis. I was an uneducated first-year medical student, writing poems myself but largely ignorant of the tradition and treasures of English literature. I was attracted, though, in my casual reading, in particular, to poems written out of personal predicament, poems that appeared to spring from urgent experience.

The following year I left my home town, Cardiff, to continue my medical studies in London where, after a few months, I found congenial digs in Swiss Cottage. Congenial they might have been but, at first, a stranger to the location and having no friends round and about, I would often feel lonely and homesick. One evening, instead of studying Gray's *Anatomy*, or Samson Wright's textbook on Physiology, or writing a letter home, or attempting to fiddle at a poem, I walked out into the February air of Swiss Cottage streets. Should I take this direction or that? I walked for the best part of a mile, all too aware that I was more than 150 miles away from family and friends and Welsh familiarity. This was London, immense, impersonal, unknowable. I had walked up a long slope of an avenue and now I turned through narrower declining streets. Eventually I turned left and before me appeared open grassy space on one side of the road. I did not know that I had reached the borders of Hampstead Heath.

Soon I came to a large pond which was overlooked by a row of tall houses, or rather the backs of houses, with many windows. No one was about, no one at all. I threaded my way to the water's edge where I crouched down, squatting the way miners do in the valleys. In half an hour it would be dark. I felt small, I felt an exile from that which I knew best, I experienced that sense of longing and loss the Welsh call *hiraeth*, and, idly, I picked up one of the twigs that had fallen from the trees around me and wrote my name in the water.

I wandered on, not knowing where I was but after a minute or so, much to my astonishment, saw a road called Keats Grove. Keats Grove? Why Keats Grove? Did Keats once live here? I was, I realised, in Hampstead. Sure enough, here in front of me now I could see the house where Keats had lived. I gazed over a wooden fence at the front garden where on a grass plot under a plum tree, in 1819, he wrote his 'Ode to a Nightingale'. I felt the cold, an icicle, at the back of my neck for I suddenly remembered Keats's epitaph. On the night of 14 February 1821, the dying Keats had asked his friend Joseph Severn that his gravestone should bear the words, 'Here lies one whose name was writ in water.'

It seemed to me then, as it still does now, that that graphic instruction might have been rehearsed in actuality – was not merely a symbol. And if Keats had written his name in water was it not likely that he had done so in a nearby pond? When I returned to my digs that evening I did not open Gray's *Anatomy* or stare at the contours of the skeleton bones I owned but took down from my sparse bookshelf my second-hand volume of Keats's poems.

I found myself reading out loud 'La Belle Dame sans Merci' and somehow it did not seem to matter that I was travelling once more in an unlikely kingdom where one encountered a knight, a faery's child and even an elfin grot! Nor was I unduly irritated by Miltonic inversions – 'anguish moist', 'honey wild'. Instead I mesmerised myself reading the poem; I found it thrilling.

O what can ail thee, knight-at-arms,
  Alone and palely loitering?
The sedge has wither'd from the lake,
  And no birds sing.

O what can ail thee, knight-at-arms,
  So haggard and so woe-begone?
The squirrel's granary is full,
  And the harvest's done.

I see a lily on thy brow,
  With anguish moist and fever dew,
And on thy cheeks a fading rose
  Fast withereth too.

I met a lady in the meads,
  Full beautiful – a faery's child,
Her hair was long, her foot was light,
  And her eyes were wild.

I made a garland for her head,
  And bracelets too, and fragrant zone;
She look'd at me as she did love,
  And made sweet moan.

I set her on my pacing steed,
  And nothing else saw all day long,
For sidelong would she bend, and sing
  A faery's song.

She found me roots of relish sweet,
  And honey wild, and manna dew,
And sure in language strange she said –
  'I love thee true'.

She took me to her elfin grot,
  And there she wept, and sigh'd full sore,
And there I shut her wild wild eyes
  With kisses four.

And there she lulled me asleep,
  And there I dream'd – Ah! woe betide!

The latest dream I ever dream'd
  On the cold hill side.

I saw pale kings and princes too,
  Pale warriors, death-pale were they all;
They cried – 'La Belle Dame sans Merci
  Hath thee in thrall!'

I saw their starved lips in the gloam,
  With horrid warning gaped wide,
And I awoke and found me here,
  On the cold hill's side.

And this is why I sojourn here,
  Alone and palely loitering,
Though the sedge has wither'd from the lake,
  And no birds sing.

It must have been over a year later, after a session in the dissecting room at King's College in the Strand, I saw on the notice-board in the foyer that the poet, Edmund Blunden, was to give a lecture on Keats and Shelley to the Literary Society. So instead of returning to my digs I hung around until six o'clock and, alone among the medical students, went to Blunden's lecture. I don't recall in any detail what he talked about but he mentioned frequently the word 'Romanticism'. I don't recall either what question I asked him after the lecture was over. He discerned evidently that I was deeply interested in poetry and he invited me to have a drink with him. He told me of a dinner party where both Wordsworth and Keats were guests. When Keats tried to make a conversational point Mrs Wordsworth, placing a restraining hand on Keats's arm, said imperiously, 'Mr Wordsworth is *never* interrupted.' Blunden was the first poet I had ever met. I told him I wrote poetry. Eventually I showed him some of my early flawed poems and he was encouraging and kind. Perhaps it was because I, like Keats, was a medical student.

II

Edmund Blunden notwithstanding, T. S. Eliot had remarked, 'Romanticism and classicism are not matters with which creative writers can afford to bother over much. It is true that from time to time writers have labelled themselves "romanticists" or "classicists" . . . These names are the delight of professors and historians of literature but should not be taken seriously.' Eliot went on to point out the confusion caused by the use of such a term as Romanticism: it having different meanings, at different times, in different contexts.

If I now ask myself the question, 'What is Romanticism?' I would have to admit that, while difficult to define precisely, it is nevertheless a useful categorisation, especially in a consideration of Keats's poetry. Romantic poets, whether of this century or the last, do share certain tendencies in common, in their degree of irrationality, in their gravity of feeling, in the musical intensity of their diction, in their explorations into the world of the imagination.

Yet the Romantic poem, however much it may reveal itself as one obviously powered from some deep internal source, cannot allow its direction to be lawless. It has to refer to things of the world we all know. It must, perforce, follow external prescriptions in order to communicate with the reader, prescriptions that are signposted, that have their own decorated logic, their sequences and concomitances, that are not arbitrary, not emancipated as the dream of one who slumbers in the night. A reverie, need I say, shaped into a poem with its purposes of rhythm is not the same as night dream. A Keatsian reverie, ordered into a compelling narrative, may have a mythopoeic resonance a night dream can never have, though their association intrigued Keats himself.

A friend of mine, Thomas Blackburn, once suggested that poets should have the double vision of the god Odin: one eye to observe the outer scene, the other blinded one to behold what is going on in the night of oneself. It could be argued that all poetry owns a romantic impulse: that even that which is now labelled as classical did not appear as such when first broadcast. One can cite Nietzsche who, in *The Origin of Tragedy*, argued that our present impression of Greek art as being calm and Apollonian is hardly resonant with the wild, corybantic, Dionysian spirit of ancient Greece; that, as the centuries have passed, so too, it seems, have Greek works of art discharged their intense, emotional, even barbaric, content to become transfigured into what we now identify as classical proportion and beauty.

In fact, I believe, as doubtless others do, and have done, that the antithesis of the term Romanticism to designate a mode of literature, is not so much Classicism as Realism. Not that any true writer can be a pure Romantic – if he were he would be dizzily unreadable. The romantic body after flight sometimes needs to be realistic, to be sedentary, to rest on the gluteus maximus. Even within the confines of nineteenth-century High Romanticism itself there are different degrees of elevation dependent on the writer's attachment to the world we all know and the truth of nature rather than that of his own fancy. One need only consider the differences in approach to subject matter and degree of linguistic decoration by the leaders of the English Romantic movement, Coleridge and Wordsworth.

Coleridge's brand of extreme romanticism with its commitment to the flying Imagination was inherited by Keats and both poets contemplated 'in thought, as in picture, the image of a greater and better world' – for Keats a world of no tortured patients, no ugly cripples, no blundering apothecaries with their ineffectual plasters, pills and ointment boxes. When Keats did take the three steps from the sublime to the tellurian, from Feathers to Iron, when he sat, if you like, on his buttocks, he sounded, at best, like a poetry-writing medical student at play. Such was his Elizabethan-like erotic song 'Oh, blush not so'.

Oh, blush not so, oh, blush not so,
Or I shall think ye knowing.
And if ye smile the blushing while
Then maidenheads are going.

There's a blush for won't, and a blush for shan't –
And a blush for having done it.
There's a blush for thought, and a blush for naught
And a blush for just begun it . . .

III

If I may talk about my own poetry for a moment . . . (as the philosopher said, 'for a poet not to talk about his own work is a very refined form of hypocrisy'). Well, when I look back to my own apprentice work in *After Every Green Thing* (1948) and most of the poems in *Walking Under Water* (1952) which I wrote while still a medical student, I recognise that I had caught the current neo-romantic mode of expression like an infection, sounding sometimes like Dylan Thomas on an off-day. Moreover, much of my early work, like so many of the neo-romantic effusions of my immediate post-war contemporaries, allowed the real world to dip beyond the curve of the horizon, out of sight.

Well, the real world had been for me, in the late 1940s, often confined to the locus of the hospital – a challenging, a disturbing, even a painful place to inhabit, as it would be for any youngster capable of profoundly empathising with sick patients. I certainly found, during those early clinical years, my confrontation with diseased patients, not the equivalent of trench warfare as the American critic M. L. Rosenthal has generously suggested, but at least strenuously uncomfortable and unpleasant. Medical students, in escaping from painful reality, are notorious for playing pranks. Did I find another escape route in playing with words? And were the three steps from Iron to Feathers facilitated by a Romantic mode of expression?

Sigmund Freud, in his 1908 paper, 'The Poet and Daydreaming', by putting forward the hypothesis that imaginative creation, like daydreaming, is a continuation and substitute for childhood play, infers that this ludic activity is a form of escape from the precipitate pressures of a present reality. It may be so. It may be that all poetry-writing is such. Or is some poetry, the most incisive poetry, not an escape from reality but rather an immersion into reality?

Freud, in comparing the imaginative writer with the day-dreamer emphasises how much of that day-dreaming contains the fulfilment of a wish. The wish to escape from the sphere of sorrow to a sort of tranquillised utopia is explicitly stated by many Romantic poets.

I have desired to go
  Where springs not fail,
To fields where flies no sharp and sided hail
  And a few lilies blow.

And I have asked to be
  Where no storms come,
Where the green swell is in the havens dumb,
  And out of the swing of the sea.

(*Gerard Manley Hopkins*)

I will arise and go now, and go to Innisfree,
And a small cabin build there, of clay and wattles made:
Nine bean-rows will I have there, a hive for the honey-bee,
And live alone in the bee-loud glade . . .

(*W. B. Yeats*)

As his poetry reveals, Keats often visited that bee-loud glade. He called it by other names. For instance, the arcadian land of the immortal nightingale where men do not know the weariness, the fever and the fret . . .

> O for a beaker full of the warm South . . . [Keats cried]
> . . . That I might drink, and leave the world unseen.

It is with such an impassioned, forlorn regret that Keats leaves his waking dream for the real world 'where youth grows pale and spectre-thin and dies'. Dies of tuberculosis and the legacy of hungry generations.

In the bee-loud glade there were no tooth-drawings, no blood-lettings, no unwrapping of stinking, foul dressings, no sordid surgical interventions the twenty-one-year-old Keats had to attend to. At Guy's, in 1816, students acted simultaneously as surgeon's assistants (dressers) while carrying on dissecting the dead bodies snatched from fresh graves. No antiseptic precautions were taken: often students quit the dissecting room to visit the operating theatre directly without even washing their hands.

IV

One essential of poetry, according to Coleridge, is that it be impassioned. He called for 'vehement feeling'. It is this exhibition of a more than usual state of emotion, of vehement feeling, that discomforts contemporary anti-Romantic critics. For instance, several of those who in the 1950s contributed to Robert Conquest's anti-Romantic anthology *New Lines*, Kingsley Amis and Donald Davie among them, shared this distaste for the display of feeling in poetry and called for 'a neutral tone'. They railed against the more lush romantic verbalisation of emotion.

But if Romantic poets could be accused of turning away from the world of our everyday, many anti-romantic critics can be arraigned for fainting away from true feeling. Of course, fear of open feeling and sensuousness is not confined to certain poets and critics of our age. Some years ago I picked up in a second-hand bookshop an anthology of nineteenth-century poetry published by Macmillan in 1883. In it I was amused to read Matthew Arnold introducing a batch of poems by John Keats. Arnold's introduction revealed a snobbish and a surprisingly anti-romantic response to Keats's sensibility. He wrote:

> No one can question the eminency, in Keats's poetry, of the quality of sensuousness; the question with some people will be, whether he is anything else. Many things may be brought forward which seem to show him as under the fascination and sole dominion of sense, and desiring nothing better. There is the exclamation in one of his letters: 'O for a life of sensations rather than of thoughts!'

Matthew Arnold then went on to criticise the publication of the *Letters to Fanny Brawne*.

> A man who writes love-letters in this strain is probably predestined, one may observe, to misfortune in his love affairs; but that is nothing. The complete enervation of the writer is the real point for remark. We have the tone, or rather the entire want of tone, the abandonment of all reticence and all dignity, of the

> merely sensuous man, of the man who 'is passion's slave.' Nay, we have them in such wise that one is tempted to speak even as *Blackwood* or the *Quarterly* were in the old days wont to speak; one is tempted to say that Keats's love-letter is the love-letter of a surgeon's apprentice. It has in its relaxed self-abandonment something underbred and ignoble, as of a youth ill brought up, without the training which teaches us that we must put some constraint upon our feelings and upon the expression of them. It is the sort of love-letter of a surgeon's apprentice which one might hear read out in a breach of promise case, or in the Divorce Court. The sensuous man speaks in it, and the sensuous man of a badly bred and badly trained sort.

Well, I won't quote Matthew Arnold's class-ridden absurdities any further. Keats, perhaps, of all the High Romantic poets of the nineteenth-century has attracted the ire of contemporary anti-Romantic critics – precisely because he both exhibits feeling and inhabits the dales of Arcady rather than the pavements of our loud streets. Thus Kingsley Amis has grumpily asserted, 'If Keats is to be the ideal poet, ideal poetry too readily becomes a tissue of affectionate description of nice things, and if any pupil should wonder what the dales of Arcady have got to do with him, then the answer is that poetry deals with "the world of the imagination", i.e. not the real world.'

That poetry, the writing of it, might have been an escape-route for Keats is hard to deny. I have confessed how, as a medical student, I was spiritually bruised by what I had witnessed in Casualty or in Outpatients at Westminster Hospital; but how much more Keats, empathising, had to endure, be wounded by – not merely bruised by – the brutal scenes within the groaning wards and screaming operating theatres of Guy's Infirmary in 1816.

Keats had been a dresser for, an assistant to, that incompetent Guy's surgeon, Billy Lucas Junior, at a time, of course, when there were no anaesthetics. Worse, Keats's capacity to identify himself with a suffering patient or with any living creature seems to have been inordinately pronounced. In a letter to Benjamin Bailey he claimed, 'If a sparrow comes before my window I take part in its existence and pick about the gravel.' He could even feel himself unified with a billiard ball, apprehend its 'sense of delight from its roundness, smoothness and the very volubility of its motion'.

Is it any wonder then that Keats arrived at the notion of Negative Capability? As a medical student, listening to the querulous narratives of the diseased, he had to annihilate self momentarily. If, at times, he was 'with Achilles shouting in the trenches or with Theocritus in the Vales of Sicily' he was also with Mrs Smith haemorrhaging to death or with Mr Robinson whose left leg, being gangrenous, had to be sawn off.

The imagination was an easier place to be encamped in, sweeter by far. Moreover, he was encouraged along the escape-route of Poetry, for in the very year (1816) he passed the examination of the Court of Apothecaries and was licensed to practise he had his first poem published. Leigh Hunt, the editor of *The Examiner*, in accepting Keats's poem, had opened a door through which the five-foot-high young gifted poet might escape and pursue the beautiful. For in nineteenth-century England there was always the possibility that that pursuit might be rewarded financially – that with luck the life of a professional poet might make economic sense. (As the composer, Berlioz, himself an ex-medical student, once quipped, 'The luck of having talent is not enough; one must also have a talent for luck.')

How much Keats turned away from his fearful experiences at Guy's can be discerned by examining his poetry which is almost free of medical references and from his letters which rarely refer to medical matters. Keats was surely one of the few medical students in history who never seemed to luxuriate in comic or tragic medical anecdotes. On the contrary, when he speaks of Medicine seriously it is only to congratulate himself on escaping from it. And there is something cheerful in his confession, 'My last operation was the opening of a man's temporal artery. [Did he mean vein?] I did it with the utmost nicety but reflecting what had passed through my mind at the time, my dexterity seemed a miracle and I never took up the lancet again.' Given the state of Medicine then – those blood-lettings! those ill-advised starvation diets! those poisonous medicines! – Keats inadvertently served humanity well by foregoing medical practice.

Medical theory was bonkers (even more than some of it is today!). For instance Keats, during a lecture he attended at Guy's, was told by Astley Cooper, and no doubt believed it, that the young who led a life of intemperance were subject to ossification of the arteries and 'that those who have been much addicted to study, from keeping up a continual determination of blood to the brain, have often the vessels of that part ossified.'

I remarked a couple of minutes ago that the imagination was an easier place to be encamped in, sweeter by far than the blood-streaked boards of a hospital. But Keats believed the imagination could be compared to Adam's dream – 'he awoke and found it truth.' In a letter to his brother George he boasted, 'You speak of Lord Byron and me. There is a great difference between us. He describes what he sees – I describe what I imagine. Mine is the hardest task.'

There would be many who would not agree that Keats's professed method of poetic attack was the harder option. As long ago as the third century BC, the philosopher-painter of Peking, Han Fei, wryly remarked, 'It's hard to paint a horse or a dog but easy to paint a ghost.' Any creativity is easy – as Proust opined – 'if we need not take reality into account.' In any case, the sensibility of Keats was such that he could not but react to the glories of the world about us, he could not keep an admiring eye closed or his grateful ears shut. Besides he had a keen sense of observation, a gift no doubt encouraged by his medical education. The painter Severn, who used to walk with him over Highgate Hill, reported how Keats noticed everything: 'The colour of one woman's hair, the smile on a child's face, the furtive animalism below the deceptive humanity in many of the vagrants – hats, clothes, shoes, whatever conveyed the remotest hint as to the real self of the wearer.'

It is true, though, that the Romantic writer works from a principle within to make thrilling secrets audible however much he may rely on accurate observation of the real world. When we read a poem by Keats, such a one as 'La Belle Dame sans Merci', we come to realise that by escaping from the real world it is possible to reach the shores of a psychic reality, moreover not a private one, but as meaningful to us as the quotidian world about us where birds do sing – even the caged creatures.

'La Belle Dame' may own literary antecedents – Burton's 'Anatomy of Melancholy' (which Keats was reading at the time of the poem's composition) and the Coleridge of 'The Rime of the Ancient Mariner':

Her lips were red, her looks were free
Her locks were yellow as gold
Her skin was white as leprosy
The Nightmare LIFE-IN-DEATH was she
Who thicks man's blood with cold.

But despite such literary echoes, Keats's quintessentially romantic poem remains, as Robert Gittings has remarked, 'a pure expression of our deepest instincts'.

'La Belle Dame', like other successful Romantic poems of this century or of the last, is patently not mere verse, not a form of rationality set to word-music. Poetry, its very nature, has to communicate its unreason. So when 'La Belle Dame' was composed it went beyond the reach of the conscious craftsman and thus remains open to several creative misreadings; but what comes through unambiguously is that though Keats believed, for most of his too-short writing career, that poetry should not dwell on 'the burrs and thorns of life' he could not help but acknowledge in this poem – as in others – those inner burrs, those inner thorns that are invisible to ourselves. The pursuit of the beautiful, that credo of Keats may well divagate across a path of thorns into the realm of tragedy.

'La Belle Dame', like any genuine Romantic poem plumbs our inner nature; it sinks to where swaggering Dionysus rules, 'that genius of the heart' – as Nietzsche called him. So what initially appears to have been a journey along an escape-route from the objective world ends finally at the terminal of inward reality – which is no escape at all.

And so we, responding to the music and to the mythic matrix of such a poem, can almost apprehend what kind of things the blind eye of Odin saw when it peered inward. Then we can, momentarily at least, believe with Novalis that the world must be romanticised so that its original meaning may again be found – that after hearing Keats's dream we may awake and find it truth.

V

Several times, after giving poetry readings in the late 1950s, I was asked, 'Why don't your poems reveal that you are a practising doctor?' I used to respond and console myself by saying that the poetry of doctor-poets much more illustrious than me, Dr Keats, for example, hardly revealed their medical experience either. The people in Keats's poems were not real, were certainly not suffering patients. They seemed more like wonderful silhouettes in a tapestry – like Madeline in 'The Eve of St. Agnes' – 'so pure a thing, so free from mortal taint'.

But soon I began to believe more and more that poetry should immerse itself in common reality, not be an escape from it. So the question put to me at poetry readings I insistently addressed to myself and, as a result, became prepared to confront my medical experience. Louis Pasteur once declared, 'Chance favours the prepared mind.' In 1962 I wrote the first of a series of poems that touched strenuously on my medical experience – 'Pathology of Colours'.

> I know the colour rose, and it is lovely,
> but not when it ripens in a tumour;
> and healing greens, leaves and grass, so springlike,
> in limbs that fester are not springlike.
>
> I have seen red-blue tinged with hirsute mauve
> in the plum-skin face of a suicide.
> I have seen white, china-white almost, stare
> from behind the smashed windscreen of a car.
>
> And the criminal, multi-coloured flash
> of an H-bomb is no more beautiful
> than an autopsy when the belly's opened –
> to show cathedral windows never opened.

So in the simple blessing of a rainbow,
in the bevelled edge of a sunlit mirror,
I have seen, visible, Death's artifact
like a soldier's ribbon on a tunic tacked.

Intermittently, over the decades, chance has favoured me with such medically coloured poems, some light and affirmative but more, I fear, of a darker hue. A few have been about very ill-beloved relatives. I'm reminded how Keats, in 1818, wrote to Dilke about his dying brother, Tom, and how, in order to escape from the awfulness of it all, he composed romantic poetry. 'I wish I could say Tom was any better. His identity presses upon me all day,' he wrote. '. . . I am obliged to write and plunge into abstract images to ease myself of his countenance, his voice and feebleness.'

In his early poem 'Sleep and Poetry' Keats would argue that poetry should be 'nought more untranquil than the grassy slopes between two hills', should minister to pleasure – 'soothe the cares and lift the thoughts of man'. His aesthetic was resonant with contemporary assumptions about art yet in the later poems he questions that aesthetic – he had become only too conscious of the contrariness between the ease of sweet dreaming and the pain of confronting the suffering in the real public and private arena. Indeed that contrariness becomes, in part, the theme in poems such as the 'Ode to a Nightingale' or 'The Fall of Hyperion'. If Keats had lived longer I suspect he may have, at least mythopoeically, called on his vivid experiences at Guy's Hospital. With the privilege of continuing good health he may have allowed emotion to be recollected in tranquillity and have used the fabric of his experiences of 1815–16 in the making of mature poems. He had dissected stolen dead bodies, walked the pus-drenched wards of Guy's, visited the lunatic house for Incurables, assisted at screaming operations. 'Nothing ever becomes real till it is experienced,' Keats once declared in a letter. 'Even a proverb is no proverb till your Life has illustrated it.' Already in 'The Fall of Hyperion' we observe a less linguistic opulence and note how his alert sensitivity, negative capability, led him to identify himself even with the dying and the dead; among them, no doubt, the corpses whom he had dissected at Guy's and, though unsaid, his dying tuberculous mother and young brother Tom, whom he had so feelingly nursed.

> . . . suddenly a palsied chill
> Struck from the paved level up to my limbs,
> And was ascending quick to put cold grasp
> Upon those streams that pulse beside the throat:
> I shriek'd; and the sharp anguish of my shriek
> Stung my own ears – I strove hard to escape
> The numbness; strove to gain the lowest step.
> Slow, heavy, deadly was my pace: the cold
> Grew stifling, suffocating, at the heart;
> And when I clasp'd my hands I felt them not.

That is a long way from the dales of Arcady, much less tranquil than the grassy slopes between two hills. Towards the end of his young life Keats resolved to write in a more realistic mode, not to be merely one of the tribe of dreamers – to be closer to Chaucer rather than to Ariosto. As Robert Gittings and others have pointed out, the new ideal of his poetry would be to emphasise reality, to be a poet who would write without fever. Alas, at 11 p.m. on 3 February 1820 Keats suffered an haemoptysis. Coming back to Hampstead on the stage-coach from Town, feeling desperately ill, he alighted near that pond where I once unthinkingly signed my name, walked coughing towards what they now call Keats Grove to reach Wentworth Place. At once he went to his bedroom where he coughed yet again. When Brown, his friendly landlord came to his room he observed Keats peering at something on the bed sheets. In candlelight, they both stared at a blob of blood. Dr Keats said calmly, as if he were making a diagnosis and prognosis, 'I know the colour of that blood, it is arterial blood. I cannot be deceived in that colour. That drop of blood is my death warrant. I must die.'

VI

The year before last on 31 October, Keats's birthday, after reading the Sunday newspapers with their shrill headlines, my wife and I drove over to Keats Grove in Hampstead. For there, at Wentworth Place, where Keats once lived with Charles Brown, a gentle ceremony was about to take place: a replanting in the front garden of a plum tree. Soon we joined an invited group of Keats's admirers, and watched as the editor of the local Hampstead weekly paper shovelled earth on to the sapling. Among the observing crowd of faces I spotted some I recognised – faces of politicians, actors, poets, and physicians. Among them Michael Foot and Glenda Jackson.

In the spring of 1819 Charles Brown had written, 'A nightingale had built her nest in my house. Keats felt a continual and tranquil joy in her song; and one morning he took a chair from the breakfast table to the grass-plot under a plum tree where he sat for two or three hours . . .' Under that long-gone plum tree Keats had composed his 'Ode to a Nightingale'. And now, here on the same grass-plot, next to the living plum sapling an actor declaimed Keats's impassioned meditation.

My wife and I stood on the lawn. Across from us the gathered upturned faces listened, under a grey orbicular sky while the actor intoned:

> Thou wast not born for death, immortal Bird!
>   No hungry generations tread thee down;
> The voice I hear this passing night was heard
>   In ancient days by emperor and clown:
> Perhaps the self-same song that found a path
>   Through the sad heart of Ruth, when, sick for home,
>   She stood in tears amid the alien corn;
>   The same that oft-times hath
> Charm'd magic casements, opening on the foam
>   Of perilous seas, in faery lands forlorn.
>
> Forlorn! the very word is like a bell
>   To toll me back from thee to my sole self!
> Adieu! the fancy cannot cheat so well
>   As she is fam'd to do, deceiving elf.
> Adieu! adieu! thy plaintive anthem fades
>   Past the near meadows, over the still stream,

Up the hill-side; and now 'tis buried deep
In the next valley-glades:
Was it a vision, or a waking dream?
Fled is that music: – Do I wake or sleep?

Even as the ode was read I could not help thinking of Keats's long, wretched dying in Rome – of his last letter to Brown in which he remarked, 'I always made an awkward bow' and of his empathic concern for Severn who finally nursed him: 'How can you bear all this . . .' he said, and 'I am keeping you from your paints . . .' The out-of-doors ceremony over, the guests trooped into the house for a glass of wine. Soon the lawn was empty; only the reduplicating litter of yellowing leaves, the colour of banana-skin, remained on the green grass, and an elegiac hole in the earth, half-filled for the baby plum tree.

The Charisma of Quacks

At the Hotel Bullion in the Rue Montmartre in 1780 scores of people could be seen sitting with their feet immersed in a large wooden tub, applying magnetised iron rods and filings to themselves. Many were moaning piteously or breathing with a sound resembling a death rattle. In the centre of this mass of people was one who belonged to what we now call The Two Cultures: that of Science and Rationalism and that of Magic and Poetry. He was the Viennese physician and showman Franz Anton Mesmer. Of course in those distant days there was only One Culture – indeed, the very word 'scientist' is an early Victorian depiction, replacing the words Natural Philosopher.

Anyway, as Mesmer darted this way and that he carried a wand and wore his famous purple cloak. Occasionally, Dr Mesmer would stop, catch hold of a patient's hands and hold them in his while he gazed deeply into wild eyes. Then the purple-cloaked figure would touch the sick person with his wand and a cure sometimes resulted.

Those panting, quivering people about him had been put into a trance, had been mesmerised by his magnetised rods – or so Mesmer claimed, for this 'poet-physician' ascribed his healing force to animal magnetism emanating from the stars which he believed he had the gift of transmitting. Mesmer was a trained doctor and sincere in his beliefs: he intuitively understood that charismatic showmanship and the awe inspired by a reputation could heighten suggestibility and aid the healing process.

Another eighteenth-century medicaster who also had been trained as a physician was Chevalier Taylor. This tall, imposing,

---

A lecture delivered at Denison College, Ohio (18 March 1980)

British oculist blatantly advertised that with his superb arsenal of gold-coloured instruments he could cure squints, corneal opacities and blindness. His self-made reputation, bolstered by a few medical successes, brought him eventually to the court of King Frederick of Prussia where he treated a number of illustrious patients – one such was J. S. Bach.

Several bungled surgical operations led him finally to be expelled from Frederick the Great's kingdom. Some, though, continued to believe in the surgical skill of this renowned oculist. Voltaire, hearing about Taylor's exile, remarked that the King had driven from his dominions the one man in Europe who could have opened his eyes!

Years later, now discredited, still dressed entirely in black, he could sometimes be discovered in one or another of London's hostelries, boasting at the table of fellow-diners how, as a result of his successes, he received many a gold coin from grateful men patients and many a voluptuous favour from women he had cured.

It has been reported that one of the diners, irritated by Taylor's insistent boasts, asked, 'Since you have told us a great many things that you've done and can do – the amazing miracles that you've performed – would you be so good as to relate to us something that you cannot do?

'Nothing so easy, sir,' Taylor replied. 'I'm unable to pay for my share of the dinner bill and that I must beg you to do.'

* * *

At least one patient in every three seeking advice and treatment from a doctor in an urban practice suffers from a functional or stress disorder, one that may be distressing, even alarming. The doctor confronted by such patients is often at a loss, and can do less well than a Chevalier Taylor or an Anton Mesmer. Indeed the ancient Egyptian conception of a healer may be more to the point: 'He who treats the sick must be expert, learned in the proper incantations and know how to make amulets.'

Doctors may believe that medical science has moved away from sortilege, from the era of magic healing by incantation, by astrology and by touch. The sicker a patient is, however, the more primitive he tends to become. Hence the massive sale of patent medicines and the continued existence of 'fringe healers' practising hypnotherapy, radiesthesia, acupuncture, faith healing, and other unorthodoxies. The Chevalier Taylors and Anton Mesmers of the twentieth century thrive to the puzzlement of many orthodox practitioners.

I am reminded of an anecdote recorded in the memoirs, dated 1787, of Major James George Semple concerning a contemporary London quack, Rock, who

> standing one day at his door on Ludgate Hill when a real doctor of Physic passed who had learning and abilities but whose modesty was the true cause of his poverty. 'How comes it,' says he to the Quack, 'that you, without education, without skill, without the least knowledge of science, are enabled to live in the style you do? You keep your town house, your carriage and your country house, whilst I, allowed to possess some knowledge, have neither, and can hardly pick up a subsistence!' 'Why, look ye,' said Rock smiling, 'how many people do you think have passed since you asked me that question?' 'Why,' answered the Doctor, 'perhaps a hundred.' 'And how many out of those hundred, think you, possess common sense?' 'Possibly one,' answered the Doctor. 'Then,' said Rock, 'that one comes to you, and I take care of the other ninety-nine.'

That the quacks of past centuries were sometimes more successful than licensed doctors is understandable. After all, bleeding, dosing, and enemas were once, not so long ago, the main armoury of orthodox practitioners. Furthermore, the quacks of yesteryear exhibited a mesmeric public showmanship that most licensed doctors eschewed. Today the manufacturers of proprietary medicines sell their products with the help of advertising agencies: ARE YOU WORN OUT WITH CATARRH – *don't delay get Mentholatum Balsam today*; or JUNO JUNIPAH TABLETS! *You can't even taste them but in no time their gently corrective action means you* CAN *taste the joy of feeling and looking your old self again.* In the old days the quacks wrote their own copy, and with much greater verve. Consider, for instance, a leaflet by Cornelius of Tilbourne, a master quack of seventeenth-century Britain. At the head of his handbill you may read a royal recommendation: SWORN CHYRUGEON TO KING CHARLES II FROM WHOSE HANDS I RECEIVED A GOLD MEDAL AND CHAIN. The text continues: *I recover and give sight to the blind. I restore sight in a moment. I cure deafness (if curable), I cure vomiting, rising of vapour, pain in the milt, stitches in the side, and all scorbutick distempers.*

With such a royal recommendation and with such unambiguous certainty about his healing abilities no wonder Cornelius, on occasions, worked certain wonders for diseases that were frequently emotionally determined. Such quacks as Cornelius, as Rock, as Mesmer and Chevalier Taylor, instinctively knew the wisdom of Aristotle, that 'the mind has the same command over the body as the master over the slave.'

Whatever method the fringe healer uses is irrelevant. For the fringe healer has a confidence in his method, be it acupuncture, faith healing or radiesthesia, or at least would seem to have a confidence, that an ordinary physician with his scientific 'ifs' and 'buts' and 'maybes' does not own. The more fanatical the fringe practitioner's faith in his method, the more he radiates confidence, the more often will his treatment be successful. In that sense he is truly a Confidence Man. The emotionally disturbed patient with his concrete symptoms – sciatica, headaches, skin phenomena, chronic lassitude, heartburn, palpitations or whatever – is more likely to have faith in an assertive, optimistic healer than in the average doctor, half-educated, worried, beset by any number of reservations, doubts. Nearly 2,000 years ago the great Greek physician Galen wrote, 'He cures most in whom most have faith.' Today many have faith in those whom many doctors label as charlatans.

Some sixteen years ago I was required by a Sunday newspaper to interview half a dozen notable medicasters, among them Professor Niehans in Switzerland and Harry Edwards, here, in Britain. Niehans, through his ridiculous 'cellular therapy'*, claimed to rejuvenate such aged politicians as Adenauer, actresses such as Gloria Swanson, writers such as wrinkled Somerset Maugham. Harry Edwards, too, had his famous patients. He was the foremost spiritualist medium in Britain

---

*Niehans injected fresh foetal liver cells (from an unborn lamb) to rejuvenate diseased livers; fresh foetal heart cells to revitalise a failing heart; fresh foetal brain cells in brain conditions and so forth and so on.

and his spirit guides, he told his patients, were no other than the ghosts of Louis Pasteur and Lord Lister.

I confess that before I interviewed such fringe-healers I believed them to be charlatans. After meeting them I realised it was more complicated than that. It may be that, secretly, they each thought themselves to be the fourth member of the Quarternity! In any event, I suspected they were – to use the jargon of psychiatrists – 'Borderline psychotics'. They seemed to be dangerously encamped near the night borders of insanity.

⋆ ⋆ ⋆

When I interviewed Professor Niehans on 14 March 1964 in his spacious home overlooking the lake at Burier-Vevey he sounded paranoid with grandiose illusions. He spoke of himself, often, in the third person as certain inmates of certain hospitals tend to do. 'Niehans is a revolutionary,' he said. 'And revolutionaries in Medicine have much opposition. That's why I kept my discoveries secret for twenty years, why I had to give 3,000 injections before I released information about what I was doing. Niehans had to be absolutely sure . . . Lately I've been working on diabetes. Ah, when I publish my results what a storm there'll be. How they'll cry out against me once more. There are many people against Niehans. *They* tried to take my clinic away from me. *They* have succeeded now in barring me from the slaughterhouse in Clarens where I obtained the fresh cells from the embryos of ewes.'

I glanced out of the window at the quivering reflections of mountain on the lake, at clouds on mountains and mountains on clouds, everything in a dream and beautiful, sheer opera, sheer fake.

My conversation with Harry Edwards was equally bizarre. It took place not in a mental ward but at his mansion in Shere, Surrey.

Edwards: I had 8,750 letters this week. Most of 'em tell me they're incurable. As a result of my meditations 80 per cent record a measure of improvement. 30 per cent of these – a complete recovery.

Me: When do you meditate?

Edwards: In the early hours of the morning.
Me: To tune into your spirit guides?
Edwards: Yes.
Me: Louis Pasteur and Lord Lister?
Edwards: Yes. It's a matter of love and compassion.
Me: You told me you treat people who suffer illnesses like leukaemia, cancer, multiple sclerosis – don't you feel worried about raising false hopes?
Edwards: The gift of healing is a divine gift, one given to me as it has been to others. We never limit the power of spirit healing however apparently intractable the illness. As a result people who've been deaf are deaf no more, hunchbacks no longer hunchbacks, cripples can now walk unaided, their crutches discarded.
Me: What of the powers of suggestion, what of . . .?
Edwards: Can you suggest things to animals? Why only this week an Alsatian was brought here for spirit healing. The dog was unable to walk. It was paralysed. But it left this Sanctuary cured.

Yes, it seemed to me that charismatic healers like the somewhat presidential Professor Niehans and the more grubby Harry Edwards needed their patients, not merely to make a living for themselves, albeit a rich living, but to save themselves from a total break with reality. Their relationship with patients was a symbiotic one. By trying to cure them and sometimes by apparently relieving them of symptoms they not only gratified their own powerful inner needs but reinforced their own delusions of grandeur.

Meeting those contemporary fringe-healers should have allowed me to judge a little less superficially the Quacks of bygone centuries. Now that I come to think again of one such as Chevalier Taylor I can no longer imagine him as a witty, benign, handsome, practical joker, fooling fools and nudging, with consummate charm, desirable women into bed. On the contrary, he probably had a psychological profile not unlike Niehans or Edwards.

* * *

It may seem strange that eye-blazing men like Niehans, like Edwards, though now differently named, can still attract to their consulting rooms so many sick people in awe of them and in devout prostration before them; but those whose desperate symptoms can hardly be ameliorated by modern medicine must be tempted to believe in random miracles. Sick men and women are likely to regress in attitude of mind to that of dependent childhood; to when they owned little critical intelligence and took so many things on faith; to the time when they accepted parental simplifications and were particularly susceptible to suggestion; to the time when certain things occurred without evident explanation – just like miracles.

Within us all, when we sleep, our pagan ancestor sleeps too. The pagan dreamer in us is ready to awaken and misworship and misbelieve. Illness often leads to the renunciation of responsibility for self, in a reduction of rationality and to theopathy. So is it surprising, after all, that those in need of miracles – hundreds of thousands each year in Britain alone – seek out charismatic fringe healers who confidently claim their healing gifts to be revolutionary or to be God-bestowed?

It is strange, this power of charisma, the extraordinary magical quality and power some people seem to possess. The other day I heard someone remark, 'Charisma? They used to call it in the old days S.A. Sex appeal.' Perhaps. True charismatics do appear to own a sensitive access to the psycho-dynamics of the opposite sex. This may be because of the marked bisexual components of such individuals. Psychoanalysts such as L. Jessner and D. W. Abse have likened them to hypnotists, remarking that the relationship of the hypnotist to his subject is both maternal and paternal. Techniques for inducing hypnosis are appeals to love (the giving mother) and to awe (the authoritative father). On one hand the hypnotist is like a mother as he soothes and strokes the patient; on the other hand he is like a father when issuing commands in an imposing manner: 'Your arm is getting lighter, it'll go into the air of its own accord, higher, higher.'

It may be that the famous 'bedside manner' some doctors instinctively own is based on this ability to be paternal and maternal to patients at one and the same time. Charismatic fringe healers certainly exhibit this ability to become, as it were, the primal father and the primal mother. Some address their patients as 'my child'. Speak to the disciples of these fringe charismatics and they speak of their 'leader' in the clear tones of love. They write tracts about them in the language of love. As for 'awe', well, every famous person is held in awe by some. The public exhibitions, the floodlights, the advertisements, the propaganda, bestow charisma on the subject featured, be he a Chevalier Taylor or a Harry Edwards.

Those official corporations such as the British Medical Association that frown on publicity for individual doctors inadvertently prevent some patients from gaining benefit from orthodox healers who otherwise might be more vulgarly famous and so more charismatic. The conditions of love and awe are necessary for the healer, orthodox doctor or quack. That those in the orthodox medical profession instinctively understand this is demonstrated in the great London teaching hospitals. To understand how the qualities of love and awe operate in this ambience it is only necessary to listen to the nursing staff talk about this or that consultant, or to go on a ward round with the consultant himself, Sir John This or Sir Charles That, and witness the attitude of his long retinue as they whisper Hallelujah, as the great one brilliantly walks half an inch above the floor. The patient observing this feels more confident. And grateful!

The glamorous aura of those who heal is significant. The white coat of healing may look clinical, antiseptic, but the purple cloak of the magician such as the one Anton Mesmer once wore can still usefully be hung on the hook behind the door of every doctor's surgery. It has been reported that the novelist Henry James kept on his desk a card on which was printed the slogan, DRAMATISE, DRAMATISE. On my desk, at the clinic where I work, I would put another slogan: MESMER & CHEVALIER TAYLOR RULE O.K. And I would keep it there though I now know that those who wear the purple cloak are somewhat mad, that in floodlight they stand one foot on a quivering rope, the other poised over a fathomless chasm of darkness.

More than a Green Placebo

At an animated dinner party, our host told us how a certain doctor, on investigating the verbal composition of articles published in the *British Medical Journal*, had discovered that, on average, 42% of the words in each issue were adjectives. After some further discussion, I asked, 'Is it worth travelling around the world to count the cats of Zanzibar?' Satisfied that I had triumphantly put all opposing discourse to an end with that propitious quotation from Thoreau, I sat back, smugly, waiting for the pudding to be served.

Then, unexpectedly, one of the guests, John Heath-Stubbs, emphatically replied, 'Yes!' He provoked laughter because of his intervention, and urgently he repeated, 'Yes, yes, it *is* worth going around the world to count the cats of Zanzibar.'

John Heath-Stubbs, besides being a poet, is a considerable scholar; and at that time I thought it was as a scholar that he had answered Thoreau's rhetorical question in the affirmative. After all, scholars, like scientists, should not prejudge the value of any harmless investigation before it is embarked upon. But I suspect others at that dinner table believed that Heath-Stubbs replied 'Yes' because he was a poet.

Most people, after all, have as little regard for the activity of writing poems as they have for the kind of scholarship that involves the counting of adjectives in successive issues of the *BMJ*. They are somewhat baffled by those who are engaged in such apparently useless activity, unless that activity brings monetary reward or is simply an expression of a hobby. Writing poetry as a central

---

The Lancet, Vol. 351 (31 January 1998)

concern, not as a marginal pastime, year in year out, putting the right words in the right order for no evident reason, neither wishing to persuade anybody nor to legislate, must seem to many a very odd occupation indeed. No wonder I'm asked, as no doubt other poets are, 'Do you really consider writing poetry important?' They are politely asking, 'Why is a grown man like you playing with words?'

In an attempt to justify one's trade as a poet, it is no longer possible to resort to arguing the moral nature of poetry. Those nineteenth-century claims that 'Poetry strengthens the faculty which is the organ of the moral nature of man in the same manner as exercise strengthens a limb' (*A Defence of Poetry*, P. B. Shelley) seem hollow now post-Auschwitz and Hiroshima. Even T. S. Eliot's 'poetry refines the dialect of the tribe' seems in all its ambiguities to be a grandiose assertion, if not a dubious one. The very multiplicity of definitions about the function of poetry proves, does it not, that most people are suspicious that poetry has no function? I know of no long essays in defence of carpentry or in defence of surgery. Everyone is convinced that carpenters and surgeons are necessary. Even so, if by chance professional poets somehow commanded, in the future, regular salaries, I suspect there would be fewer essays in defence of poetry; and if that salary were substantial, no longer would poets be thought of as playing childish word-games, a sort of Radio Three Scrabble.

However, poetry does have several uses. For instance, lately I have been reading an interesting, vulnerable, often touching anthology of verses that have been written out of, or about, mental disorder. The anthology is called *Beyond Bedlam*[1] and originated with a group at the Maudsley Hospital, London, who had asked, among other questions, what role can poetry have in alleviating symptoms of mental distress? One knows that patients can be consoled by reading poetry, and many doctors have no doubt seen, as I have, a volume of poems at the bedside of a terminally ill patient. But what the editors of *Beyond Bedlam* were interested in was how the act of writing poetry by patients themselves can be beneficial.

In 1973–74, I was privileged to be writer-in-residence at Princeton University. One of my duties for that American academic year was to preside over a small class of aspiring student-writers.

Each week they presented me with their new-minted poems, most in foetal condition, and these were discussed, closely examined, winked at, criticised, and not entirely dismissed, for as Johnson once pithily remarked, 'The price of reading other people's poetry is praise.'

I did feel sometimes that these weekly sessions seemed more to resemble group therapy than the routine enterprise of a literary workshop. One of the students, an anxious, very bright, young woman had been having periodic weekend migraine attacks, but these almost always failed to keep their appointments during that academic year. Was it a coincidence? One day, she laughingly remarked, 'Reading and writing poetry is a green placebo, Dr Abse.'

I was interested that she had defined poetry as such. A 1972 editorial in *The Lancet* referred to the power of placebos: 'Although it is more satisfying to the practitioner to ascribe a favourable response to his wise choice of pharmacological agent, it is sadly true that up to three-quarters of patients with affective disorders improve with placebo alone.'[2] That hardly surprising assertion went on to discuss, among other matters, less well-known facts such as the importance of tablet colour in the prescribing of a placebo. Though depression responded most favourably to yellow tablets, the green ones worked their magic with greater proficiency in treating anxiety than either those coloured yellow or red.

Of course, poetry is more than a green placebo because, apart from any questionable therapeutic use, it can metastasise in major and minor ways. W. H. Auden was defeatist when he cried out: '. . . poetry makes nothing happen: it survives/In the valley of its saying where executives/Would never want to tamper'.[3] He wrote those lines under a benign government.

Once poets sat at the Prince's right hand and praised the Prince. Their lies, if beautiful enough, may have contributed to the myth-making of history. Now poets, especially those who live in authoritarian societies, no longer sit at the Prince's right hand but, like others, may suffer the decisions of that powerful figure and are almost obligated to bear witness as best they can. Writing out of their own personal predicament, they may affect others who share that predicament or who are in sympathy with that predicament. No one can measure the small detonations of poems that have in their own idioplasm a sociohistorical implication. Poems can become, according to social circumstances, subversive documents.

But what of the value of exposing medical students to literary texts in general and poetry in particular, as happens with ever greater frequency at medical schools in the USA? Those who teach literature and medicine claim, with some justification, that by reading poems and stories about people afflicted mentally or lowered by physical illness, the student, on occasion, is better able to respond to patients. The best healers are thought to be those who are sensitive but tough and who can, to a degree, empathise with their patient's predicament. The patient's point of view, ventilated through an anecdote poem or a portrait poem, or through a prose narrative, can lead students to be more aware of parallel real-life situations such as they may encounter in the future.

Then there are texts that lend themselves to a debate about medical ethics. One such is 'The Use of Force',[4] a pre-war short story by the poet-physician William Carlos Williams. It is a fine piece of writing that is frequently introduced into the literature-and-medicine classrooms of US medical schools. It concerns a young girl with a fever who possibly has diphtheria. The girl will not allow her throat to be examined and resolutely closes her mouth. The attending physician, increasingly frustrated and erotically aroused, finally engages in what can only be called oral assault.

Literary texts by doctors, because of their authenticity, prove to be especially useful teaching tools, whether they are by Anton Chekhov, William Carlos Williams, or such American contemporaries as the ex-Yale surgeon Richard Selzer or the poet John Stone, a cardiac specialist currently at Emory University Medical School, Atlanta. Two books I would recommend to all readers of *The Lancet* and that I would introduce to a literature-and-medicine syllabus are *The Private Life of Islam*,[5] a diary that reads like a novel, written by Ian Young when he spent a summer while a medical student in a provincial maternity unit in Algeria; and *Doctor Glas*,[6] a Scandinavian classic by the novelist Hjalmar Söderberg.

Some poems, *inadvertently*, can also become didactic instruments. When I was young, some poems of the German poet Rainer Maria Rilke, became guru-lessons for me. I think I am someone who tends to talk too much, to display rather than to listen – not a useful characteristic for a medical student or a doctor at a hospital bedside or in a consulting room. The ideal is to listen solely to patients, never having to silence the clamour that one's own senses might make. That I have done so often enough was helped by reminding myself of these religious lines by Rilke[7] that, in Babette Deutsch's translation, I learnt by heart as a student:

> If only there were stillness, full, complete.
> If all the random and approximate
> were muted, with neighbours' laughter, for your sake,
> and if the clamour that my senses make
> did not confound the vigil I would keep –
>
> Then in a thousandfold thought I could think
> you out, even to your utmost brink,
> and (while a smile endures) possess you, giving
> you away, as though I were but giving thanks,
> to all the living.

Other poems and prose have influenced me as they would many medical students if the latter were allowed to escape from the merely technical education they receive in the UK that leaves too many of our doctors largely ignorant of literature. I am not suggesting that a doctor open to and pleasured by literary texts is likely to be a better doctor than the most blatant philistine with a stethoscope. The latter, gradually, will doubtless become wiser with life experience; the former, though, does have an initial start in being awakened to his or her future patients' life stories. 'What is there good in us,' said Goethe, 'if it is not the power and the inclination to appropriate to ourselves the resources of the outward world, and to make them subservient to our highest ends.'[8]

The prose of Rilke, as well as his poems, intrigued me when I was a medical student. Denise Levertov, now a celebrated American poet, but who, when young, was a nurse in wartime London, confesses in her autobiographical book *Light Up the Cave*[9] that her first lesson from Rilke was to '*experience* what you live'.

Most of us hardly question what influences us and do not observe our barely fathomable metamorphosis steadily. We merely mark how our life situation may be changed or how our interests have developed; how our children have grown up, how others we love have become older or died. All authors, though, have visible, concrete evidence of their own internal changes: they can turn to their artefacts – in my case to my plays and novels as well as to my poems – and see how these give witness to altering attitudes, preoccupations, arguments with oneself. They recall debts to other writers; transient experiences, some medical, some not; successes and failures; occasions and relationships. Poems on the page lie there and do not lie: their own progenitor can scrutinise them as if they were spiritual X-rays.

And here's the curious thing: after decades of writing poems, every poet, I believe, if he takes his own work seriously, as he should, comes under the influence of it. When a poet begins to write a poem there is no reader; but as he concludes his poem he himself becomes the first reader. Sometimes the last! He receives his own words. Thereafter, in subtle ways, his poems, even as they may recede for others, remain for him strangely active. They help to determine not only how he will continue to write but how he will live. Some may argue that poetry is a useless thing, an activity that can rival the counting of the cats of Zanzibar. But whatever else poems do, or do not do, at the very least they profoundly alter the man or woman who wrote them.

References

1. K. Smith and M. Sweeney, eds., *Beyond Bedlam* (London: Anvil Press, 1997).
2. Anon., 'Drugs or placebo', *The Lancet* ii (1972), pp. 122–123.
3. W. H. Auden, 'In Memory of W. B. Yeats', *Collected Shorter Poems* (London: Faber and Faber, 1950), p. 65.
4. W. C. Williams, 'The Use of Force', *The Doctor Stories* (London: Faber and Faber, 1987), pp. 56–60.
5. I. Young, *The Private Life of Islam* (London: Pimlico, 1991).

6. H. Söderberg, trans. A. Britten, *Doctor Glas* (Boston: Little Brown, 1963).
7. R. M. Rilke, trans. B. Deutsch, *Poems from the Book of Hours* (London: Vision Press, 1948).
8. J. P. Eckermann, trans. J. Oxenford, *Conversations with Goethe* (London, Everyman's Library, 1970).
9. D. Levertov, *Light Up the Cave* (New York: New Directions, 1981), p. 284.

The Experiment

1

We are told by Plutarch that Julius Caesar surpassed all other commanders for in his campaigns in Gaul, over a period of a decade, he stormed 800 cities and subdued 300 nations. He slaughtered 1,000,000 men and took another 1,000,000 prisoners. We may be taken aback by the sheer size of these figures but we feel very little. All that suffering, for which, of course, we were in no way responsible, occurred such a long time ago. We can neither respond deeply to the plight of Caesar's victims nor enthusiastically admire Caesar's victories. History has become a storybook, albeit bloody, but all that blood has rusted, is too old, ancient. Indeed the crucible of centuries has transformed it into mere theatrical red paint: great distance, the long perspective, the blurring of faraway scenes, makes even the worst savagery appear ritualistic, almost decorous.

We feel otherwise about the wars and victims of our own century. Some men become hoarse shouting about them. In *The Times* today, I read that Senator George McGovern has made a speech in Beverly Hills, California. Despite the location, despite the proximity of the synthetic dream factories of Hollywood, he most earnestly shouted, 'Except for Adolf Hitler's extermination of the Jewish people the American bombardment of defenceless peasants in Indo-China is the most barbaric act of modern times.' In 1947, Jung had already maintained, echoing others, that 'in Germany, a highly cultured land, the horrors exceeded by far anything the world has ever known.'

Preface to Abse's play *The Dogs of Pavlov* (Vallentine Mitchell, 1973)

But, of course, there is no competition: the man-made catastrophes of our times have only different names. Wherever modern man has been a wolf to modern man, whatever the roll call, call it Buchenwald or Vietnam, whatever the name of the horror, there we are involved and there we must respond.

Even the First World War has not yet become an opera or a prettified musical like, say, *Fiddler on the Roof*. We could not accept quite such a vulgarisation or trivialisiation of that piece of our history yet. *Oh, What a Lovely War* at least owns a sardonic bite and is indeed a moral piece of theatre. After all, our fathers or grandfathers kept their heavy rainbowed medals in the bottom drawer of the bureau. We remember too the anecdotes they told us and the songs they hummed or whistled – the same songs that assault us so poignantly when we hear them today, played by some blind or crippled accordionist amongst the muffling traffic of a busy metropolis: 'Roses of Picardy', 'It's a Long Way to Tipperary', 'Smile, Smile, Smile'. We are moved by the silly heroism recounted in such First World War books as Robert Graves's *Goodbye to All That*, or Edmund Blunden's *Undertones of War*; and the poems of Siegfried Sassoon, Wilfred Owen and Isaac Rosenberg continue to engage us in a meaningful, contemporary way. In short, the suffering of the First World War is still real to us – is not merely an epic tale told in a dark shadowy hall to the accompaniment of a melancholy harp. The pain and the suffering, though not our own but our fathers', or our fathers' fathers', was an expensive matter. So we hold on to it like a possession and we want no one to change it, to tarnish it.

If the public calamities of our fathers' time are dear enough to us, our own seem barely supportable. We hardly think about them but they are always with us. We are all involved, every one of us, however far removed from those scenes of bleak, pale crimes. We are, metaphorically speaking, survivors because of them. We have lived through Auschwitz and Belsen, Hiroshima and Nagasaki and we did not know the enormity of the offence. We were not there. But with the passing of the years these catastrophes do not recede into history, do not become a tale in a storybook. On the contrary, something odd happens, the reverse happens, they come nearer and nearer, they become like scenes in a dream advancing towards us, on top of us, big, huge.

For with the passing of the years we hear more and learn more significant details. The actual survivors tell their terrible stories of gold from teeth and lampshades from human skin and so gradually the abstract geography of hell becomes concrete: we see the belching smoke of the chimneys, we hear the hiss of the gas and the dying cries of the murdered. We may not be able to hold steady, in the front of our minds, the enormity of the offence for very long, the picture slips away in the silence between two heartbeats; we cannot continually retain in our minds, as we perceive the natural beauty of the earth, or as we are touched by the genuine tenderness of lovers and friends, the psychotic savagery of our twentieth-century life. We have to shrug our shoulders finally or make a grim joke like Cioran – 'What would be left of our tragedies if a literate insect were to present us his?'

No, we cannot look too long at the searchlights of Auschwitz or at the coloured, intense flash of light over Hiroshima. We repress the horror. It becomes a numb disaster. In order to continue living as happily as possible, the more capacity we have for empathy the more we need to make it numb. It is not wrong to do that, indeed we have no choice. All the same we do have a continual headache that we rarely discern.

So who can tell what psychic devastation has really taken place within us, the survivors, especially for those of us who were brought up in an optimistic tradition, heirs of the nineteenth century, who believed in the inevitability of human progress, and who thought that the soul of man was born pure? Norman Mailer has said, 'Probably, we shall never be able to determine the psychic havoc of the concentration camps and the atom bomb upon the unconscious mind of almost everyone alive in those years.' And he goes on to ask, as others before him have done, remembering the millions killed in the concentration camps, 'Who can ignore the more hideous questions about his own nature?' For Mailer has apprehended, as others have also done, that it was not the German people alone who were capable of such stupendous crimes.

Social psychologists may point out that the 'typical' German may be self-important, insecure, over-respectful to authority, over-docile to superiors, and a little tyrant to his inferiors in the social scale, but we are not convinced that their faults are peculiar to them alone. The Germans may have that unattractive gift for planning meticulously, they may have a need for obsessional organisation – and this, analytically speaking, does point down to suppressed powerful forces within of anarchy and division. Because of such suppressed forces, needing order, they may well have responded with a particular facility to Hitler's confident promise of A New Order. It is true that when the horns of the hunters were blowing in the dark the German nation of eighty millions, with terrible banners unfurled, followed their raving, hysterical Führer with 'a sleep-walker's confidence.' But despite their so-called national characteristics, their particular institutions, their history, despite Hitler and the Nazis, whose jackboots left footsteps trailing away from Auschwitz and Buchenwald, despite all this, of course they are not a special people with different chromosomes any more than the Jews, or others are, whom they butchered.

To read Hannah Arendt's book on the trial of Adolf Eichmann is a depressing experience if only because we learn that, with a few important exceptions, nation after nation turned on its scapegoats with a mercilessness and brutality that sometimes shocked in its openness even the German SS. The willingness of apparently ordinary people to obey evil commands is not a specifically German phenomenon but the record of Germany remains, and it is a shameful one. Some will forgive and most will feel no longer vengeful, if only because, with Heine, they may say, 'Mine is a most peaceful disposition. My wishes are: a humble cottage with a thatched roof, but a good bed, good food, the freshest milk and butter, flowers before my window, and a few fine trees before my door; and if God wants to make my happiness complete, he will grant me the joy of seeing some six or seven of my enemies hanging from those trees. Before their death I shall, moved in my heart, forgive them all the wrong they did me in their lifetime. One must, it is true, forgive one's enemies – but not before they have been hanged.'

2

We have no inborn tendency, Germans and non-Germans alike, to obey orders. On the contrary, we are born saying 'no' to civilization's imperatives. But from babyhood on, we are conditioned to say 'yes', to obey. We are trained by punishment and reward, by threat and promise.

When we were small our parents proscribed our instinctual actions because they wished us not to be antisocial or because they were worried lest we damaged ourselves. If we obeyed them no harm would befall us; we would be rewarded; our parents would smile upon us and love us. If, however, we rebelled, atrocious things might happen to us physically and we would lose the love of those two people we most needed. There was no actual choice of course. We, the little barbarians, had to become civilised or else.

Or else we would be unloved, castrated, killed. 'If you touch that,' the six-foot high voice said, 'you will be electrocuted. Come away, this minute. I'll beat you. I will not love you any more. Come away I tell you or you will be killed.' Or more simply, bluntly, to the point, 'Stop that. It will come off!' That six-foot high voice knew best. It was omnipotent and respectable. It was law and order. It was the voice of spoilsport bearded Moses coming down the mountain, barefooted, with the Ten Commandments slipping from his hand, shouting 'don't' as we danced so happily, with such clear vivacity and happiness around the golden calf.

From the beginning, then, disobedience is associated in our minds with fearful consequences, even death. No wonder most people hardly operate their consciences as they react to a command – they do not think of its moral coloration. The conflict is not there, necessarily. Besides, the effect of an imperative may be too remote, too abstract. So we press down a lever or turn up a switch, obey this order or that order in My Lai or in Ulster. Consciences even where they are in operation are remarkably soluble. Worse, too often evil commands allow us to satisfy certain instinctual aggressive needs. Can we be sure that even without fear of the punitive consequences of disobedience there would have been neither the searchlights of Auschwitz nor the intense light over

Hiroshima? Could we say simplistically with Alex Comfort, 'For the lack of a joiner's obedience the crucifixion will not now take place'?

Some years ago a play of mine, *In the Cage*, was produced at the Questors Theatre, Ealing. In it, I had peripherally touched on this question of obedience to an evil command. More recently I had wanted to take up that theme again, in dramatic terms again, but in a different way, and more centrally. So when the Questors Theatre offered to commission another play from me for their New Plays Festival, I accepted and told them how I would like to set *The Dogs of Pavlov* in a psychological laboratory.

For I had, not long before, read about a most remarkable experiment that had taken place at Yale University. This experiment had been devised by a Professor Stanley Milgram who was interested scientifically in 'the compulsion to do evil' and how men would obey commands that were in strong conflict with their conscience.

In my view, it is dubious whether his simple but brilliant and terrible experiment should have been carried out. I would like to take up this point later. For the moment, I merely wish to comment on how the strategy of his experiment led to fascinating and disturbing results – results which may instruct us and warn even the most sanguine of us about our natures. The conclusions we must draw from the experiment underline for us again the ironic, indeed holy, practice of James Joyce taking for his slogan Satan's '*Non Serviam*' ('I will not obey').

3

Supposing you, the reader, had agreed to take part in Professor Milgram's experiment. You had seen an advertisement in a New Haven newspaper. It seemed volunteers were required to participate in a study of memory and learning at Yale University. So you had volunteered – glad to be of use, to be used in the service of a scientific inquiry; besides, it would probably be interesting and, moreover, they even offered to pay each volunteer a small sum of money which would amply cover expenses. Others had already responded to that advertisement – high-school teachers, engineers, salesmen, clerks, labourers. All these people were between twenty and fifty years of age.

So one evening you had arrived at the laboratory in Yale and, along with another volunteer, a forty-seven-year-old accountant, you had been introduced to a younger man in a technician's grey coat. He evidently was a scientist. Imposingly he explained to you both, 'We know very little about the effect of punishment on learning. No truly scientific studies have been made of it in human beings. For instance, we don't know how *much* punishment is best for learning. We don't know how much difference it makes as to who is giving the punishment – whether an adult learns best from a younger or older person than himself – many things of that sort.'

The accountant nodded his head and you too, no doubt, listened attentively as the youngish scientist in the grey coat sternly continued, 'So in this study we are bringing together a number of adults of different occupations and ages. We're asking some of them to be teachers, some to be learners. We want to find out what effect *punishment* will have on learning.'

Perhaps, at this juncture, you had vaguely thought that, on balance, you would have preferred to be the teacher, the one who doled out the punishment, rather than the learner who received it. However, you made no awkward objections, did not say, 'I want to be one rather than the other.' After all, you had freely volunteered and everybody had been so courteous and you wanted to do your best to help them in this worthwhile experiment that was being carried out at such a *fine*, such a reputable university.

The scientist pushed forward a hat in which there were two slips of paper. It seemed like a child's game, a lottery. You pulled out one slip of paper; the other volunteer, the accountant, extracted the other. You opened your slip; he opened his. You read the word on it, 'TEACHER', smiled, then both of you were taken to an adjacent room. There, the accountant was strapped into an electric chair while you were being placed in front of an impressive shock generator which had a formidable row of lever-switches.

The accountant was given 'a learning talk'. He had to remember a series of paired words. When one word was spoken, the paired word had to be supplied by the accountant in the electric chair. If he made a mistake you were to give him an electric shock by pulling down one of the levers. *With each successive mistake you were to give him a stronger shock.*

You looked down at the thirty levers of the shock generator – these levers were set in a horizontal line and each of them was clearly labelled fifteen volts, thirty volts, forty-five volts and so on, going up in fifteen-volt increments to the extreme right-hand side of you where the last lever was labelled four hundred and fifty volts. You also noticed that these levers were arranged so that, in addition to the voltage label underneath, different groups were marked SLIGHT SHOCK, MODERATE SHOCK, STRONG SHOCK, VERY STRONG SHOCK, INTENSE SHOCK, EXTREME INTENSITY SHOCK, DANGER: SEVERE SHOCK. And, finally, the two levers on the extreme right-hand side had been designated, minatorily, with the symbols XXX.

'Before we start, we'll have a run through,' said the scientist in the grey coat. 'And also perhaps the teacher had better have a shock to feel the kind of punishment he is doling out.' So you were given a forty-five-volt shock when the Yale scientist pulled down the third lever of the generator. It was hardly of consequence, still it no doubt reinforced your feeling that you were lucky to have pulled out the slip of paper on which was written the word *teacher* rather than *learner*.

The accountant had been firmly strapped into the electric chair and he was having electrode paste applied – 'to avoid blisters and burns,' the scientist said. It made you feel apprehensive though you noted that your accountant colleague seemed relatively calm. Perhaps you were somewhat reassured when the scientist remarked, 'Although the shocks can be extremely painful they cause no permanent tissue damage.'

Because the experimenter apparently wanted to study the effect of punishment on memory you were going to be commanded to pull down successive levers which would cause the man in the electric chair an increasing amount of pain every time he made a mistake. How far along those levers do you think you would have gone? Each time you pulled down the lever a pilot light of bright red came on, an electric buzzing could be heard, an electric blue light labelled 'voltage energizer' flashed, the dial on the voltage meter swung to the right and various relay clicks sounded, and all the time the accountant in the chair objected more and more.

'Whether the learner likes it or not,' the scientist said sternly, 'you must go on until he has learned all the word pairs correctly. So please go on.'

At seventy-five volts the accountant had grunted, at one hundred and twenty volts he had complained verbally, at one hundred and fifty volts he demanded to be released from that chair, indeed from the experiment.

But the scientist had commanded you emotionlessly to continue nevertheless, and had added, 'The experiment requires that you continue,' and later, 'It is absolutely essential that you continue.'

You pulled down the levers, the shocks escalated, the protests of the accountant became louder, increasingly strident, more urgent, even desperate. He was pleading, 'Get me out of here! I won't be in the experiment anymore! I refuse to go on,' until at two hundred and eighty-five volts he had screamed in agony.

Would you have stopped then? You are absolutely sure you would have stopped then, if not before, though the Yale scientist was again calmly ordering you to continue, urging you with the positive commands of a hypnotist, 'You have no other choice. You *must* go on.'

I suspect that you the reader, even if you had agreed to volunteer for such an experiment in the first place, believe that you would never have cooperated to any great extent with the experimenter, would never have really hurt the accountant, that mild stranger strapped in the electric chair. You are sure, I know you are sure. But what about your next-door neighbour? Supposing you were in that electric chair, are you certain that your next-door neighbour would not have responded to those clear commands? Would he have said, '*Non Serviam*'?

The results of the experiments carried out at Yale are hardly reassuring. Let Professor Milgram speak for himself. 'The initial reaction a reader might have to the experiment is: why would anyone in his right mind even bother to administer the first shocks at all? Why would he not simply get up and walk out of the laboratory? But the fact is, no one ever does. Since the subject has come to the laboratory to aid the experimenter he is quite willing to start off with the procedure. There is nothing very extraordinary in this, particularly since the person who is to receive the shocks seems initially cooperative, if somewhat apprehensive. What is surprising is how far ordinary individuals will go in complying with the experimenter's instructions. Indeed, the results of the experiment were both surprising and dismaying. Despite the fact that many subjects experience stress, despite the fact that many protest to the experimenter, a substantial proportion continue to the last shock.'

The reader may be startled that so many submitted to the commands of the Yale scientist in a technician's grey coat and that when the experiment was repeated at other places, at other American universities, the results were basically the same. It may be equally incredible to the reader that scientists at Yale, and elsewhere, could allow volunteers to be so grossly shocked, to endure such dangerous levels of electric current. Well, they didn't. You the reader were had, hoaxed, fooled. That electric chair was never really wired up. Right from the beginning you were taken in. That accountant was collaborating with the Yale scientists. He was in on the secret. He was an actor. They were not a bit interested in the relationship of learning and punishment. That was bullshit, a cover story. They were intent on devising a laboratory situation where *you* had increasing conflict as you were commanded to electric-shock (or so you thought) a fellow human being. You, not that accountant-actor, were the victim. They wanted to know how much, to what degree, you would submit to a respectable, apparently reasonable authority – despite the pain and agony of your 'victim' and your slowly awakening conscience. They discovered that you often expressed disapproval – you even denounced, sometimes, the experiment as absurd, stupid. Yet, frequently, you obeyed even to the last lever for you could not be defiant enough to disengage.

Consider again what happened. The so-called accountant and you both chose a slip of paper from a hat. You did not know both pieces of paper had written on them 'TEACHER'. You were cheated. You were taken to a shock generator – but despite its elaborate dials and general convincing construction, it was a fraud. Only when the third lever was pulled could it generate a shock, a small shock, a forty-five-volt shock. You were the one who was shocked, you remember. It was you who were cheated. The accountant in the chair had been smeared with a grease to stop burns, the man in the grey coat had said. That too was a lie, part of the pretence. You were cheated. Those lines the accountant spoke were part of a prepared script. Those groans, those screams, were all counterfeit. You were cheated. Like any man conned, in my view, you have a right to feel angry. Yet, you may say – when your anger settles to leave a nasty little scar, a small infarct in the soul – thank heavens anyway that accountant was only an actor, that nobody really did get hurt. Or did they?

4

To have a play on, in front of strange juries in rows of plush chairs, is a time of self immolation, even martyrdom. Each time I have watched, from some inconspicuous seat in the back row of a theatre, a first performance of one of my own plays, I have, when it is a comedy, laughed more than anybody else in the auditorium; when a tragedy I have cried more than anybody else; and, either way, when the curtain has come down and the house lights have gone up, I have been more exhausted than anybody else. I have always staggered backstage feeling shot at, anaemic as a St Sebastian. Then, arrows barely removed, I have gone through the usual theatrical routine of brushing my lips against the cheek of the leading actress, 'Thank you . . . sweetie . . . wonderful,' shaking hands with the leading actor, 'Thank you, terrific . . .' and then the others, 'Thank you, superb, thank you, marvellous, you certainly gave me a plus, thank you, ta, I told you they'd laugh at that, thank you all,' to end up hugging the bastard director who actually had the impertinence to cut some of the best lines. 'Well you really pulled it off, Ted, Bill, Peter, Ken, Ronnie, thanks, thanks.' At the same time the few compliments returned are accepted gratefully like so many pints of pure blood.

The New Plays Festival at the Questors Theatre takes place annually. Each night, after each performance, there is a discussion about the play. The chairman who leads the discussion is someone well thought of in the theatre, someone like E. Martin Browne or Martin Esslin. The author is expected to attend these discussions and sometimes they can prove to be an ordeal in themselves – especially if the play has not had good notices; for even theatrically informed audiences on such occasions tend to form group attitudes. They like or do not like; they attack or praise. A pack formation does seem to occur and whether they bite or lick depends not only on what went on inside the theatre itself but what has happened outside – the reviews, the word-of-mouth, the attitude of the chairman to his own personal experience of the play, and so on.

Oscar Wilde once remarked that he knew his play was a success – but the question was, would the audience be one? The audience at the Questors Theatre for *The Dogs of Pavlov*, though it included some friends and relations, passed with distinction. Soon after the opening night, the 'FULL UP' signs appeared and I found all kinds of people began telephoning me at my home to see if I could wangle them seats. This small 'success' was helped by the fact that a couple of respected critics on national newspapers had trekked out to Ealing and had been kind to the play. Also BBC2 had filmed a scene from it and a tangential discussion had followed afterwards. I mention all this mainly, of course, in order to boast – but also to indicate reasons why the nightly discussions after the performance of *The Dogs of Pavlov* were not too much of an ordeal – not as they had been, for instance, for an earlier play of mine that had been performed at the Questors.

The after-performance discussions would focus initially on the play itself, on the characters in the play, their interrelationships, on dramatic devices in the play, on such matters as tension and pace and density, on other technical matters such as the film sequences and lighting and so on. But, after a while, the themes touched on in *The Dogs of Pavlov* were grittily engaged and attitudes about power and manipulation, racial prejudice and victimisation, and even scientific experimentation itself were ventilated. I discovered more things in my play than I had thought I had put in.

Yet people on the whole preferred to discuss things other than the gut-aching historical outcome of man's willingness to submit to evil orders. 'Human kind cannot bear very much reality.' Certainly, there were those who amazingly saw only a very indirect relationship of the laboratory experiment (as played out on the stage) to what had happened so recently in Europe. I remember one articulate member of the audience in particular, who brilliantly enlarged on one man's need to dominate others and who did not see the relevance of that to anti-Semitism or colour prejudice. He quoted amusingly Dr Jean de Rougemont: 'If my neighbour is stronger than I, I fear him; if he is weaker, I despise him; if we are equal, I resort to subterfuge'; he pointed out (correctly) how I had been influenced by W. H. Auden's essay on Iago, 'The Joker in the Pack'; he touched on other academic points with great clarity and intelligence – yet he seemed to think the Nazi holocaust an irrelevance to the play that he had just seen performed. He was not alone in this.

I have said at the beginning that the worst savagery of our own time has not yet become blurred to a more ritualistic pattern as centuries old violence has done. 'We are all involved,' I argued, 'every one of us, however far removed from those scenes of bleak, pale crimes. We are, metaphorically, survivors because of them.' I exaggerated. There are many who know little about Auschwitz or feel utterly estranged from that 'foreign' happening. We cannot feel ourselves to be survivors unless we feel some empathy for the victims of these pale crimes, unless we have, too, some sense of history. 'According to the wishes of the Reichsführer SS, Auschwitz became the greatest known extermination factor of all time,' wrote Rudolf Höss, the Auschwitz commandant. 'When in the summer of 1941 he gave me personal orders to prepare a mass extermination site in Auschwitz and to carry out this extermination, I could not in the slightest degree imagine its extent and consequences. . . I didn't waste time thinking it over then – I had received the order – and had to carry it out. Whether the mass extermination of the Jews was necessary or not, I could not allow myself to judge. As the Führer himself had ordered the "Final Solution of the Jewish problem" there was nothing for an old Nazi to think about.'

Question: Who was Rudolf Höss? Answer: Not a monster but a man like you and me. That is the kind of question and answer that triggered off Professor Milgram's experiment at Yale. It is the question that has nagged many contemporary writers – some Jews, others not – into writing novels, film scripts, poems and, very occasionally, plays. It was the same question and answer that is, as far as I am concerned, the central theme of *The Dogs of Pavlov*.

If, sometimes, the after-performance debates about this central theme seemed hesitant, the sub-topic, the rights and wrongs of using humans as guinea-pigs for a scientific inquiry, generated much confident dialogue and passion. This was particularly true the night Michael Billington of *The Times* chaired the discussion for he seemed to think that human guinea-pig experimentation was the dominant proposition of *The Dogs of Pavlov*.

It is a subject, in any case, that interests many people. It is relevant to them not so much because they recall how doctors in Nazi Germany experimented vilely on concentration camp victims but rather because of publicity, more recent, about human guinea-pig experimentation at major teaching hospitals. There have been disquieting headlines in the newspapers and feature programmes on television. People are quite properly shocked and feel angry when they hear of doctors transgressing the spirit of the Hippocratic oath. Certainly, at the Questors Theatre, there were those who felt strongly about even such experiments as those carried out at Yale. 'Not ethical,' one man at the back thundered.

I do not know whether actual criteria exist for judging whether any particular human guinea-pig experiment is deemed to be ethical or not. I am not a lawyer nor a philosopher but surely commonsense dictates that these experiments should be judged to be ethical or not according to (a) the conscious motives of the experimenter; (b) the free consent of the subject experimented on; and (c) the harmlessness or likely harmfulness, physical and mental, that results from the experiment on the subject.

(a) *The conscious motives of the experimenter.* The scientist will usually maintain that his quest is to seek out new knowledge that can be used in the service of humankind. Or as Francis Bacon (who should be first in the pantheon of social psychologists) wrote once, 'The end of our foundation is the knowledge of causes and secret workings of things . . . to the effecting of all things possible.' Supposing though, instead, the experiment has been primarily devised for personal gain or publicity or for the personal advancement of the experimenter (to secure, say, promotion, through publication of a scientific paper) would we not judge the whole experiment rather more harshly?

(b) *The free consent of the subject experimented on.* Obviously to choose *freely* to participate in an experiment the subject must be old enough, intelligent enough and sane enough to make that choice after the facts of the experiment have been explained to him truthfully. He must not, therefore, be hoaxed.

(c) *The harmfulness or harmlessness of the experiment on the subject.* The interests of the patient experimented on cannot be casually ignored. He must not be used as a counter. It is true that the outcome of an experiment is not always foreseeable but this does not mean that, should harm result, the experimenter can disclaim responsibility.

Let us turn for a moment to an undisputed case of unethical human guinea-pig experimentation that took place in New York in 1965. On that occasion, highly qualified medical specialists, experts in cancer and viruses, had injected live cancer cells into debilitated patients without their knowledge. When live cancer cells are injected into a healthy human being the body rejects these cells as they do other foreign transplants. The medical researcher wanted to ascertain whether a debilitated human body, debilitated by chronic disease other than cancer, would also be able to reject the foreign cancer cells.

Laudably, the research doctors were trying to find a means of immunising patients against cancer. But the patients injected with live cancer cells would not have agreed to such a measure – so they were lied to. They were told that the injections were simply a part of the treatment they needed.

On hearing of this experiment, three other doctors on the staff of the same New York hospital resigned in protest. An investigation followed. The research doctors were found guilty of unethical conduct and the investigatory committee recommended that their medical licences be suspended. We are not surprised by such a judgement because though (a) the conscious motives of the experimenters were impeccable, (b) the patients did not give their free consent to the experiment and (c) there was a distinct possibility that the outcome of the experiment would be harmful to them.

To be sure, the experiments that are taking place in psychological laboratories all over the world are not unethical like that New York medical experiment cited above. Yet it seems right, and in the public interest, that the spotlight be shone from time to time not only on experiments going on in the sick wards of hospitals but also on those in psychological laboratories so that their usefulness and ethical content can at least be questioned. Diana Baumrind, a research psychologist at the University of California who has written aggressively about the Yale experiment in the *American Psychologist*, has also commented, 'It has become commonplace in sociopsychological laboratory studies to manipulate, embarrass and discomfort subjects.' Isn't it time then that the general public knew about these studies?

When we spotlight the experiment that took place at Yale I suspect many will be grossly offended by the hoax element necessary for the experiment to take place in the first instance. They may feel that in order to demonstrate that subjects may behave like so many Eichmanns the experimenter had to act the part, to some extent, of a Himmler. Others may even believe that the documents of history can teach us the consequences of destructive obedience better than any laboratory experiment, however cleverly conceived.

Of course, Professor Stanley Milgram, in setting up his experiment, was actuated by the highest of motives. He had hopes that his work would lead to human betterment. Besides, as he has put it, 'enlightenment is more dignified than ignorance,' and 'new knowledge is pregnant with humane consequences'.

Nevertheless, the volunteers who came to the Yale laboratory were placed under formidable stress and were divested of their human dignity. As the scientists stared through their one-way mirrors at the guinea pigs responding to the commands of the man in the technician's grey coat, they saw highly charged, dramatic conflict occur. I quote directly from Milgram's paper, 'Behavioral Study of Obedience': 'Many subjects showed signs of nervousness in the experimental situation and especially upon administering the more powerful shocks. In a large number of cases the degree of tension reached extremes that are rarely seen in sociopsychological laboratory studies. Subjects were observed to sweat, tremble, stutter, bite their lips, groan and dig their fingernails into their flesh. These were characteristic rather than exceptional responses to the experiment. One sign of tension was the regular recurrence of nervous laughing fits. . . . The laughter seemed entirely out of place, even bizarre. Full blown uncontrollable seizures were observed in 3 subjects. On one occasion, we observed a seizure so violently convulsive that it was necessary to call a halt to the experiment.'

Here is a further description of another subject by an observer other than Professor Milgram: 'I observed a mature and critically poised businessman enter the laboratory smiling and confident. Within twenty minutes he was reduced to a twitching stuttering wreck who was rapidly approaching a point of nervous collapse. He constantly pulled on his ear lobe, and twisted his hands. At one point, he pushed his fist into his forehead and muttered, "Oh God, let's stop it." And yet he continued to respond to every word of the experimenter, and obeyed to the end.'

Prior to the laboratory experience neither Professor Milgram nor his colleague could envisage that their experiment would induce such harrowing and startling effects on their volunteer subjects. When they could foresee what might happen they were confronted with the choice of continuing their experiment or stopping it. They decided to continue. Professor Milgram felt there was no evidence of durable injurious effects on the subjects. 'In my judgment,' he has written, 'at no point were subjects exposed to danger and at no point did they run the risk of injurious effects resulting from participation. If it had been otherwise, the experiment would have been terminated at once.'

Indeed Stanley Milgram believed that some of his volunteers had been enriched by the experience. By musing on their ugly performances in that Yale laboratory they might have received valuable and startling insights into their own personalities. To be sure, if Socrates' absolutist command of 'Know thyself' is invariably a wise one who can quarrel with Professor Milgram's conclusion? Still, isn't it also plausible that for some people, partial self knowledge, anyway, could be the knowledge forbidden to Adam and so its revelation could lead to the re-enactment of the Fall, and to a personal, living damnation? Who can be certain? Montaigne once inscribed on his mantelpiece, 'Que sçaise-je?' ('What do I know?')

Statements by the human guinea-pig subjects do suggest that a number of them subjectively felt they had benefited from the experiment; others seemed pleased that they had helped along a piece of scientific research. It should be mentioned, too, that after each experimental session the volunteer-subject was informed that the electric shock treatment had been a hoax and, apparently, friendly reconciliations then took place between the subject and the accountant-actor who had once sat in the unwired chair. 'The experiment was explained to the defiant subjects,' Milgram has written, 'in a way that supported their decision to disobey the experimenter. Obedient subjects were assured of the fact that their behavior was entirely normal and that their feelings of conflict or tension were shared by other participants.'

It is evident that post-experimentally Professor Milgram was most concerned for the welfare of his human guinea-pigs. Hence those reconciliations, those lengthy talks about the experiment after each session and so on. He even sent the volunteers a follow-up questionnaire about their participation in the experiment so that they could express their thoughts and feelings about how they behaved. 92 per cent returned the questionnaire. Of these, 84 per cent maintained they were pleased to have participated; 15 per cent were neutral; and 1.3 per cent 'indicated negative feelings'. Professor Milgram found reassurance in the answers to that questionnaire. 'The replies to the questionnaire confirmed my impression that participants felt positively towards the experiment,' he wrote replying to Diana Baumrind's earlier attack on the Yale study in the *American Psychologist*.

Professor Baumrind had written: 'From the subject's point of view procedures which involve loss of dignity, self-esteem and trust in rational authority are probably most harmful in the long run and require the most thoughtfully planned reparations, if engaged in at all. . . I would not like to see experiments such as Milgram's proceed unless the subjects were fully informed of the dangers of serious after effects and his corrections were clearly shown to be effective in restoring their state of wellbeing.' I would go further than Professor Baumrind because I for one, even if I was certain that post-experimental reparations were 100 per cent effective in 100 per cent of the subjects, would still feel most uneasy about the Yale experiments – as I would feel about any experiments based on a hoax, that causes men to lose their dignity, to twitch, to suffer seizures, to reach the point of almost nervous collapse. How can such experiments be happily sanctioned by an informed public though carefully conducted, though supervised by men of impeccable morals, though performed for the most idealistic of reasons? Certainly such experiments would not have been sanctioned by those disinterested people who were articulate in the after-performance discussions of *The Dogs of Pavlov* at the Questors Theatre.

6

At the last after-performance discussion of *The Dogs of Pavlov*, one lady, concerned about the morality of human guinea-pig experiments, gently asked why I was not absolutely accurate about the details of those experiments as outlined in my play. 'For instance,' she asked, 'why did you make the minor characters of Dr Daly and Dr Olwen Jones research doctors instead of research psychologists?' I told her that I was marginally happier writing about doctors – since I was one myself – than about psychologists but that, in any case, I was interested in writing a fictional piece of theatre with fictional characters. Indeed, I was more interested in how these fictional characters related to each other in human terms rather than in any abstract idea – even if that idea was about the destructive consequences of obedience. For a play is not an essay nor, for that matter, a dramatised moral tract.

Prior to writing *The Dogs of Pavlov* the only thing I had read on the Yale experiment was an interesting essay by a Stanley Milgram called 'The Compulsion to Do Evil' in the journal *Patterns of Prejudice*. This essay I found suggestive but *The Dogs of Pavlov* is, of course, a work of imagination as is the experiment outlined in it. But when asked to write this introduction I read for the first time

Professor Milgram's original papers, 'Behavioral Study of Obedience' (*Journal of Abnormal and Social Psychology*) and 'Some Conditions of Obedience and Disobedience to Authority' (*Human Relations*) and in the process of discovering additional details about the Yale experiment and its variations I found the results even more profoundly disturbing.

Professor Milgram speaks of a painful alteration in his own thinking as a consequence of his Yale laboratory studies. Far too frequently, he witnessed good people 'knuckle under to the demands of authority' and these same people perform actions that were utterly callous. 'What is the limit of such obedience?' he asks. 'At many points we attempted to establish a boundary. Cries from the victim were inserted: not good enough. The victim claimed heart trouble: subjects still shocked him on command.'

Nobody can feel sanguine about the statistics of the Yale experiments. These statistics, like the recent documents of history, are red lights warning us how a coercive government today could command its subjects to perform evil acts, and these subjects would not feel themselves to be morally guilty in obeying such commands. Rather they would regard themselves as innocent agents of a legitimate authority. In Milgram's post-experimental interviews, when asked why they continued to shock the accountant in the chair 'all along the board' they characteristically replied, 'I wouldn't have done it by myself. I was just doing what I was told.' We have heard that story before – not only at Nuremberg – and, alas, we shall hear it again. For as Professor Milgram says, 'It would be wrong to think of it as a thin alibi concocted for the occasion. Rather, it is a fundamental mode of thinking for a great many people once they are locked into a subordinate position of responsibility.'

On the other hand, we ought to remind ourselves, for it is the same part of the truth, that over one-third of the participants did not fall into the category of 'obedient' subjects. There were those who were utterly defiant. There were those, also, who managed to 'cheat' the experimenter in a humane way: thus they assured the experimenter (not wishing to offend him) that they were progressively raising the voltage shock level whereas, in fact, they surreptitiously continued to pull the first lever of the generator giving the accountant, they thought, only the mildest of shocks! Even those who did pull down all the levers – at least many of them – did exhibit high levels of conflict, as has already been indicated. This demonstrates, at least, that their consciences were being strenuously exercised. Hardly true solace, you may think, for any real victim!

Perhaps for small solace one should go back to the actual documents of history – to Berlin, for example, in 1942, to the Gestapo headquarters at Prinz-Albrechtstrasse. There a Gestapo official said to Dr Baeck who was President of the Representative Council of German Jews, 'Surely not even you can deny that the whole German nation is behind the Führer's measures regarding the Jews?' Dr Baeck replied, 'I wouldn't like to be dogmatic about that. I would, though, like to say one thing. When I go home from here . . . with my yellow star, nothing bad will happen to me. . . . On the other hand, here and there someone will try and push his way over to me, a stranger; he will look around nervously and press my hand. He might even push an apple into my hand, a bar of chocolate, or a cigarette. Apart from that, nothing will happen to me. I don't know whether the Führer, in my place, would have the same experience!'

There is the parable of the three wise men who walked past a dead dog. The first uttered, 'What a terrible sight!'; the second, 'What a terrible smell!'; but the third, who was the wisest of all, remarked, 'What beautiful white teeth has that dead dog!' We must find our consolations where we can.

2

Ninian Park Blues

In the silence of the house, upstairs in my bedroom, long past the fidgety tick of midnight, I lie horizontal under the sheets, my head on the pillow. The curtains are drawn. My wife, inert, asleep beside me. I stare at the back of my eyelids. This is the Waiting Room of Sleep. Before I am called to the other side of the adjoining door's frosted window something needs to inhabit the restless mind.

I confess that during those last wakeful moments which stretch and elongate with advancing age like shadows moving away from a night lamppost, I frequently summon eleven blue-shirted Cardiff City football players, along with three substitutes, into the now crowded Waiting Room to autograph Sleep's Visitors' Book. I have done so intermittently over many decades. Different players file in, one by one. All wear the Bluebird shirt. Some announce their famous names: Trevor Ford, John Charles, Mel Charles, Ivor Allchurch, all of whom played for Cardiff City in their declining football years.

What a pathetic confession! What a ridiculous obsession! Am I a baby needing a sort of dummy before I can fall asleep?

Here I am, a grown-up man, indeed an old man, still dreamily involved with a relatively down-and-out Division 3 soccer team. More than that, I'm hungry for Cardiff City news: who's asked for a transfer? who's injured? who's in, who's out? what happened to X and will Ryan Giggs really sign for Cardiff?

In recent years I have become friendly with Leslie Hamilton, the Cardiff City doctor. Sometimes, when the Bluebirds play in or near

---

From *Perfect Pitch No. 1*, ed. Simon Kupes (Headline, 1997)

London where I spend three-quarters of my life, he invites me to join him in the Directors' box and enjoy the backstage pre-match and half-time hospitality of the Home side. Always first, though, a sighing admonition: 'You can't come like that, Dannie. You have to be suitably dressed.' The short-haired business men who populate the boardrooms of football are stuffily rank conscious. Some Saturdays I wear a tie.

I must irritate my friend, Dr Hamilton, not only sartorially. Because I want to hear the latest Cardiff City gossip, the behind-scenes misdoings and machinations, the comings and goings, the resignations and aspirations, the betrayals of the last manager, the style of the new one, I sometimes clutch Dr Hamilton's lapels and cross-examine him. He, alas, remains, as a doctor should, invincibly discreet. Or I display my own swanking medical knowledge and query the constituents of the team's pre-match diet or propose, 'Given the absence of joint changes on clinical and X-ray examination; given normal laboratory findings, maybe it's just a psychogenic arthralgia?' How often he diverts my penetrative suggestions or diagnoses by telling me that he met someone who writes poetry. 'One of the players?' I ask hopefully, remembering the forgettable verses of ex-Cardiff City centre-forward, John Toshack.

I learn more about happenings at Ninian Park by reading *The South Wales Football Echo* which I have sent to me at my London home all season. Even when I worked as Writer-in-Residence at Princeton University, New Jersey 08540, USA for the 1973–74 academic year, I ensured that the pink newspaper regularly reached our rented home in Pine Street. I did not subscribe to *The Times Literary Supplement*, the *New Statesman*, *The Listener*, or *The Spectator*. I needed to keep in touch only with vital news.

More important, of course, than football chatter is watching the actual games. This I did and this I do for I am a season-ticket holder. I arrange my frequent sojourns in South Wales to coincide with Cardiff's home fixtures. If invited to give a poetry reading at Hereford or Northampton or Scunthorpe or any other sad Division 3 town I scan the Bluebirds' fixture list to suggest a particular Saturday evening date so that I can be rewarded by watching my team play on that same away day afternoon.

Once upon a youthful time I often shared a platform or stage at a provincial Town Hall, Theatre, Library or Pub, with Laurie Lee. When we were offered a tandem gig somewhere in the United Kingdom it used to worry me that Laurie would consult his address book to see if he had a girlfriend there, in this or that town, whereas I merely fumbled yet again for the City fixture list. Dummy. Dummy. Cider only with the Bluebirds and not a Rosie in sight.

* * *

'If you want to go, you're on your own,' insisted my seventeen-year-old brother, Leo.

'The *Echo* reckons they'll do better than last season,' I said, trying to persuade my big brother to take me to Ninian Park.

'They couldn't do worse.'

'They've eight new players,' I mumbled.

Almost a year earlier I had seen my first game. Leo had allowed me to accompany him to watch the Bluebirds play Torquay United. We had joined 18,000 jugular critics for that Division 3 (South) match. City had only lost 0–1, so I was hooked!

That 1933–34 season when I first became a fan, Cardiff City's ponderous and awkward defence leaked 105 goals. If they, surprisingly, scored first then the headlines in *The South Wales Echo* would inevitably read BLUEBIRDS FLATTER TO DECEIVE. They finished bottom of Division 3 and, pleadingly, had to seek re-election – the worst season in their history. Only a few years earlier, in the previous decade, The Bluebirds had been Division One League Championship runners-up, F.A. Cup Finalists and F.A. Cup Winners. But since 1929 they'd slid down the League Tables as if greased. How are the mighty fallen! Tell it not at the Kop, publish it not in the streets of Highbury, lest the daughters of Swansea Town rejoice.

Though I had never seen them in their prime, they were still my heroes. When I kicked a football in Roath Park or a tennis ball in the back lane with villain Philip Griffiths I underwent a wondrous metamorphosis. I wore an invisible royal blue shirt and I responded to the name of speedy Reg Keating, the City centre-forward, a blur of blue, who was known to have once scored a goal. So I was very disappointed that on Saturday 25 August 1934, Leo would not take me to Ninian Park because, as he said, they lost all the time.

So what? We always seemed to back losers in our house. We sided with the workers but the Capitalists continued to water the workers' beer. Hadn't he, himself, taught me an alternative rhyming alphabet which began – A stands for Armaments, the Capitalist's pride, B stands for Bolshie, the thorn in their side? We voted Labour, didn't we? But around our patch they always lost the elections. Leo drummed into me that the Red Indians were the good guys not the imperialist Cowboys. It was true too: Saturday mornings at the Globe Cinema, the cowboys, led by Tom Mix, always won. And hadn't I heard my mother muttering, shaking her head, 'Your Dad's a loser.' Was she, I wonder, only talking about horses and greyhounds?

It was my gentle and beloved father, though, who one Saturday of late August sunlight financed me – pennies for the tramcar journey, sixpence for the game – so that I could go ON MY OWN, for the first time, to Ninian Park. Still only ten years high, I set out on this daring expedition from our semi-detached house in Albany Road. I don't remember my farewell in the hallway but I bet my mother fussed and kissed me goodbye as if I were going on a trek to the North Pole.

An hour or so later I stood outside the Ninian Park stadium disconsolate. I searched through my pockets once more only to find the used tram ticket, pennies for my return journey and the handkerchief that my mother had pushed into my pocket before I left the house. The sixpence had vanished, the little silver sixpenny bit, so generously given to me despite business being so bad and Australia winning the final Test match by 562 runs, had become invisible.

All around me people filed through the turnstiles. Someone was shouting, 'Programmes, getcher programme,' and another fellow with a strange Schnozzle Durante croak attempted to sell the converging crowds this or that differently coloured rosette. There were policemen on foot and policemen on horses and amidst all the whirl of movement a few stood lazily in front of an unhygienic-looking van whose owner in a white coat purveyed sizzling sausages and onions.

I listened glumly to the conversations of those standing at the van. I don't recall what they were saying. Perhaps they spoke fondly of the old days, of the great players who wore the royal blue shirt – Fred Keanor, Hardy, Ferguson and Farquharson, legendary figures before my time. I did not know what they were saying and soon, in any case, they moved off. No one loitered near the sausage van. Gradually the crowds in Sloper Road thinned out, to join the flat-capped masses swaying in the swearing terraces. I could hear the military band playing within the ground. I stood there, close to tears, knowing the misery of the world and that Outside is a lonely place.

How did I lose that sixpence? On the way maybe, upstairs in the smoke-filled tram? Had I pulled the handkerchief out of my pocket and inadvertently sent the sixpenny bit rolling beneath one of the varnished wooden seats? Surely the pipe-smoking pensioner sitting next to me wasn't an evil, clever pickpocket? What would I tell them all when I returned home? Mama, I sat next to Bill Sykes.

A sudden, barbaric roar from the crowd within the stadium signalled that the teams had appeared from the tunnel. The game would soon begin. Still some stragglers hurried towards the turnstiles as I waited there, unwilling to retrace my steps down Sloper Road. Soon there were no longer any late-comers. I stood in solitary vigil listening to the crowd's oohs and resonant aahs, coming and fading now that the game had begun. I must have been crying for suddenly a gruff voice said, 'Whassermara, sonny?' He bent down, he was a policeman so he sided with the oppressors of the workers – Leo had told me. But when I confessed that I had lost my sixpence he advised, 'They let the unemployed in near the end of the game. They open the gates at the Grangetown end. You could slip in then, sonny.' He began to walk away. Then he changed his mind. He came back and gave me sixpence.

I joined the 20,000 spectators in Ninian Park who attended the first Division 3 (South) game of the 1934–35 season. In the crowded Grangetown area between the goal posts I, umbilicus-high, tried to struggle through the massed supporters so that I could see my heroes. Suddenly, as was the custom with small boys, I was elevated by benign hands and passed down good-naturedly over capped heads to join other pygmies near the front. We beat Charlton Athletic 2–1 and Keating scored one of the goals. Though we won those early late summer matches we ended that season 19th in the League. As so often City 'flattered only to deceive.'

★ ★ ★

I am trying to recall in more detail how it used to be at Ninian Park before and after the old wooden Grandstand, one evening in 1937, lit up with incandescent fury as it burned on and on and to the ground. The Canton Stand had not then been surgically abbreviated to render it safe to sit in. The Grangetown end, now open to the frequently raining Welsh skies, used to be steeper and higher and owned a long oblique roof. The Division 3 crowds averaged 20,000, not the current 3,000.

Before the match a brass band, a uniformed platoon, would march around the touchlines, hoompa hoompa, as they played rhythmic military airs. Bollocks. And the same to you. Bollocks. A man pregnant with a huge drum would trail behind the platoon, while leading them an ostentatious conjurer would, at intervals, throw a somersaulting pole high into the air before catching it in his croupier-white gloves. How the crowd would have loved to observe that Clever Dick lose and drop it.

Just before kick-off the brass band would assemble outside the Players' Tunnel. When the team spurted on to the turf the band would strike up Cardiff's inappropriate, inanely optimistic, signature tune: HAPPY DAYS ARE HERE AGAIN. The crowd's welcoming shout to the emerging players would zenith to such decibels that the pigeons which, at one time, thrived under the roofs of the Stands would fountain up and out and away.

In those sepia days before the war, season after season I, alone or with school friends, used to observe this pre-match ritual from behind the goalposts at the Grangetown end. Opposite, the length of the green pitch away, loomed the slanting roof of the Canton Stand on which was painted an advertisement for Franklyn's

Tobacco. Beneath it, in the depths of the posterior darkness, small sparks of light would transiently appear here and there, above and below, to the left and to the right – evidence that the advertisement had been effective for the spectators were lighting up their pipes or cigarettes.

Before the commencement of the game, a flotilla of motorised wheelchairs carrying cripples of the First World War would settle below the wings of the Grandstand behind the touchlines near the corner flags. By 1939 these odd, closed, ugly vehicles had become scarce but after the Second World War, out of the smoke as it were, in an unhappy reincarnation, new wheelchair vehicles appeared. Years passed before they vanished from the scene.

So often have I visited Ninian Park in fine, wet, or wind-blown weather, have stood on the terraces, sat in the Stands, been comfortable or bloody cold as I observed football fashions changing: the prolegomenon and the tactics on the pitch. Everything so different and so much the same. I see the brown ball become white, see it passed back to the goalkeeper who picks it up, though directed from his own team-mate. I hear a referee's long whistle blow from a bygone year. How does the song go? I remember it well. And 1952 was a very good year: City returned (briefly, alas) to Division 1 and over 50,000 attended the final 2nd Division game against Leeds.

> Memory of faded games, the discarded years,
> talk of Aston Villa, Orient, and the Swans.
> Half-time, the band played the same military airs
> as when the Bluebirds once were champions.
> Round touchlines the same cripples in their chairs.

In those lean, utility, post-war years, before the introduction of flood-lighting, fixtures began at 2.30 p.m. and the kick-off was even earlier mid-winter. Often, late in the game, the players in the smoke-brown, thickening gloom, would become, at the distant Canton end, anonymous astigmatic figures drifting this way or that without evident purpose. At the confusion of the final whistle, whatever the score – win, lose or draw – hordes of youngsters would invade the pitch. Some would bring on a ball and incompetently kick it into the empty Grangetown end goal with amazing delight, others would seek the players' autographs. They were hardly chased off. They had become part of the Saturday afternoon ritual.

Nor did one experience feelings of incipient threat as the crowds dispersed into and through the dusk of Sloper Road. Because money was scarcer, trains slower, motorways not yet built, Away fans did not usually attend the game in numbers. The Home crowd, being more homogeneous, shared the same gods (who failed them), chanted the same chorus. They belonged to the same defeated tribe.

Like many of the youngsters near the barrier behind the goal-posts I held back at the end of the match in order to avoid the crush of the crowds converging through the big gates of the Grangetown end. How quickly Ninian Park became empty, forlorn, abandoned, as the unaccompanied small boys patiently waited there. Outside the lampposts jerked into luminous activity and somehow emphasised the oncoming darkness of a December night.

How many occasions did I see City lose; how often the thin, damp, Welsh rain descended in melancholy sympathy at lighting-up time as I quit the ground into Sloper Road to progress under the hoardings, to re-enter real life. 'South Wales Echo, sir. Last edition. NAZIS ENTER RHINELAND. Echo. Echo. Echo.'

> Silent the stadium. The crowds have all filed out.
> Only the pigeons beneath the roofs remain.
> The clean programmes are trampled underfoot
> and natural the dark, appropriate the rain
> while under lampposts threatening newsboys shout.

⋆ ⋆ ⋆

In 1944, most weekdays, you could have found me in the precincts of King's College in the Strand, more often than not on its fifth floor in the long Dissecting Room where, on slabs, anonymous dead human beings awaited medical students' scalpels. I cannot say I enjoyed studying the anatomy of the human body. Like other students I laid bare muscles, tendons, arteries and nerves until tissue-sections resembled the coloured plates in the anatomy text-book. At night, we had to take turns fire-watching on the roof of King's College. It was not always unfathomably dark. Sometimes the moon transformed the fluent Thames below into a long, twisting slug of mercury; or long searchlight beams probed the arena of the sky; sometimes, too, the chug chug of a doodlebug, a pilotless rocket, alarmed the fire-watchers below. So it was a relief to escape into the calm of a Saturday afternoon and *play* football.

In *A Poet in the Family* I confessed how much I enjoyed those afternoons: 'I gained pleasure from playing rugby or cricket or tennis or squash – but soccer was something else. That season 1943–44, when I played for King's first eleven along with those other medical students, I enjoyed my soccer more than ever before. I can remember the details of some games with disturbing clarity. I am sure it sounds kinky, and I have never thought of myself as kinky, but I enjoyed my soccer then, at least on some days, as much as I have sexual intercourse on some nights with the right person.'

A few of the King's College team were chosen to represent London University. That was how I met Wyn Griffiths, a veterinary student based in Reading, a goalkeeper who also played for Cardiff City. (Later, after the war, he had games for Arsenal and indeed played in that smog-dense famous fixture against the Moscow Dynamos.) Just before Easter, after a London University match, Wyn Griffiths suggested I trained, during the holiday break, with the City team, 'Cyril Spiers, the manager, welcomes guest players,' Wyn told me.

So that springtime, excited, I ran too slowly over the green holy grass of Ninian Park and tried to pass the ball to players I admired, among them the winger Beriah Moore and the future Welsh International, Alf Sherwood. Afterwards, Cyril Spiers asked me if, the following Saturday, I should like to play for the Reserves in the Welsh League home match against Oswestry.

I returned to our house in Cathedral Road my chest stuck out for medals. Because my elder brothers, Wilfred and Leo, one in the Army, the other in the RAF, had both been posted abroad I could not boast to them. So, casually, I informed my father that I would be turning out for Cardiff City Reserves. 'Christ, they must be bloody short of players,' he opined. My mother, though, consoled me: 'Never mind, son, not everybody can play for the first team.'

That Saturday afternoon I did not wear the blue shirt of Cardiff City Reserves. Cyril Spiers took me aside in the Dressing Room and explained that only ten of the Oswestry team had turned up. 'Would you,' he continued politely, 'be good enough to play for them?' Oswestry? What could I say? I had never been to fatuous Oswestry, didn't want to go there either though I knew they had a renowned orthopaedic centre and, come to think of it, wasn't it the place where Wilfred Owen was born? But I wanted to play for Cardiff not Oswestry.

Soon I was in the visitors' Dressing room pulling over my head the red shirt of Oswestry Town and minutes later following strangers in other red shirts as we ambled on to the pitch. How daunting the deserted terraces and the emptiness of the stadium: 50 people, not 50,000, were about to observe my inept display.

What I remember best about the game is an incident half way through the second half. Minutes beforehand, I had experienced a cramp in my calf muscle so, instead of falling back into our own half, I doodled upfield in the centre-forward position. When the Oswestry right full back blasted an oblique long ball in a high trajectory to my left, I found myself clear and I was able to steer the ball towards the penalty area.

Here I was, this no day dream. Good God, this was Ninian Park. The game so far had been goalless. I could be a hero. The goalposts were advancing towards me and I was being chased by some fast bugger in a blue shirt. In my dreams I would smash the ball high into the net beating the goalkeeper, as the *Football Echo* would put it, 'all ends up'. 50,000 frenetic supporters would scream, 'Goal.' My mouth tasted, 'Hallelujah.'

It did not turn out like that. I wore a red shirt, not a blue one. I heard not the voice of multitudes but the clear solitary cry of Cyril Spiers from the touchline: 'Now's your chance, son.'

The goalposts continued to advance towards me. At my heels the Cardiff City player was becoming intimate. The Cardiff City goalkeeper was leaving his area as if to welcome me. He narrowed the angle and the goalposts shrank to hockey size. 'Now's your chance, son.' A cry hanging in the air. I had not time to switch the ball from my left foot to my more certain right. I was running too fast. Surely I would be tripped up by the pagan, burly cipher behind me? But now I was in the penalty area and the undeceived goalkeeper, half crouching, still advanced. '. . . chance, son.' I prodded at the ball with my left foot as, almost simultaneously, I crashed into the green-jerseyed keeper. I saw the ball slither across the pigmented green turf and scrape the wrong side of the far talcum-white goalpost. The Grangetown Stand behind and above the crossbar yawned darkness and silence.

The goalkeeper, winded, soon revived, but I discovered that the patella of my right knee had been displaced upwards. It did not hurt, but after I'd pushed it down into its normal position I limped for the rest of the game. I merely loitered, in those days of no substitutes, more or less one-legged on the right wing until the final whistle blew.

I did not tell my father that I had played for Oswestry Town. Nor anybody else. My secret; even when my Uncle Sol, obviously briefed by my Dad, asked me how I got on playing for Cardiff City Reserves.

Often, when I sit in Block D, row M, of the Grandstand at Ninian Park my eyes stray towards the Grangetown end goalposts. Or rather, to the left upright. To be exact, to the foot of the left upright where an invisible X marks the spot where a ghost ball still scrapes its outer side.

⋆ ⋆ ⋆

Decades ago, for one whole winter, I did not watch Cardiff City. A friend of mine, having been offered a temporary University teaching job in Connecticut, lent me his Grandstand season ticket for the Spurs. The football proved to be much more classy, of course, than the scrappy long ball, adrenalin kick-about evident at Ninian Park. Some of the spectators were classy too. I sat next to Lewis Greifer, an old friend, script editor of the television series *Love Story*, and peered over the tidy parting of philosopher, Freddie Ayer and the non-existent one of music critic, Hans Keller. Behind me, though, camped a more conventional soccer fan who, on several occasions, brought with him a pre-puberty, diminutive boy who used to call out in his high pre-puberty voice to Cliff Jones or Danny Blanchflower, 'Well done, my son.'

The man himself, like the boy, all through the match sucked boiled sweets and every time Spurs scored I had to extract a sticky lump of orange, or raspberry, or lemon-coloured carbohydrate from the back of my neck. If I had shut my eyes for ninety minutes I could have known how many goals Tottenham had scored simply by counting the half-sucked acid drops that had unerringly landed above my collar. That could hardly happen at Ninian Park because our forwards usually suffered from a goal famine.

The game that progressed below might have been a dramatic, mobile, altering diagram of subtlety and excellence, of Glory, Glory, Nice One Cyril and Hallelujah, but I did not feel partisan as I did and do when watching the Bluebirds' rare skills and common errors at Ninian Park. Academic appreciation is not enough. Visceral engagement spices even a bland routine game.

After that one season betrayal in following a Rolls-Royce London team I invested, for the first time, in a Cardiff City Grandstand season ticket. That year, I think it was 1963, the Bluebirds had been promoted temporarily to Division 2 and City had signed John Charles from Roma for £25,000. The so-called Gentle Giant, on his debut, scored from 75 yards.

A season or two later, after an injury, he could not get back into the side. I recall sitting next to him in the Stand as he glumly observed his team mates' endeavours. Generally, whenever this or that one made a blatant mistake he would remain silent, impassive; but when young Don Murray, who had supplanted him at centre-half blundered, he would groan audibly!

The Welsh crowds of thirty and more years ago remained relatively benign. Many had journeyed from the Valleys – blue-scarved coal miners in their flat caps among them. They have disappeared into the shiny grey photographic plates of a Welsh social history book. Decades have passed since the respectable, more posh spectators in the Grandstand were astonished when one of their kind, sitting close to the Directors' box, rose to his feet and screamed

'FUCKIN' UNGENTLEMANLY BE'AVIOUR.' Even the disreputable gifted Welsh poet, John Tripp, who once accompanied me to Ninian Park, could only yell at the referee from time to time in a small voice, 'Go back to Hong Kong.' The referee hailed from Bristol so perhaps it was the rhyme of Hong and Kong that so entranced my companion. Then the crowd never cried out, as they regularly do now, 'THE REFEREE IS A WANKER.' Masturbation was still a taboo word.

I did eventually switch my season ticket seat from Block C to the present Block D. In my old seat, no spectator experiencing an oral orgasm would ejaculate boiled sweets on to the back of my neck; but a new pipe-smoking ticket holder parked himself next to me. I had only recently given up smoking myself. I did not wish to inhale second-hand tobacco smoke relentlessly through ninety minutes. Besides, another season ticket holder nearby irritated me by hurling abuse, week after week, at one particular player. First his wrath lasered on Derek Showers, a somewhat clumsy centre-forward. 'YOU ARE A SHOWER, SHOWERS. CRAAAP.' When Showers was dropped from the team he chose his next victim, the central defender, Albert Lamour, whose ability to kick into touch could have been the envy of many a rugby player. Almost every time Lamour received the ball he would be ready with his monotonous, repetitive, snarled abuse: 'YOU CART-'ORSE YOU. CRAAAP.'

It is customary to upbraid the referee's apparent diabolism. How often have I listened to the Ninian Park grumble: 'It's always an uphill struggle. We never 'ave a Welsh ref, see. Always a prejudiced Englishman.' But choosing to scapegoat one of our own players so regularly annoyed me. The following season I breathed the fresher air of Block D and now I still sit there next to a pleasant school-teacher whose only unfavourable habit is to favour me charitably with an occasional religious tract.

True, at certain key matches, against Swansea for example, I sometimes believe that that Block C Ku-Klux-Klan-like character who needed to focus on a victim, has been cloned and cloned and cloned again. Quitting Ninian Park there have been occasions when I needed to move quickly to the safety of my parked car because of a sudden stampede of agitated running feet, raw shouts of rival supporters, over-alert policemen and police dogs barking. But the first time I encountered *real* malignant crowd menace was in the 1970s at a Millwall away match.

Even before the game began a whole mass of razor-headed yobs began to scream in unison, 'KICK THEIR FUCKIN' 'EADS IN, KICK THEIR FUCKIN' 'EADS IN.' They brandished their right fists rhythmically to this threatening cry which was orchestrated by no evident Oswald Mosley. To be sure, I had experienced milder displays of mindless crowd aggression but this was something else. Crowd rage. After the game that cancerous destructive violence metastasised around and about the mean streets of Cold Blow Lane.

Nowadays, unalloyed mass frenzy, barely suppressed, has ceased to be remarkable at soccer games. These battalions of ranting, lead-irritable, broken-homed, frustrated youths are but a legacy and symptom of our unhealthy, uncaring Thatcher-fashioned society where even TV football is stolen from the people by the fattest cats of this world. May they all drop dead.

Still, lethal crowds or not – and, fortunately, mostly not at Ninian Park – I enjoy my Bluebird Saturday afternoons. I like joining the crowds converging with sanguine expectation towards the turnstiles of the City ground. Men and blue-jeaned youths mainly, some wearing blue-and-white Cardiff City scarves or sponsored T-shirts, all walking purposefully in the same direction past the stragglers outside the Ninian pub, past the waiting, stern,distrustful police and their vans, to pass under the shabby railway bridge into Sloper Road itself with the looming Stands and high, unlit floodlights of Ninian Park.

I feel the same old pleasurable anticipation as I take my place in Row M, Block D. No brass band entertains the relatively sparse spectators but the tannoy inaudibly gives out the team changes in what sounds like Serbo-Croat. No matter, I look towards the Grangetown Stand and I see a prewar boy who answers to my name. I hear him singing, 'Roll along, Cardiff City, roll along, To the top of the League where you belong. With a little bit of luck, you'll win the F.A.Cup, roll along Cardiff City, roll along.' But now a 1997 whistle blows. Car-DIFF. Car-DIFF.

Pegasus and the Rocking Horse

Notes on Originality and Imitation in Poetry

1

I should confess, ladies and gentlemen, confess immediately, that I was somewhat puzzled when I was invited to address you here this evening for I have as little, and as much, interest in your discipline as I suspect some of you may have in mine. I am reminded of the prolegomenon to a lecture given by Robert Bridges in 1917, one dreary night in rain-swept, gas-lit South Wales. He said to the bemused members of the Tredegar and District Cooperative Society, 'I am here to talk about poetry and you little think how surprised you ought to be. I have refused many invitations to lecture on poetry; but most of us nowadays are doing what we most dislike.'

It is sibling rivalry, no doubt, that brings me here, that explains why I accepted your kind invitation: both my brothers are seriously preoccupied with depth psychology and would feel more at home in this Ernest Jones room than I. Indeed, I have been here once before. On that occasion, two years ago, I attended a lecture delivered by my psychoanalyst brother, Wilfred. So, as you see, I am in some measure imitating him. As for my other brother, Leo, he is, as some of you may know, the very original MP for Pontypool who relentlessly speculates on the psychodynamics of politics and the psychopathology of his Parliamentary colleagues – much to their chagrin.

My interest in psychoanalytic literature has been much more sporadic, much more confined, than that of my brothers so for this

---

A lecture delivered to the Institute of Psychoanalysis in London (1981)

second Tolkien lecture I could only offer to compose for you some notes on originality and imitation in poetry, a subject that interests *me*. This theme, however, was welcomed as being appropriate and, further, it was generously suggested that I could illustrate what I had to say by referring to my own texts, my own poems.

2

Indisputably, during the twentieth century, there has been, in the judgement of artistic works, an italic emphasis on the value of originality. Many feel that to imitate another is somehow a fraudulent exercise, that imitation stales the imagination rather than provokes it. Yet such imperious slogans as 'Keep It Spontaneous' and 'Make It New' are frequently misunderstood. At best, the artist can only engage in a deception: his work must *appear* spontaneous however many versions, drafts, rehearsals, have been gone through in its maturation; his work must *appear* new though the old, the traditional, have been called upon to be vividly refurbished.

In the autumn of 1971 there was an exhibition in London, called *Art into Art*, that illustrated the influence of earlier artists on the imagery and stylistic modes of later artists. In the exhibition's catalogue, Keith Roberts acknowledged that the activity of copying and imitating is not admired nowadays as once it was, that the spirit of the age is very much 'to do your own thing'. One impetus then, it seemed, for this exhibition was to act as a corrective: to dispel popular prejudice against imitation.

No one, I imagine, would have recommended that exhibition to his students – had they and he been alive – more than Sir Joshua Reynolds who, in his Sixth Discourse on Art, urged that novitiates and master craftsmen alike should engage themselves in the continual activity of imitation. 'Invention,' Reynolds suggested, 'is one of the great marks of genius; but if we consult experience we shall find that it is by being conversant with the inventions of others that we learn to invent; as by reading the thoughts of others we learn to think.' He then went on to describe and prescribe the means whereby admired inventions can be truly known – in short, by assiduously copying them. 'No man,' Reynolds dogmatically averred, 'can be an artist, whatever he may suppose, upon any other terms.'

Blake, no admirer of Reynolds – he felt he'd spent 'the vigour of his youth and genius under the oppression of Sir Joshua and his Gang of Cunning Hired Knaves' – even Blake, annotating Reynolds's Discourses, commented, 'The difference between a Bad Artist and a Good One is the Bad Artist seems to Copy a Great Deal. The Good One Really does Copy a Great Deal.'

To be sure, Reynolds's advice to painters was by no means unambiguous. By imitation he meant something far more than a mere mechanical copy, which he censured for being inferior, for being barren and servile. We today readily assent to such a censure. Tom, Dick and Harry will declare that a slavish copy lacks the genius of the original. Yet, pause for a moment: why shouldn't a forgery by a master craftsman be as powerful as its model?

One modern explanation of this conundrum has been supplied by Anton Ehrenzweig in his book, *The Psycho-Analysis of Artistic Vision and Hearing*, where he stressed the importance of unconscious perception in our appreciation of works of art. He argued, for instance, that when we look at a painting we are blind to certain details in it, we repress certain significant and disturbing forms that feed the painting with active energy. Copies, he asserted, are emotionally sterile because the unconscious has played little part in the making of them. But let me quote him directly: 'The conscious imitator of a great work,' he wrote, 'misses the chaotic, inarticulate structure of technique and the emotional impact of the original. He fails because he reproduces by a conscious effort what the master has created unconsciously. As he copies the erratic brushwork of the original, the gestalt process ruling his conscious form perception will inevitably straighten out and regularise what he sees; he will overlook the little gaps and vaguenesses as accidental and insignificant in which, however, the master's unconscious has symbolised itself most powerfully.'

Ehrenzweig reminds us how when we recollect a dream we disremember its incoherence, its vagueness, as we conjure it up in a more orderly manner. 'As our mind lingers on the dream memory,' he continues, 'it gains in clarity and compactness and those details which drop out first are sure to be the most important. Freud had only to observe which details would be suppressed first in order to know where he had to start his analysis.' In short, if we think of the original masterwork as the dream of the artist, then the imitator, because of the safeguarding reaction of his superego, cannot copy the dream itself, only the dream, as it were, that he remembers.

This argument seems to me to be almost persuasive – almost, not totally, because, in the history of art, forgeries, criminal and legitimate, are not always, *inevitably*, discernible. Certain copyists become so skilled, so in empathy with the original artist, that their mimetic gifts amaze and dazzle – to such an extent, indeed, that the viewer becomes blind to which is the original and which the copy. For instance, no critic more than John Ruskin knew so thoroughly the works of Turner or appreciated them as much or championed them more; but he insisted that those two extraordinary Turner copyists, William Ward and Isobel Jay, sign their 'Turner' watercolours (and he countersigned them) lest, at a later date, their versions be mistaken for the real thing, strange.

Nevertheless, despite the copyists' skills, in our judgement of them as works of art, we properly take into account the fact of primacy, we uphold the value of primacy. Offered a gift of a Turner watercolour or a Ward or Isobel Jay copy we would choose the Turner – and not only for monetary reasons. There is something in us, prim and primitive, childlike perhaps, that makes us respond to an imitation, albeit sub-vocally, 'Copycat, copycat!'

If we profoundly admire an original work of art and can discern the difference between it and its imitation, then we come to *resent* the copy. It is as if, in some curious way, it cheapens the model that inspired it. When one man's powerfully individual voice or style is caught like an infection – and usually just as unwittingly – often the imitator seems ill; his work has not the energy of health. Even if we should admire an imitation at first, not knowing it to be one such, when we do discover the original, immediately the copy becomes diminished for us. We experience a puritanical sense of outrage that one artist or poet has gone to another, if not like a thief in the night, at least like an absent-minded, plundering sleepwalker. Soon enough the imitation we admired and thought so fine becomes in our minds merely a derivative object.

Perhaps this is what Blake meant by saying, 'The Bad Artist seems to Copy a Great Deal,' and why Reynolds warned, 'Borrowing or stealing . . . will have a right to the same lenity as was used by the Lacedemonians who did not punish theft, but the want of artifice to conceal it.'

3

To become conversant with works of art, to copy them, may well be a part, and a good part, of the education of an apprentice painter. But what of an apprentice poet? Does he similarly need a wide knowledge of poetry? Should he also take models and imitate them consciously?

While no education in verse can enlarge a dwarf talent, it is certain that no man or woman can make a real poem who has not read seriously the works of his contemporaries and something of that tradition which informed them. As the American poet William Cullen Bryant remarked in a lecture he gave in 1826, 'Whoever would entirely disclaim imitation, and aspire to the praises of complete originality, should be altogether ignorant of any poetry written by others, and of all those aids which the cultivation of poetry has lent to prose. Deprive an author of these advantages, and what sort of poetry does anyone imagine that he would produce? I dare say it would be sufficiently original, but who will affirm that it could be read?'

I remember some years ago talking to Stephen Spender about a biography of Robert Frost. Spender wondered, somewhat wickedly but not too seriously, whether Frost had wanted to be the only poet in the world.

'Would *you* like to be the only poet in the world?' Stephen Spender suddenly asked me.

I don't think he expected a reply but I said, 'Of course not. If I were, I would soon be locked up in a mental hospital. Besides, I would miss reading my contemporaries too much.'

In fact, all poets, apprentice ones as well as those somewhat riper, would be unlikely to be writing poetry unless, for years, they had enjoyed reading the stuff. Young aspiring writers know that their lives would be much poorer, much more threadbare, if poetry was not available to them. So they seek it out, to enjoy it, to be enlarged by it, and unconsciously they are influenced technically by what they read. They hardly need to be persuaded to read poems nor to write parodies as conscious exercises.

These days writing schools abound (in the USA they are illiterately called 'creative writing programs') and in some of them students are urged not merely to tackle forms – sonnets, sestinas, villanelles – but to 'write in the manner of . . .'. It would appear that whole classes, hordes of young men and women, are in strenuous training to win prizes in those competitions hebdomadally set in the back pages of the *New Statesman*. I suppose there is nothing wrong in committing parodies. They prove the author's esteem for certain originals even as he gently mocks them. There have even been poets, Swinburne among them, who have deliberately parodied themselves, this act of narcissism neutralised by a humorous self-ridicule. The whole thrust of making a parody is to produce something comical. Even when composed by one as skilled as Wendy Cope, parodies are no more than music-hall impersonations – and I doubt whether many aspiring poets long to become the Mike Yarwoods of verse.

Besides, it's only the surface manner and the metre that can be *consciously* imitated, not the hidden inner lining of a great poem, not even the real sound of that inner lining. The real sound, its sum of cadences and silences – the musical matrix of a poem in which even punctuation plays a part – defies rational analysis. A metre allows us to know only the rough caricature of a poem's sound. Blake's line, 'Tyger, Tyger, burning bright' may own the same metre, have the same number of syllables as, say, Auden's 'Lay your sleeping head, my love,' but we do not have to be a Schoenberg to recognise that these two lines differ musically.

Whether an apprentice poet is urged to write parodies or not, soon enough he will become *unconsciously* influenced by what he admires, and in most cases overwhelmingly possessed by another man's voice. He may be unaware of having become a dummy to a great ventriloquist. He may believe he speaks with his own voice when others listening hear only the intrusive accents of Hardy or Yeats or D. H. Lawrence or Eliot or Dylan Thomas or someone else equally distinctive. It may take years before such dominant hauntings are recognised by the possessed aspiring poet and exorcised. Meanwhile he will 'sway upon a rocking horse and think it Pegasus'.

I look at the early work of my favourite contemporaries and recognise who possessed them. I go like a detective with a magnifying glass to find they are covered blatantly with the fingerprints of older, famous poets. I see in their verse crude transplantations, bloodstains from the underside of poems not theirs. I look at my own first published book – and wince. Some poets, genuine minor poets, even as they mature never entirely escape from the thraldom of their first masters. Recently, over breakfast, I glanced at the current issue of the *Times Literary Supplement* and read a review of a posthumous volume of poetry by Thomas Blackburn. The reviewer, a friend of Blackburn's, John Heath-Stubbs, justly praised his friend's talent, but remarked:

> At times Blackburn had a lazy habit of quoting verbatim from other poets and not, as did Eliot, placing the quotations in a context which gives them a new dimension. Thus we find well-known phrases from Yeats and Eliot and even Ezra Pound's grammatically incorrect *contra natura*. Blackburn would have defended this practice by saying that other poets had expressed what he wanted to say so precisely that he could not alter it. But this will not do: the poet has always to 'make it new'.

But why is a distinctive voice in *poetry* so important to us in the enjoyment of it; or why, conversely, are recognisable imitations so irritating? The same criteria apply as in painting, not least the territorial claims of primacy. Consider for a moment those majestic lines of *English* poetry in Ecclesiastes that many of us may have known and valued for years – valued as literature, I mean.

> . . . Or ever the silver cord be loosed, or the golden bowl be broken, or the pitcher be broken at the fountain, or the wheel

> broken at the cistern. Then shall the dust return to the earth as it was and the spirit shall return unto God who gave it. Vanity of vanity, saith the Preacher, all is vanity.

In the New English Bible of 1972 we find a different translation from the Hebrew which the editors believe to be clearer, more readable, more accurate:

> . . . before the silver cord is snapped and the golden bowl is broken, before the pitcher is shattered at the spring and the wheel broken at the well, before the dust returns to the earth as it began and the spring returns to God who gave it. Emptiness, emptiness, says the Speaker, all is empty.

It is not possible for those of us attached to the older version to accept the recent rendering as anything but a paste copy of less value. Apart from its sense, 'Emptiness, emptiness' has a passable sound relationship to 'Vanity, vanity' but the final 'all is empty' seems faintly ridiculous because we hear a distinct aural error as we, reflexly, echo what we already know and admire. Only those totally new to both versions are able to make a more objective judgement about which is the better poetry; they, unlike us, have not to contend with the power of primacy. Translations, like original poems, if they are really fine, can inhabit us and, once accepted, all other versions, all other translations, whether objectively better or not, are dismissed by us as imposters.

Sir Joshua Reynolds's advice to apprentice-painters was complex: he warned them of the dangers of imitation though he recommended the practice of it. In poetry these dangers are even more acute. The power of primacy and therefore the importance of originality remain paramount. Certainly no metamorphosis of the wooden rocking horse can occur unless a new-made poem is active with originality, and paradoxically this originality can only subsist where there have first been models.

It is obvious that the work of some poets appears to be more original than that of others. Some, by being least imitative of the fashionable modes of the period – poets absorb generic modes as much as individual models – seem eccentric when they first attract the public's eye. They have been more rebellious, have adopted a more confident, pugnacious posture towards the dominant literary tradition than most of their colleagues. I recall Freud believed that 'a man who has been the indisputable favourite of his mother keeps for life the feeling of a conqueror, the confidence of success that often induces real success'. The aetiology of artistic confidence, a poet's risk-taking and adventurousness in technique, may indeed reside in early developmental entanglements.

I dare say a number of you would consider that some of, if not all, the hidden roots of a poet's technical rebelliousness – his overturning of models, his striving for marked originality – may find nourishment in the darkness of his Oedipus complex. Be that as it may, the general reader's initial response to blatant originality is one of hostility, a degree of hostility of greater moment than that directed against blatant acts of imitation which I commented on earlier. Poets who remark metre in an original way are particularly likely to irritate most poetry readers. What Robert Bridges declared about metre still obtains: 'It offers a form which the hearers recognise and desire, and by its recurrence keeps it steadily in view. Its practical working may be seen in the unpopularity of poems that are written in an unrecognised metre and the favour shown to well established forms by the average reader.'

It may be that Bridges privately, with a too complacent satisfaction, was thinking of his own fame – he was Poet Laureate – and of the contrasting neglect of his innovative friend Gerard Manley Hopkins. The irony, of course, is that with the passage of time it is Manley Hopkins who has found favour with poetry readers rather than Bridges whose diction, if not metre, seems stale to us. Yes, Bridges perhaps was too imitative of the poetic conventions of his day, while we can now see to what end Manley Hopkins confessed, 'The effect of studying masterpieces makes me admire and do otherwise.' In short, it is not a matter only of models becoming part of a poet's natural disposition like his heart that beats and his blood that throbs; he may go further, he may inventively react against such models so that the rocking horse gallops up the mountain and takes wing.

4

I should like to return to the reasons why some writers feel compelled to be innovative in an extreme way whereas so many others seem content to work within the constraints of a dominant literary convention. It may be that psychoanalysts have news to give us about this enigma other than the old headlines on page one about Oedipus. One text I discovered to be particularly audacious and rewarding is *Thrills and Regressions* (1959) by the analyst Michael Balint. To be sure, he does not concern himself with the nature of originality, that is not his central theme, but I believe his propositions to be relevant to it.

A baby, Dr Balint suggests, may respond to the early traumatic discovery that important objects lie outside himself in one of two ways: (a) he may create a fantasy world where firm objects, though having now an independent existence, are deemed to be still benevolent and reliable; or (b) he may recreate the illusion of the world prior to the trauma – when there were no hazardous, independent objects at all, when there were only free, unobstructed, friendly expanses.

It seems the direction of these early responses persists, to a greater or lesser extent, into adult life. So there are those who, when their security is threatened, would *cling* to objects. These are the so-called ocnophils. Then there are those who are their antithesis – the so-called philobats who, finding objects hazardous, would reach for the free spaces between them. For the extreme philobat, objects are indeed objectionable whereas for the extreme ocnophil they are objectives.

In describing adult behaviour patterns, Michael Balint spotlights the philobat as one who prefers to be solitary, devoid of support, relying on his own resources – indeed, the further he is in distance (and time) from safety, from *mother* earth, the greater the thrill he experiences in proving his independence. That is why, Dr Balint suggests, some find it attractive to undertake solitary crossings of the Atlantic or remain aloft in gliders for long periods. Clearly the philobat, or rather the extreme philobat, for there are all kinds of mixtures and gradations, would be perceived by most of us as having the character of a hero. Such men live dangerously. They are, though, according to Dr Balint, bolstered by their feelings of their own potency by holding on to phallic objects, to a magic penis: the tight-rope walker carries his pole, the lion-tamer his whip, the skier his stick, and yes . . . the poet his pen!

It is odd that the poet, the true poet, should be conceived to be, like the trapeze artist or lonely mountaineer, or racing motorist, a philobatic hero. Michael Balint infers as much. Other analysts too have done so in the past and will continue to do so in the future. How romantically one such as Jung discusses the Poet with a capital P. 'Art', he writes in *Modern Man in Search of a Soul*, 'is a kind of innate drive that seizes a human being and makes him its instrument. The artist is not a person endowed with free will who seeks his own ends but one who allows art to realize its purposes through him. . . . To perform this difficult office it is sometimes necessary for him to sacrifice happiness and everything that makes life worth living for the ordinary human being.'

'Tosh,' one might say, but the fact is that this view of the poet as tragic philobatic hero-figure is commonplace and poets themselves have contributed to the making of this myth. 'Why,' asked Yeats, 'should we honour those that die upon the field of battle, a man may show as reckless a courage in entering into the abyss of himself?' And here's Rainer Maria Rilke pronouncing in a letter, 'I feel myself to be an artist, weak and wavering in strength and boldness. . . . Not as a martyrdom do I regard art – but as a battle the chosen one has to wage with himself and his environment.' As Robert Graves has justly remarked, 'Despite all the charlatans, racketeers, and incompetents who have disgraced the poetic profession an aroma of holiness still clings to the title "poet" as it does to the titles "saint" and "hero", both of which are properly reserved for the dead.' Nor does Mr Graves demur from this popular belief.

It may be inferred from my remarks that I do! I certainly would not subscribe to the notion that the poet is a hero, that the writing of poetry is an heroic act. That notion seems absurd to me; yet when I look back at the poems I myself have written and at the few in particular that have taken as theme the creative process itself, I am surprised to see that my rational belief is contradicted by those very poems. I am even startled to discover that one of them, a poem written some years before the appearance of Michael Balint's *Thrills and Regressions*, actually spotlights the poet as trapeze artist, the very same figure Dr Balint characterises as an extreme philobat.

I called my poem, 'Go Home the Act is Over'. It was written soon after Dylan Thomas died in 1953 and I had Dylan Thomas very much in mind when I wrote it. I subsequently suppressed the poem. I did not, for instance, include it in my *Collected Poems* (1977) because I did not think it good enough. However I should like to read it to you now for it does lucidly define what I am saying:

Go Home the Act is Over

Roll up, roll up, the circus has begun
and poets, freaks of multilingual Time, perform.
Fingers, ten dwarfs, beat thunder on a drum
and whizzing spotlights flash as in a storm.

Look, like a trapeze artist he flies with wires
above pedestrians who with iambics freeze.
To those with cold hands he offers fires
and sings the catastrophes.

Play gaudy drums then, let the lions roar,
the circus crowd is ready. You others
is it his death you're waiting for?
Where any poet sings, the vulture hovers.

Electricians above the balcony point the light.
Against the roof his two shadows dance
and somersault. He sings for our delight
but seeing gold he trips and loses balance.

The audience is hushed. The sawdust ring
is empty except where that singer lies.
Still, high in the air, two trapezes swing.
Does that last image leak from his two eyes?

Return now to that place. The grass, instead,
the wind and stars where once the spotlights shone.
His funambulists and jugglers are dead.
The show is over. The big tent gone.

It seems that each generation needs to create a martyr-poet: in the fifties when I wrote 'Go Home the Act is Over', it was Dylan Thomas, a generation earlier Wilfred Owen. More recently, Sylvia Plath has been cast for that role. There are those who feel romantically – common reader, analyst, sometimes, as you see, the artists themselves – that somehow the poet soars to forbidden heights, steals the ambrosia of the gods, illicitly brings heavenly fire to earth. What has been said of the public's attitude, in another context, about drug addicts could equally describe general feelings about the *poète maudit*: 'Prometheus, having illicitly brought the fire to earth, is condemned to a millennium of being eaten alive; Tantalus, having stolen the ambrosia of the gods, suffers a fate that makes his name a symbol of an exquisite form of torture; Icarus, having sought the forbidden heights, suffers the inevitable consequence of plummeting to the depths.'

And so the poet too, receiving merciless justice, becomes sacrificial martyr and then is glamorised: Alec Guinness, incongruously wearing a red wig, a curly red wig, impersonated a libidinous Dylan Thomas on a Broadway stage; Glenda Jackson, of luscious proportions, transformed slight, angular, flat-chested Stevie Smith in a British film; and even as I'm speaking now, they are preparing in Langholm, a small border town in Dumfriesshire, to erect a sculpture-monument to honour their locally born Hugh MacDiarmid. When MacDiarmid was alive, by the way, his poetry was of less consequence to members of the Langholm council who declined to grant him the freedom of the town – instead they honoured Neil Armstrong the astronaut, whose connection with Langholm was somewhat more cosmic. In any event, dead, it seems MacDiarmid has become as philobatic a hero as any astronaut alive.

Indeed it is not unusual that the poet, elevated to a pedestal after his death, may have received scant attention from the public at large during his lifetime, especially if his work has been conspicuously original. The analyst, Phyllis Greenacre, in describing an individual's reactions to strange events – events not poems – wrote, 'Any experience which is so strange that there is little in his life to which he can relate it, is felt as inimical, alien and overwhelming. On the other hand, an experience which is only somewhat or a little bit new is pleasantly exciting.' As with external events, so with poems: if too strange (original) the poems may be felt to be inimical, if 'a little bit new' they may be welcomed as 'pleasantly exciting'. But I should like to qualify Dr Greenacre's proposition: the intensity of the experience, the poem's effect, depends surely not only on the gradation of its strangeness (originality) but on the ocnophilic or philobatic temperament of the individual, the particular reader. A strange experience, whether an event or a poem, may provoke in one person, at first, inordinate hostility or fear; in another it may merely promote curiosity or unease.

Most people have ocnophilic leanings. Accordingly they prefer that the pattern of any new poem be not too strange, the cadences and images and syntax not too strange, the organisation, structure and theme not too strange. The word *ocnophil*, by the way, was suggested to Michael Balint because it stems from the Greek verb meaning to shrink, to hesitate, to cling. So the reader, with his ocnophilic tendencies, *clings* to the nourishing breast of proved traditional modes, to that with which he is most familiar. The avant-garde writer apprehends this: he expects resistance to his way-out inventions. William Wordsworth in his day, publishing the *Lyrical Ballads*, certain of the marked originality of his poems in style and theme – poems that were so different from those currently receiving general approbation – expected more derision than praise. And he was correct in this assumption. Thirty years after the publication of the *Lyrical Ballads* the common ocnophilic reader in England thought Wordsworth to be a fool who could write forty dull sonnets on one streamlet or go berserk about linnets, red-breasts, larks, cuckoos, daisies and 'the scenery of the English Switzerland'. That was generally the blunt response to a particularly original poet. Later in the nineteenth century, the same reader, or at least his great-nephew, would have been more comfortable with the poems of Robert Bridges than those of Manley Hopkins.

The paradox is that though the common reader may hanker for the familiar he also inwardly desires the poet to take heroic creative risks. This conflict is resolved eventually: strangeness endured ceases to be strange. As Dr Greenacre has pointed out in another context, the fear an individual may experience as a result of a strange event may in time give way to the triumph of recognition. It is sad that this recognition, in connection with fresh poetry, is so often postponed until after the poet's death.

Earlier I suggested that we are likely to resent an imitation of an admired model. I spoke of the claims of primacy, I remarked that something in us, prim and primitive, leads us to whisper, 'Copycat, copycat,' derisively. Perhaps at this point I can partially identify that something in us. For if we do, consciously or unconsciously, conceive the artist as hero, as one who takes philobatic risks, we will, with some irritation, discount the efforts of those who merely make replicas and imitations. For these imitators have not truly adventured, have avoided the thrilling risks that we admire, or will in time admire. We recognise that the imitator is no more philobatic than we are and so cannot, must not be acknowledged as poet-hero. On the contrary, he is a pretender and impudent. He is an imposter, and scorn, not honour, should be accorded him!

I Accuse

The early twentieth-century artists' slogan of *Make It New*, uttered hypnotically like a mantra from generation to generation, has led, in our time, to an ever more frenetic quest for innovation for its own sake. Given the accelerating pace of scientific discovery and technological invention it may seem appropriate that artists, those out in front, dare the rapids of the imagination. Besides, the peregrine spirit of artists, some more than others, can never be utterly still. As T. S. Eliot put it succinctly in 'Little Gidding':

> Last season's fruit is eaten
> And the fulfilled beast shall kick the empty pail.
> For last year's words belong to last year's language
> And next year's words await another voice.

Alas, daring the rapids does not, in itself, lead to an artistic language that is individual, significant and accessible. Too often, instead of language we are offered baby-babble as I was to find out when I caught up with *The British Art Show 4* at Manchester. Though I had approached the show expecting little I was curious. I had read reviews of it, some of which suggested that the work of these (to me) unknown young artists was weird and wonderful, that the Show itself was provocative, entertaining, disappointing, fun, predictable, significant, scatty, a triumph of hype, fetching, the very spirit of the age.

As I inspected different installations I remembered how, in 1916,

---

From a Hayward Gallery pamphlet (1996)

during the bloody catastrophe that was the First World War, Tristan Tzara and his mates in neutral Switzerland produced their own post-Futurist manifesto and called it, with nursery aplomb, Dada. Like the original Futurists, they would abolish the tradition of the past, decry the worth of bourgeois family morality and affirm that which was absurd. The one emotion they hoped to provoke was that of disgust.

As I stared at the pubic vision of Jordan Baseman, at his baby bib drooping with human hair, or at the baby pieces by Permindar Kaur, I thought how these so-called artists, like so many others grouped in this show, seemed to be Neo-Dadaists, defeated by the brilliant but crushing weight of our genuine artistic past. All they seemed able to do, in lucid absurdity, was to offer us gimmicks and daft performance. Worse, sometimes they leaned on titles for significance. E.g. *Manifest Destiny*. Get it? The baby has arrived at puberty. Somebody in the art schools of Britain and the U.S.A. should teach their students that genuine art is never merely an illustration of an idea.

The one young artist I had heard of before I set out for Manchester was Damien Hirst. I had read how he had won in 1995 the laughable Turner Prize. The winner laughs all the way to the bank while we laugh at the judges. The eminent art critic, William Feaver, had written that Hirst received this prize 'for his panache and effrontery, for livening things up by gracing them with impact, in yes, formaldehyde.' Wow!

Many years ago I was a medical student at King's College in London. There on the fifth floor, the large desolate Dissecting Room with those naked human corpses lying on slabs awaited our scalpels. Perhaps entering that room for the first time I did feel the Dadaist emotion of disgust. I know a fellow student, one more sensitive than me, did so and could hardly stay. But I doubt even he, given back his first innocence, would have felt any emotion – no disgust, nothing – when confronted by a nice stuffed sheep in a glass case. At best he might have admired the taxidermist's skill, and thought how this was one mild beast that would not worry even Lord Howe.

Damien Hirst, remarks Richard Cork, the distinguished art critic and one of the three guilty perpetrators of this exhibition, 'insists on confronting us with the brute fact of mortality . . . He presents the viewer with the incontrovertible reality of extinction . . . forces us to think queasily about the part we play in the extermination process . . . utterly serious about the need to acknowledge and somehow come to terms with the unfathomable transience of life.' Wow again! Perhaps I should take Mr Cork to a medical school's Path Lab museum – those bottles of diseased kidneys, that foetus monster pickled not for aesthetic delight. If Richard Cork has had an artistic experience surveying Hirst's sheep he would froth at the mouth in a Dissecting Room in the Pathology Museum. I cannot remember the name of the philosopher who remarked that farting through a keyhole was a clever thing to do, but was it art?

In fact, from the evidence of this Show, Damien Hirst does not even possess a colour sense. One respected critic, David Lee, would persuade us that Hirst allows us 'a fetching range of pastel shades'. Look at that awful bedroom pink which Cork suggests is 'deceptively festive' on which those dead souls we call butterflies are attached. Or that Hirst companion piece titled 'I Feel Love' with its glossy household paint of a pale green. Fetching? Retching, I think. Festive? Well, I suppose some feasts make you nauseous.

We have learnt from Freud that our appreciation of painting and sculpture does not rely simply on surface perception, but also on the power of hidden symbolism. But what most of the artists – Hirst, Baseman, Ofili, Wiltshire, etc. – offer us are emblems of surface ideas. The symbol, x, nameless, mysterious, ineffable, has become named, translated into banality. Take Hermione Wiltshire's *Casanova*. Mystery is absent. OK. The Computer animation offers us, undisguised, an emblem of male erection. I am reminded of the famous physiologist, Joseph Barcroft, who, on giving lectures on the function of the spleen, would begin by saying, 'Ladies and Gentlemen, with exception of the penis, the spleen alters its size more than any organ of the body.' Did Hermione Wiltshire attend such a lecture or is her simple, almost funny joke, a result of penetrating experience?

In Manchester, as I did my gallery rounds, I overheard better jokes from some of the sparse spectators. One woman commented compassionately, 'Maybe this lot were not allowed to play with paints when they were kids.' In Anya Gallacio's room, the walls of which had been coated apparently in 20 kgs of white chocolate, another woman remarked, 'Well, this takes the chocolate biscuit!' That this smelly excremental vision, like so many of the other infantile installations, should be taken seriously by some serious art critics is a treason of artistic standards and one that is despicable and depressing.

3

Playing to the Gallery

During the 1950s the middle-brow *Spectator* spokesmen of the Movement poets delighted in deflating cultural pretentiousness. 'Filthy Mozart' might have been a joke cry but the Movement's sincere suspicions of High Culture led a number of them to pose as outrageous Philistines. Among their anti-cultural interdictions, 'No more poems about paintings' seemed to have point since so many inert post-war pieces about sculpture and paintings had been published. There were other arguments offered elsewhere. The American poet, James Merrill, declared in 1960, 'I'm somewhat prejudiced against poems written about existing works of art. A certain parasitism is involved, I'm afraid: riding on someone else's coat-tails. Not that there aren't some beautiful ones . . .'

With galleries being increasingly visited by the general public, travel abroad more commonplace, and the ubiquitousness of colour reproductions, not a few twentieth-century poets have indeed contributed 'beautiful ones'. In 1986, when I was privileged to co-edit *Voices in the Gallery*, sponsored by the Tate, we were able to include eighty such poems, chosen from literally thousands of twentieth-century poems about paintings. We eschewed poems that were purely 'parasitical' and merely descriptive but chose those where the painting was *experienced* by the poet, inhabited by the poet, and thus survived the distance from their source: poems in their own right. However, we trusted that with the adjacency of poem and picture an illuminating synergy would result to allow serious entertainment for the reader, if not by

---

Review of Paul Durcan's *Give Me Your Hand*, from *Poetry Review*, Vol. 84, No. 2 (Summer 1994)

setting his/her imagination free, then at least by temporarily and profitably confining it.

Now the National Gallery has sponsored a similarly elegant book, having commissioned the quirky, talented Irish poet, Paul Durcan, to write about 50 of their paintings. Interesting as some of these poems are, few of them would survive the distance from their source. One that does so is 'Portrait of a Lady in Yellow'. Here Durcan imagines that a profile portrait of a young woman by Baldovinetti represents a victim of an IRA explosion in a Charing Cross Road bookshop. The father (mother?) has been summoned to London to identify the daughter and the poem itself is a monologue by the parent. I am reminded of the great lament by the fifteenth-century Welsh poet, Lewis Glyn Cothi for his dead son. Cothi wrote: 'The death of Sion stands by me/Stabbing me twice in the chest./My boy, my twirling taper,/My bosom, my heart, my song,/My prime concern till my death,/My clever bard, my daydream,/My toy he was, my candle/My fair soul, my one deceit . . .' Durcan writes:

> O my daughter.
> My mandolin in the window.
> My bedroom door.
> My ikon.
> My handkerchief under my pillow.
> My snake.
> Three feminine vowels.
> I miss you.

Most of the poems lack this serious tone and aspire to be humorously vernacular. When Paul Durcan does not self-indulgently divagate too much from the subject of the painting, when he keeps to the wit of brevity, then his humour which so often depends on the aggression of satire – 'taking the piss' – allows the reader to chuckle genuinely instead of groan as one does after an unfunny joke or a pun. Alas, for the most part Durcan presents himself as the Dave Allen of Poets who, like that Irish comedian, delights in funny blasphemy. Nothing wrong with that; nothing wrong with spouting monologues with inveterate flippancy, providing you don't happen to have a reverence for a particular painting, if not for theological dogma.

Though there are occasions when one might wish to salute the wildness of Durcan's inventive fancy, one is too often aware that these cabaret performances, monologues spoken by characters in the pictures, allow an untutored reader to opine that modern poetry is just prose cut up into arbitrary line-lengths. I take at random a half dozen lines. Durcan ventriloquises for Jesus:

> Mother was comprehensively insignificant
> In the scheme of things in Belfast city.
> She had no position on or in anything
> Nor did she read newspapers
> Except the odd tabloid or watch TV
> Except for *Coronation Street* . . .

Why are these undistinguished lines not continuous? Why do the lines begin with the presumption of capital letters? The above passage is not atypical.

Sophisticated readers, irrespective of whether the monologues are prose or poetry, will protest that trawling through most of this book is like being in an art gallery with an anecdotal companion maniacally trying to be funny. Worse, that as one looks at a painting long known and admired one's vision is soiled by the flippancy of a too proximate chatterbox. I felt like that when I turned the page to a reproduction of Rubens's *Samson and Delilah*, a painting I've long thought to be wonderful. In it Samson is asleep on Delilah's richly brocaded lap and a Philistine is cutting Samson's hair. Durcan gives the 'barber' these lines about Delilah:

> She whispers to me: He make the big love.
> I whisper: He what?
> She whispers: He make the big love . . .
> She whispers: He do the whole intercourse –
> Not just middle
> But beginning end middle . . .

And so on. Somehow, because I revere the painting I resent the cheap tone of the 'barber's' monologue. I resent, too, that Durcan's poems rarely pay true homage to the painting he writes about, unlike so many of the 'beautiful ones' of our best twentieth-century poets. On the other hand, it should be remembered that these monologues are all commissioned – and commissioned poetry, even by gifted poets, as one knows from the lamentable efforts of successive poets laureate, is only occasionally memorable.

The Dread of Sylvia Plath

Now as penalty for her skill,
By day she must walk in dread
Steel gauntlets of traffic, terror-struck
Lest, out of spite, the whole
Elaborate scaffold of sky overhead
Fall racketing finale on her luck.

from 'Aerialist', a poem of Sylvia Plath's Juvenilia

The notion that poets must suffer in order to produce their 'magical' artefacts, that they are other, mentally deranged, endowed with special powers as a result of this derangement, is one that has a long tradition. But it was a particularly popular notion during the nineteenth century and one fostered by the nineteenth-century writers themselves. Emile Zola, the novelist, was in no way put out by the conclusion of a jury of scientists that his genius owed its origins to the neurotic aspect of his nature.

Twentieth-century critics have largely endorsed these romantic ideas. Some suggest (quite wrongly in my view) that 'Only a maladjusted psychotic personality can faithfully interpret the maladjusted psychotic personality of the age in which we live.' They have seen in the Philoctetes legend of 'the wound and the bow' the allegorical predicament of the artist who, while owning special gifts (the bow) is alienated from his fellow men by his suffering psyche

---

A lecture delivered to the Poetry Society in London, 1972; later published in *Sea-Legs*, No. 1 (1978)

(the wound). Philoctetes, it will be remembered, was that famous Greek archer who owned Hercules' bow and magical arrows but who had to live in isolation because of an offensively odorous wound caused by a serpent's bite.

The lives and writings of a number of modern American poets in particular, have been illustrative of the Philoctetes predicament. It has been pointed out how even that apparently impersonal great poem of the twentieth century, 'The Waste Land', was written while the author, T. S. Eliot, was recovering in Switzerland from a nervous breakdown. Some of the recently prominent American poets have been altogether less reticent than T. S. Eliot about their personal mental suffering. Poets such as Robert Lowell (in *Life Studies*) and Sylvia Plath (not only in her later poems) and Anne Sexton have written insistently about their mental derangements with power and direction. Indeed, on occasions, they have almost boasted of their breakdowns and suicide attempts as warriors might of their war wounds. In a poem called 'Lady Lazarus', Sylvia Plath writes of her earlier attempts at suicide with a curious mixture of boastfulness and self-mockery:

> The first time it happened I was ten.
> It was an accident.
>
> The second time I meant
> To last it out and not come back at all.
> I rocked shut
>
> As a seashell.
> They had to call and call
> And pick the worms off me like sticky pearls.
>
> Dying
> Is an art, like everything else.
> I do it exceptionally well.
>
> I do it so it feels like hell . . .

The Dread of Sylvia Plath

When Sylvia Plath successfully committed suicide in 1963, her friend Anne Sexton wrote as if that final destructive act was something to be envied. She took literally the idea that 'Dying is an art' – a consummation devoutly to be wished for. Her desire to know all about the suicide act some may find a little obnoxious, necrophiliac:

> (Sylvia, Sylvia,
> where did you go
> after you wrote me
> from Devonshire
> about raising potatoes
> and keeping bees?)
>
> what did you stand by,
> just how did you lie down into?
>
> Thief! –
> how did you crawl into,
>
> crawl down alone
> into the death I wanted so badly and for so long,
>
> the death we said we both outgrew
> the one we wore on our skinny breasts,
>
> the one we talked of so often each time
> we drowned three extra dry martinis in Boston . . .

It seems that each generation needs to create a martyr-poet: twenty years ago, Dylan Thomas; a generation earlier, Wilfred Owen. More recently some have cast Sylvia Plath for that role. There are those who feel, romantically, that somehow the poet soars to forbidden heights, steals the ambrosia of the gods, illicitly brings heavenly fire to earth. And is punished as a result.

All this, of course, has little to do with prosaic truth – but nor has the machinery of myth-making which has certainly been at work on the reputation of Sylvia Plath. After her suicide, she became a cult figure and many, I fear, were attracted to her work not because of its own intrinsic worth but because of her suicide, or because in some quarters she had suddenly become a feminist heroine. Even a sophisticated critic like Ronald De Feo confessed (in *Modern Occasions*) that one reason he read Sylvia Plath was because he wished 'to share the poet's grief, know what it's like to suffer a steady painful breakdown, to reach the end of the line.' That may seem to be a most unhealthy reason to read an unhealthy poet. Certainly there is no gainsaying that, as Mr De Feo has pointed out, 'With other poets or writers who have taken their lives – Hart Crane, Virginia Woolf, Hemingway, for example – it is easy enough to lose ourselves in their work. But it is quite difficult to read Sylvia Plath's poetry and fiction and not think of her suicide. So often she herself is the subject of her own creations.' No doubt Mr De Feo was thinking of such later, raging poems as 'Daddy' where the enunciating protagonist resembles Sylvia Plath herself, or of her novel *The Bell Jar* where Esther Greenwood is but a pseudonym for Sylvia Plath who suffers a mental breakdown and attempts to kill herself in her twentieth year. That Sylvia Plath's work is half-nakedly autobiographical is plain, but does this mean, Q.E.D., that Ronald De Feo is correct when he adds, '*Ariel* is a work to be analysed rather than experienced, a psychological gold-mine rather than a work of art'? He continues, 'When we approach Miss Plath as a fascinating case we should feel ashamed but I'm afraid we cannot help ourselves . . . here we have the record of a strange, gifted young woman who not only thought about suicide but committed it. I can't help but wonder if Miss Plath would have become so widely known had she survived the writing of *Ariel*.'

I think there are enough genuine poetry readers more interested in Sylvia Plath's poetry than in Sylvia Plath's legend than perhaps Mr De Feo credits. An earlier, well-known woman poet, Edith Sitwell, may have belonged more to the history of publicity than of literature; I do not think this is true of Sylvia Plath. For leaving all the sentimentality and all the theatrical hoo-ha aside, it is translucently evident that her talent was extraordinary, that her work though limited by neurotic elements in her nature, was vibrant and arresting partly because of those same elements. Whatever the criticisms that can be levelled against her work, Sylvia Plath has written poems that are likely to be durable.

She was born in 1932 in Boston, Massachusetts, of Austrian and German parentage. Her father was a professor of biology and an international authority on bumble bees. His death in 1941 seems to have left her with a permanent emotional wound – one that like the serpent bite was as terrible for her as for Philoctetes in legend. Indeed the spirit of her father – almost always, incidentally, malevolent – inhabits many of her poems. 'A man in black,' she calls him, 'a man in black with a Meinkampf look.' He became for her an imaginary Nazi.

Sylvia Plath had begun to write as a child. 'I wrote my first poem,' she said, 'my first published poem when I was eight and a half. It came out in *The Boston Traveller* and from then on, I suppose, I've been a bit of a professional.' Her first book though, *The Colossus*, was not published until 1960. By then, much had happened to her. At Smith College, where she had been a brilliant student, she suffered a nervous breakdown and attempted suicide. Afterwards, recovered, she won a Fulbright scholarship, came to Cambridge, England, and met the English poet, Ted Hughes, whom she was to marry in 1956.

The poems in *The Colossus* were written during the first few years of her marriage. It was an impressive first book though two years after its publication, on being asked by Peter Orr of the British Council whether she wrote her poems to be read aloud she replied, 'This is something I didn't do in my earlier poems. For example, my first book, *The Colossus*, I can't read any of the poems aloud now. I didn't write them to be read aloud. They, in fact, quite privately bore me.'

Some critics agree with Sylvia Plath's self-deprecating attitude towards her first book. For example, Edward Butscher sees no relationship between *The Colossus* and her later work: in fact, finds it difficult to believe that the same poet wrote *The Colossus* and *Ariel*. It is true that some poems in the first book do read as apprentice work; but even those poems which are somewhat derivative of Dylan Thomas ('Hardcastle Crags' or 'I want, I want') or the animal poems such as 'Sow' or 'Medallion' which echo D. H. Lawrence and compete directly with the animal poems of her husband, Ted Hughes, have their own intrinsic interest and merit. It is also true that the poems in *The Colossus* are rarely as urgent at the later ones – though there are a few that seem to be indistinguishable from those she wrote later. For instance, that intense sensual poem, 'The Beekeeper's Daughter', with its incestuous undertones (Otto Plath was, after all, a beekeeper*) not only engages us on the page but, despite Sylvia Plath's protestations, can be successfully read out loud. It begins:

> A garden of mouthings. Purple, scarlet-speckled, black
> The great corollas dilate, peeling back their silks.
> Their musk encroaches, circle after circle,
> A well of scents almost too dense to breathe in.

After that unsecretive sexual introduction it continues:

> Hieratical in your frock coat, maestro of the bees,
> You move among the many-breasted hives,
>
> My heart under your foot, sister of a stone.
>
> Trumpet-throats open to the beaks of birds.
> The Golden Rain Tree drops its powders down.
> In these little boudoirs streaked with orange and red
> The anthers nod their heads, potent as kings
> to father dynasties. The air is rich.
> Here is a queenship no mother can contest –
>
> A fruit that's death to taste: dark flesh, dark parings

And we are forced to think of guilty sex and death and perhaps how the male bee dies after he has finished clasping the queen.

---

*Adolf Hitler's father, Alois, also kept bees as a hobby. I don't know whether Sylvia Plath knew that fact.

If many of the poems in *The Colossus* are not so luxuriantly intense as this or as urgent as later ones it is because, generally, the poet has allowed a comfortable distance between the texts and the reader even when they are cast in a transparently autobiographical mode. What is evident is that Plath's poems, even in this first book, are rarely translations of concepts, of ideas into words. It seems that more often than not she began her poems with the words themselves. Most of Sylvia Plath's contemporaries, especially other women poets in England – for example Patricia Beer and Fleur Adcock – frequently make words serve their ideas or use them discriminately to relate narratives of experience; in Sylvia Plath's case the reader is more linguistically enmeshed for the words appear to be primary – the ideas and her feelings, her old psychic wounds, in short, her own predicament, service the words. One is not utterly surprised to discover that Sylvia Plath – according to Lois Ames, her friend from Smith College days – would sit, on occasions, with her back to whomsoever entered the room as she circled words over and over in the red leather Thesaurus which belonged to her father, Otto Plath. Her lexical and ludic drives are already evident in *The Colossus* and, as always, word-originated poems, though often overstrained, do tend to discharge a heavy word-energy. (One only has to think of Dylan Thomas or the early George Barker and W. S. Graham.)

In any event, Sylvia Plath's first book contains a number of notable successes besides 'The Beekeeper's Daughter'. Let me name some of them: 'Black Rook in Rainy Weather', 'Watercolor of Grantchester Meadows', 'Night Shift', 'All the Dead Dears'. The latter two poems, along with others in the book less successful, focus concretely on that sense of dread and threat manifest in many of Plath's poems, early or late. I mean the threatening dread that cannot be defined or is named so variously that the very multiplicity of names given it betrays the fiction on each occasion of naming.

NIGHT SHIFT

It was not a heart, beating,
That muted boom, that clangor

Far off, not blood in the ears
Drumming up any fever

To impose on the evening.
The noise came from outside:
A metal detonating
Native, evidently, to

These stilled suburbs: nobody
Startled at it, though the sound
Shook the ground with its pounding.
It took root at my coming

Till the thudding source, exposed,
Confounded inept guesswork:
Framed in windows of Main Street's
Silver factory, immense

Hammers hoisted, wheels turning,
Stalled, let fall their vertical
Tonnage of metal and wood;
Stunned the marrow. Men in white

Undershirts circled, tending
Without stop those greased machines,
Tending, without stop, the blunt
Indefatigable fact.

The source of dread is named in this realistic poem yet even here the men in white undershirts become more than real: they have now become symbolic and something dreadful.

Martin Heidegger in *What is Metaphysics?* has well described this sense of dread which so many of us share and which seemed to assail Sylvia Plath so acutely. 'Dread,' wrote Heidegger, 'is always a dreadful feeling *about* but not about this or that. The indefiniteness of *what* we dread is not just a lack of definition: it represents the essential impossibility of defining the *what*.'

But defining the *what* is something some poets, Sylvia Plath among them, have tried to do. Of course to name the nameless, or rather the unnameable, is bound to be an unsuccessful enterprise but it may lead to the making of successful poems. 'Night Shift' is one such poem where definition is attempted in a curiously thrilling and uplifting way. In later poems the delineation of that sense of dread becomes more oppressive and approximates that description of dread by Heidegger where he pronounces:

> In dread, as we say, 'one feels something uncanny'. What is this *something* and this *one*? We are unable to say what gives *one* that uncanny feeling. *One* just feels it generally. All things, and we with them, sink into a sort of indifference. But not in the sense that everything simply disappears; rather in the very act of drawing away from us, everything turns towards us. This withdrawal of what-is-in-totality, which then crowds round us in dread, this is what oppresses us. There is nothing to hold on to. The only thing that remains and overwhelms us whilst what is slips away, is this *nothing*. Dread reveals Nothing.

Again in 'All the Dead Dears' Sylvia Plath attempts to discover the aetiology of the dread she feels. What crowd around the living, she suggests in this poem, are the predatory dead. These have insurmountable and ravaging claims upon the living as the living will have in turn when they die on those in the cradle:

> How they grip us through thin and thick,
> These barnacle dead!
> This lady here's no kin
> Of mine, yet kin she is: she'll suck
> Blood and whistle my marrow clean
> To prove it. As I think now of her head,
>
> From the mercury-backed glass
> Mother, grandmother, greatgrandmother
> Reach hag hands to haul me in,
> And an image looms under the fishpond surface
> Where the daft father went down
> With orange duck-feet winnowing his hair -

All the long gone darlings: they
Get back, though, soon,
Soon: be it by wakes, weddings,
Childbirths or a family barbecue:
Any tough, taste, tang's
Fit for those outlaws to ride home on,

And to sanctuary: usurping the armchair
Between tick
And tack of the clock, until we go,
Each skulled-and-crossboned Gulliver
Riddled with ghosts, to lie
Deadlocked with them, taking root as cradles rock.

If this poem lacks the oppressiveness of later poems it is not only because dread here is, as it were, named and its cause made explicit – it lacks the emotional desperation of the later poems. Sylvia Plath may write, 'she'll suck blood and whistle my marrow clean' but her tone is cool, resigned so that the reader is not persuaded that the poet believes necessarily in what she is saying. And despite all the sucking of blood and the whistling of the marrow clean, the dead, though predatory, are not presented as wildly malevolent. Endearments, whether ironic or not – 'all the long gone darlings' – also contribute to turn malignancy into something more benign.

Though Sylvia Plath's later poems of *Ariel* and *Winter Trees* reveal her to be more threatened, under greater pressure, and are written in a voice more consistently her own, one can still admire the early poems for what they are even while agreeing with say, a critic like A. Alvarez, a friend of Sylvia Plath, when he attributes greater importance and worth to those poems she wrote in 1960 after the birth of her daughter, Frieda. 'It is as though the child were proof of her identity,' Alvarez remarks interestingly, 'as though it liberated her real self. I think this guess is borne out by the fact that her most creative period followed the birth of her son two years later.' There are intimations in Sylvia Plath's work that her sense of her own identity was far from secure. Perhaps she felt most existentially herself when she was at work on a poem. In her early, successful

'Black Rook in Rainy Weather' she talks of the 'rare, random descent' of the inspirational angel who allows her to 'Patch together a content/Of sorts', to gain – and this is the point here – 'A brief respite from fear/Of total neutrality.'

There is no doubt that she felt herself, on one level, to be possessed by the malevolent ghost of her father. 'I am', she wrote in one strange poem, 'The Bee Meeting', 'the magician's girl who does not flinch.' She conceived herself to be a passive victim manipulated by a magician's power, or a Hiroshima victim, or a kind of Jew who survived a concentration camp. Of her poem 'Daddy' she wrote for a BBC programme (never actually broadcast) 'Here is a poem spoken by a girl with an Electra complex. Her father died when she thought he was God. Her case is complicated by the fact that her father was also a Nazi and her mother was possibly part Jewish.' Whether Sylvia Plath interpreted 'Daddy' in this way after she had written it, or had conceived its drift and thrust early on, consciously, as a slightly disguised persona-poem, a dramatic monologue, by one like her but not her, is a moot point. And a point finally irrelevant. What is clear is that Sylvia Plath, through such fantasies, attempted to make her own inward devastation a mirror of recent European history. Her private dream, or the private dream of her *doppelgänger*, became anchored to our common historical reality:

> I could hardly speak.
> I thought every German was you.
> And the language obscene
>
> An engine, an engine
> Chuffing me off like a Jew.
> A Jew to Dachau, Auschwitz, Belsen.
> I began to talk like a Jew.
> I think I may well be a Jew.
>
> The snows of the Tyrol, the clear beer of Vienna
> Are not very pure or true.
> With my gypsy ancestress and my weird luck

And my Taroc pack and my Taroc pack
I may be a bit of a Jew.

I have always been scared of *you*,
With your Luftwaffe, your gobbledygoo.
And your neat moustache
And your Aryan eye, bright blue.
Panzer-man, panzer-man, O You –

It seems to me that in 'Daddy' Sylvia Plath has borrowed blatantly the rhyming cadences used by T. S. Eliot in 'Sweeney Agonistes' – 'I gotta use words when I talk to you'. But what has irritated or even shocked so many critics and readers about 'Daddy' is not this borrowing of Eliot's rhythms – incidentally any 'Electra' would have been gripped by the Orestes, paranoid-like epigraph to 'Sweeney Agonistes', 'You don't see them, you don't – but I see them: they are hunting me down, I must move on' – no, rather it is the larger moral dilemma which exercises critics, that dilemma which inheres in George Steiner's powerful question: 'In what sense does anyone, himself uninvolved and long after the event, commit a subtle larceny when he invokes the echoes and trappings of Auschwitz and appropriates an enormity of ready emotion to his own private design?'

Mr Steiner has argued that 'the world of Auschwitz lies outside speech as it lies outside reason' – that the cry of silence is the most appropriate response to the fact of the Holocaust. And Irving Howe, speaking specifically of Sylvia Plath's poem 'Daddy', has pronounced, 'There is something monstrous, utterly disproportionate, when tangled emotions about one's father are deliberately compared with the historical fate of the European Jews.'

One cannot but sympathise with those views. Yet it is also true that silence sometimes itself can be a crime against humanity and no one can deny that true transcendent literature of the camps – certainly neither Steiner nor Irving Howe would do so – has been created by survivors of the Camps. At once, Paul Celan's 'Death Fugue' comes to mind. But what gives that poem its legitimacy? Is it that we know that Paul Celan himself was a victim of the concentration camp and that it was not a persona-poem written by one searingly imaginative, living all his life in comfortable Hampstead? Is it only the biographical fact that gives 'Death Fugue', that fine poem, its authenticity?

Of course one is offended by poems, novels, plays, films, that would *exploit* large historical, catastrophic events in order to make themselves more important, more significant. A film, for instance, like *Hiroshima, Mon Amour* which retailed a cheap, romantic love affair against what seemed to be the adventitious background of Hiroshima deserves nothing but contempt – though for all I know the man who made the film could have been a survivor of Hiroshima. What matters in our judgement of an artistic artefact is the seeming authenticity of it, not the truth or fiction of the biographical footnote – though often these authenticities or inauthenticities may be resonant with each other. Perhaps one must join finally with M. L. Rosenthal who admitted, 'It is perhaps begging the question to suggest that a genuine confessional poem (such as 'Daddy') has to be superbly successful artistically if it is to achieve fusion of the private and the culturally symbolic. . .'.

Fusion. However much Sylvia Plath played out roles in life one cannot believe her when she remarked to George MacBeth that she had a concentration camp in her mind. Simply she felt she was going through hell. Amongst all those surprising, sedative letters to her mother there is a passage where her voice rasps through with a naked directness: 'Don't talk to me about the world needing cheerful stuff. What the person out of Belsen, *physical or psychological* [my italics] wants is nobody saying the birdies go tweet-tweet, but the full knowledge that somebody else has been there and knows the *worst*, just what it is like. It's more help to me, for example, to know that people are divorced and go through hell than to hear about happy marriages.' Some may baulk at Sylvia Plath comparing her bust marriage to the torment of Belsen yet nobody can quantify what sends one person to the depths of hell and another only to its antechamber.

Many of her late poems do seem to be messages, sometimes incoherent ones from close to the furnace. Many of them have an oneiric quality. Perhaps it is not surprising that they should be dream-like given the time of night when they were written. 'These new poems of mine have one thing in common,' she wrote. 'They were all written at about four in the morning – that still blue, almost eternal hour before cockcrow, before the baby's cry, before the glassy music of the milkman settling his bottles.' They were also written apparently when she was lonely, separated from her husband and, because of her own mental make-up resulting from childhood experiences, clearly desperate. It would seem that Sylvia Plath was a prey to overwhelming, separation anxieties. She had been separated from her father when she was a small girl. Her good, loved father became a menacing father in her poems. Perhaps this was because – though he could not help it – by dying he had abandoned her.

A. Alvarez in his book *The Savage God* writes, 'As the months went by her poetry became progressively more extreme . . . the last weeks each trivial event became the occasion for poetry: a cut finger, a fever, a bruise.' But to go a little deeper, it is obvious that these 'trivial' events had enormous significance for her. They represented her deepest feelings and her most central resentment. She wrote a poem called 'Contusion'. She felt bruised spiritually. She wrote a poem about a cut finger calling it 'Cut' – and surely that's how she felt herself to be, her whole being, cut. Cut and bruised and wounded.

Besides, the feeling she had resulting from the cutting of her thumb – 'the top quite gone', she wrote, 'except for a sort of hinge of skin' – was no doubt related to her feelings of separation. The separation of a bit of her own body was resonant with her long held, submerged separation anxiety. Of course, all this may be a wild guess, and it may not be proper to hazard guesses of this kind which have, after all, little to do with literary criticism. Nevertheless, the nature of her late poems is such that one is tempted to look at her poetry as evidence of a state of mind. For her desperation is so clearly touching and so painful even when encapsulated in genuinely wrought poems which do more than express a private terror.

'The true poet dreams being awake,' wrote Lionel Trilling in his most persuasive essay, *Art and Neurosis*. 'He is not possessed by his subject but has dominion over it.' This was not always true of Sylvia

Plath. It needs to be said loudly that a number of her poems fail, that more often than not her vision remained too inward, too recondite, too private, that she did not always have dominion over her material. She herself disliked poetry that was a mere effusion of the unconscious, that was disordered, arbitrary, corybantic. 'I think my poems immediately come out of the sensuous and emotional experiences I have,' she declared to Peter Orr in that British Council interview. 'But I must say that I cannot sympathise with those cries from the heart that are informed by nothing except by a needle or a knife or whatever it is. I believe that one should be able to control and manipulate experiences, even the most terrifying like madness, being tortured this sort of experience, and one should be able to manipulate these experiences with an informed and intelligent mind. I think that the personal experience is very important, but certainly it shouldn't be a kind of shut box and mirror-looking narcissistic experience. I believe it should be relevant and relevant to larger things such as Hiroshima and Dachau and so on.'

The personal experiences that most engaged Sylvia Plath were, for the most part, extreme ones – hence her talk of madness and of being tortured. M. L. Rosenthal invented the useful term 'Confessional Poet' to categorise those, like Plath, who broadcast the drama of their disordered emotional lives and made their 'Psychological vulnerability and shame' an embodiment of our history and civilisation. This is quite different from being simply an autobiographical poet who, to quote another American, Daniel Hoffman, is not 'trapped by emotional illness, in sufferings brought on by unresolvable crises'. He is able to 'use more of his life in his work and even when the poet's subject is similar to the confessional poet's, that subject may be viewed with perspective, detachment, humour.' In short, the unhealthy confessional poet, compared with the healthy autobiographical one is likely to be much more limited. Who can dispute that? All the same, the jet-energy force of a poetry like that of Sylvia Plath's resides precisely in this very same narrowness of bore.

Not that all Sylvia Plath's poems are couched in the vocabulary of atrocity, or reflect her extreme unhappiness and personal terror. Those poems to do with her young children, for instance, express small, joyful affirmations. She wonders at the strangeness of them. She displays a delicate tenderness that involves the reader in no sentimental way. She can begin a poem with the word 'Love' – 'Love set you going like a fat gold watch.' But painful pressures were always there and she was encouraged to express them nakedly in poetry because of the example of Robert Lowell in *Life Studies* where he wrote about his experiences in a mental hospital, and because of the views of the influential critic, A. Alvarez. She admired particularly Alvarez's introduction to his Penguin anthology *The New Poetry* where he suggested that after the horror of the concentration camps and the hydrogen bomb 'the makers of horror films are more in tune with contemporary anxiety than most of the English Poets' and he praised poets, like Lowell, who 'coped openly with the quick of their experience, experience sometimes on the edge of disintegration and breakdown.' Alvarez believed that *Life Studies* was 'as brave and revolutionary as *The Waste Land*'. If Sylvia Plath admired Alvarez's criticism, he in turn admired her work, her late work particularly, and encouraged her verbally – she would read her poems to him – and by publishing her poems in the *Observer.*

Not that she needed his encouragement to write poems that were dominated by suggestions of abnormality. She could do no other. Soon, too soon, we are given the news that Electra is dead: soon, finally, we are returned to that cool, detached vision of herself, finished and marmoreal, where alas,

> The woman is perfected
> Her dead
>
> Body wears the smile of accomplishment
> The illusion a Greek necessity
>
> Flows in the scrolls of her toga
> Her bare
>
> Feet seem to be saying:
> We have come so far, it is over.

In such a poem Sylvia Plath envisages her own death as something decorous, perfected. There is no stink of putrefaction there. Her dead body is on stage: a theatrical transfiguration has taken place and this dramatic romance is no less powerful for being unhealthy. Moreover, this play-acting not only augurs her suicide but, in some small measure, contributes to it. It signals, as it were, that the curtain can now come down and her myth may begin and grow.

Without Self-Importance

Here is a roll-call of some enjoyable British poets of the mid-twentieth century: W. H. Auden, Louis MacNeice, Dylan Thomas, John Betjeman, Keith Douglas, Bernard Spencer – but already some may well be interrupting this partial register with a 'Bernard who?' It is curious how some poets 'star' while others as gifted as Spencer remain neglected. In 1963, for instance, Sylvia Plath, who since has become notorious, gassed herself; that same year, the 54-year-old Bernard Spencer, sick and febrile, fell to his death from an open door of a train that perhaps he had opened mistakenly, but his poems continue to be largely unread despite spirited attempts by admirers such as Lawrence Durrell and Alan Ross to draw attention to them. As Roger Bowen remarked in his introduction to Spencer's *Collected Poems*, published by Oxford University Press in 1981, 'Spencer lived in the margins of literary reputation, an unassuming and, at times, almost anonymous figure.'

Even those in the habit of reading contemporary poetry tend not to know more than two or three Bernard Spencer poems, those that have adorned this or that anthology. They associate him vaguely with Geoffrey Grigson's gritty *New Verse* of the 1930s. Older readers may have even contemporaneously read the brief, too brief, obituary in *The Times* of Friday 13 September 1963. The anonymous obituarist remarked, 'few poets have had a subtler or profounder feeling for the inward character of place and of situation' and went on to praise his 'deeply-felt poems that have a haunting tone far more

---

Poetry Review, Vol. 85, No. 3 (Autumn 1995)

effective than display or rhetoric.' Many may have read that obituary; few pursued the poems.

At present, it is not the 'difficult' poets who are most likely to suffer fashionable neglect. On the contrary, those who advance wilful and riddling obfuscations or who salt their poems with studied esoteric information are seized upon, particularly by academic critics. It gives them professional work to do. Bernard Spencer does not lean on scholarly sources – he is no David Jones, nor is he a phrase-maker, one confusingly arbitrary like John Ashbery. But his work is not over-direct either, over-explicit. It does not name everything and suggest nothing. Sometimes the poems seem to be, not so much allusive, as slant, because of his thinking in long sentences and his use of an elliptical syntax. The whole poem may consist of one or two long sentences only, as in the straightforward 'In an Auction Room' (20 lines; one sentence) which gives itself up to the reader without even the smallest obstruction until we come, perhaps, to the concision of the very last line, 'what has no name; or growing old.'

> How many deaths and partings spilled
> this jumble in an upper room;
> and every chair or mirror filled
> with elbowing and smell of lives:
> the gloom
> of this tall wardrobe stopped the sun
> entering a home; the great brass bed
> stood in its throne-room, and its springs
> and shining arms are crammed like mines
> with regal illness and with love:
> the terrible settee
> with worn red flowers, the table de nuit,
> the picture with the little man
> walking the infinite road
> to a West of gold;
> these have all been (and are to be)
> loves truer than our human mould,
> or desperate walls

flung up against the shock of things,
what has no name; or growing old.

'In an Auction Room' exemplifies another of Bernard Spencer's stylistic habits: the cataloguing of objects: 'the tall wardrobe', 'the great brass bed', 'the terrible settee', 'the picture with the little man/walking the infinite road/to a West of gold'. If this pre-Larkin poem reminds one of Philip Larkin perhaps it is because of the way Spencer moves from the listing of *concrete* details to a final five-line *abstract* conclusion, and the snapping of that conclusion tight with a closing rhyme.

I do not know whether Philip Larkin was influenced by Bernard Spencer's work, which first appeared in book form in 1946. I do not know if Larkin even read him diligently. He allowed him only one poem in his anthology, *The Oxford Book of Twentieth Century English Verse* (1973). Yet there are other poems that may remind the reader of Larkin, not least Bernard Spencer's 'Passed On':

Some of his messages were personal
almost as his lost face; they showed he knew
about their pets, the life that went on beating
in desks and scrapbooks, and each particle

of the family language: the young engineer,
who had put khaki on and died in the mud,
at times would almost touch them.
Yet he was
(But how?) the sing-song spirit-gospeller;

the irrelevance, the baby-talk and spout
of 'Vera', the Control; and stagey things,
a bell, a violin, an Indian chief;
even what crashed the furniture about.

But then he was their son. That love, that birth
made the old couple blind enough to bear
the medium's welcome, taking no offence,
and haunt his room that opened clean off earth.

Both 'In an Auction Room' and 'Passed On' were included in Bernard Spencer's initial volume, *Aegean Islands* (1946). It contained sixteen poems written before 1940 and twenty-two completed between 1940 and 1942. It has to be admitted that it was an uneven book. Spencer included too many pieces that read like occasional jottings rather than poems resonant with their own inward nature. But *Aegean Islands* does contain, apart from the two poems already quoted, others that, having been read, stay around in the memory – among them 'Yachts on the Nile', 'Peasant Festival' and the matchless 'Part of Plenty':

> When she carries food to the table and stoops down
> – Doing this out of love – and lays soup with its good
> Tickling smell, or fry winking from the fire
> And I look up, perhaps from a book I am reading
> Or other work: there is an importance of beauty
> Which can't be accounted for by there and then,
> And attacks me, but not separately from the welcome
> Of the food, or the grace of her arms.
>
> When she puts a sheaf of tulips in a jug
> And pours in water and presses to one side
> The upright stems and leaves that you hear creak,
> Or loosens them, or holds them up to show me,
> So that I see the tangle of their necks and cups
> With the curls of her hair, and the body they are held
> Against, and the stalk of the small waist rising
> And flowering in the shape of breasts;
>
> Whether in the bringing of the flowers or the food
> She offers plenty, and is part of plenty,
> And whether I see her stooping, or leaning with the flowers,
> What she does is ages old, and she is not simply,
> No, but lovely in that way.

Apart from a small private press edition, the only other book of his to appear during Bernard Spencer's lifetime was *With Luck*

Lasting in 1963. Roy Fuller reviewed it in *The London Magazine.* 'Bernard Spencer has not in fact had the best of luck with his collection,' he wrote. 'He was one of the brightest of the poets who grew up under the shadow of Auden and Spender but he published no books in the thirties. His wartime poems did not come out until 1946 when the boom in verse was really over . . . Thereafter silence until 1960 when twenty-five poems were published in a tiny edition by a private press. Let's hope his new book will properly consolidate his position . . .'.

It did not 'consolidate his position'; but the poems in *With Luck Lasting* were successful even if Bernard Spencer was not. Over the years Bernard Spencer's style and the character of his texts did not appreciably change. He asserted what A. T. Tolley has called in *The Poetry of the Forties* 'the primacy of the particular'. The same mannerisms inhered in the late poems as in the early and he continued to focus, with greater confidence, on solitariness, on moody exotic places haunted by their own past – he was an admirer of the poetry of George Seferis – on people and things (especially boats), on his own past too, memories re-inhabited, and on mature love. Perhaps, after the publication of *Aegean Islands* the tone of his poems, as Roger Bowen suggests, became more elegiac and reflected increasingly 'an enclosing sense of alienation'. In any case, *With Luck Lasting* offered its too few readers a rare attribute in contemporary books of verse: a sure-fire serious pleasure.

In 1940, unfit for active service because of a 'bad lung', Bernard Spencer joined the British Council and was posted first to Greece and then, later, to Egypt. In Cairo he became friends with such writers as Keith Douglas and Lawrence Durrell, with whom he shared a first floor flat and co-edited a poetry magazine called *Personal Landscape.* After Spencer's death, Durrell accurately remarked that Spencer was very much a poet of place and mood. Indeed it is impossible to escape the context of Mediterranean countries as one reads his poems. The reader continually has a sense of reading a nostalgic and lonely expatriate – one who owns the acuteness of observation which belongs peculiarly to a wide-awake stranger. Even when Bernard Spencer returned to London, his cataloguing of sounds heard from his temporary home in Regent's Park Terrace seems to be the habit of one forever a foreigner, of a man not fatigued by too familiar surroundings:

> The noises round my house. On cobbles bounding
> Victorian-fashioned drays laden with railway goods;
> their hollow sound like stones in rolling barrels:
> the stony hoofing of dray horses.
>
> Further, the trains themselves; among them the violent,
> screaming like frightened animals, clashing metal;
> different the pompous, the heavy breathers, the aldermen,
> of those again which speed with the declining
> sadness of crying along the distant routes
> knitting together weathers and dialects.
>
> Between these noises the little teeth
> of a London silence.

Over and over again Bernard Spencer brought into his poems the noises things make – the sounds of insects, plants, animals:

> Against my bedside light
> a small green insect flings itself with a noise
> tiny and regular, a 'tink, tink, tink'.
>
> *'In a Foreign Hospital'*

> When she puts a sheaf of tulips in a jug
> And pours in water and presses to one side
> The upright stems and leaves that you hear creak. . .
>
> *'Part of Plenty'*

> Alone on a building site a watchdog stalks by the fire,
> wooed and repulsed by the jump-away flames, or raises its head
> at a barking that chips a hole in distance.
>
> *'From my Window'*

Yet despite Bernard Spencer's remarkable ability to evoke with such precision the sound of things, despite his self-evident auditory sensitivity (as if he were someone suddenly cured of a chronic deafness) his poems depend very little on their rhythmic quality to gain their effect. The rhythm of Spencer's poems is related without ostentation to an ordinary, though sophisticated, speaking voice and is constant from the first poem to the last. There is little flexibility in the aural matrix of his poems. The cadences serve Spencer's purposes adequately and, indeed, all his poems can be read out loud without difficulty. Yet they are not memorable on this account. When Spencer wishes to heighten an effect at the end of a poem he does so by the simplest aural tricks – by a concluding rhyme or by the urgency suggested by repetition. Here are the concluding lines of four poems:

> Two elms and their balanced attitude like dancers,
>   their arms like dancers.
>
> *'Allotments: April'*

> and if I am lucky, find some link, some link.
>
> *'In a Foreign Hospital'*

> human to ask, but cold. But cold.
>
> *'The Administrator'*

> which we painted out. Which we painted out.
>
> *'The Empire Clock'*

Again, the mannerisms remain constant: 'Allotments: April' was written in 1936 whereas 'The Empire Clock' was written after he left for Vienna in October 1962 and after he had sent *With Luck Lasting* to the publishers. What remained constant, too, is the 'respect for the object' which, matched with and allied to something darkly inward in himself, gives so many of Spencer's poems their energy, their force. Bernard Spencer commented that 'more sophisticated poetry if it has to have any force has also to be rooted in the uncivilised layers of the mind, where what is ugly and what is beautiful can both be contemplated and do not exclude each other.'

A number of Spencer's poems, despite their rootedness in a common external reality, infer a mystery, lead the reader to the fringes of the uncomfortable and achieve, or even describe, a certain aloof dream-like quality. Of an audience of upturned faces watching trapeze acrobats under the circus tent, Spencer writes:

> Theirs are like faces sleep has drained. The dark
> communion of dream which holds them world-aloof
> is splashed with light from an arc. All their dear care
> goes whispering and yearning
> high above the sweep of circus benches
> there where two mannikins under the great bell roof
> walk down a hair;
> he, prancing and masterful in his red-slashed shirt
> and slight and hesitant,
> she like a twist of paper turning.
>
> *'Watchers'*

In this description, external reality and the dream almost merge as one. The description is masterly and only flawed by 'all their dear care' which one feels was only inserted because of the rhyme with the perfectly just and surprising 'walk down a hair'.

In 'Table-Tennis' the dream quality is more directly described, becoming macabre:

> Because the heavy lids will not drag up
> I am playing table-tennis with eyes closed,
> asleep, and striking at the sound;
> with what a grovelling score may be supposed.
>
> In my dream I am tired and long to stop.
> Pit-ponies, sex-fiends, gypsies' bears have found
> mercy, I hope, in sleep.
>
> Each thump, each kick
> or chastening of my day crowds back in this
> unskilful ghostly tournament of poc-pic.

I know my Opponent; Who he is I miss.
The ordeal turns wilder than before;
now serve and smash must fly through a shut door.

Here the Ingmar Bergman-like Opponent has, as it were, risen from the Chess Board to play a different game.

The critic Martin Dodsworth maintains that Bernard Spencer achieves 'an extreme objectivity in his verse that almost squeezes personality out of the poem.' This does not seem to me to be true. Spencer is not a camera. His descriptive poems, while appearing to be objective, are infused with his own subjective outlook. It is as true to say that personality is *never* squeezed out of his poems. For instance, if with extreme objectivity he describes a view from his window and speaks with accuracy – I quote again:

Alone on a building site a watchdog stalks by the fire,
wooed and repulsed by the jump-away flames, or raises its head
at a barking that chips a hole in distance.

Spencer is also bringing to the scene his own feelings of solitariness. In fact he identifies himself with the dog. The dog is alone. Bernard Spencer is alone at the window. Another dog is barking in the distance emphasising that the dog beneath his window is solitary. The barking noise as invoked thus becomes extraordinarily *sad*. This anthropomorphic tendency in Spencer's descriptions and his empathy with things and animals – see also 'The Leopards' and 'Cripples' – work against an 'extreme objectivity' in his poems and make them more personal.

All Spencer's poems that refer to his own loneliness or rather to his sense of being solitary – and there are a number of these – are infused with feeling:

IN A FOREIGN HOSPITAL

Valleys away in the August dark the thunder
roots and tramples: lightning sharply prints
for an instant trees, hills, chimneys on the night.

We lie here in our similar rooms with the white
furniture, with our bit of Death inside us
(nearer than that Death our whole life lies under);
the man in the next room with the low voice,
the brown-skinned boy, the child among its toys
and I and others. Against my bedside light
a small green insect flings itself with a noise
tiny and regular, a 'tink; tink, tink'.

A Nun stands rustling by, saying good night,
hooded and starched and smiling with her kind,
lifeless, religious eyes. 'Is there anything
you want?' – 'Sister, why yes, so many things:'
England is somewhere far away to my right
and all Your letter promised; days behind
my left hand or my head (or a whole age)
are dearer names and easier beds than here.
But since tonight must lack for all of these
I am free to keep my watch with images,
a bare white room, the World, an insect's rage,
and if I am lucky, find some link, some link.

In the last year or so of his life, apparently happily remarried and working for the British Council in Vienna, he completed a further ten poems including one addressed to his new-born son. They are no different in mode from those in *With Luck Lasting*. Along with the poems from *Aegean Islands* and *With Luck Lasting* they can be found in his *Collected Poems* which Oxford University Press re-issued in 1981. It was sensitively introduced by Roger Bowen who included in this volume previously uncollected and unpublished poems, a number of which, alas, are inferior and which Bernard Spencer himself might have suppressed – not least his juvenilia. The posthumous inclusion of embryo notebook poems by an over-enthusiastic editor dilutes the impact of a poet's work for future readers – whether that poet be Bernard Spencer or Philip Larkin. Nevertheless, Spencer's book is one that will allow pleasure and illumination to those who care for poetry and who have the will to seek it out. As Roger Bowen asserts, Bernard Spencer was one who lacked any desire for self-advertisement and was a 'witty, self-deprecatory, sombre, and humorous man who wrote excellent poetry and died before his time.' Indeed it was as if he knew he would be neglected and anonymous. He identified himself with one of these boats which from harbour

> will have gone with no hooting or fuss,
> simply absent from its place among the others,
> occupied, without self-importance,
> in the thousands-of-millions-of sea.

John Ormond, a Neglected Poet

Twenty-five years ago, the star of Dylan Thomas shone with such a dazzling intensity that few could discern, on the post-war Welsh scene, any other poets at work. The only exception, perhaps, was Dylan Thomas's friend, Vernon Watkins, but no young Welsh poets, at that time, attracted attention. The Anglo-Welsh poets born in the 1920s form, as Leslie Norris has remarked, 'almost a lost generation'. Worse, these poets were heavily influenced by Dylan Thomas. They caught his fury of romantic sound and they used derivative metaphors that were overblown, over-ripe, mildewed.

One such poet was John Ormond, who was then just beginning to publish in the literary magazines. Ormond, or Ormond Thomas as he was then known, was born in Dunvant, a village near Swansea, in 1923. He sat literally at the feet of his older Swansea neighbours, Vernon Watkins and Dylan Thomas, and listened to their talk of poetry and of poets as if to holy writ. His own poetry was compounded, not unexpectedly, out of the wordy mannerisms of his literary heroes at their worst. Hardly a promising beginning; and, indeed, John Ormond's struggle in writing poetry ever since was a shedding of these powerful influences and the discovery of his own unadorned, authentic voice. Or, as Glyn Jones has put it, 'Throughout his career as a poet, it seems to me, he has exhibited an unrelenting struggle to find his own true subject matter and a way to deal with this subject matter in his own personal manner.'

From *Modern Poets in Focus* (1973)

His development then has been, in part, a reaction against the windy gesturing of his early derivative work, and this development has been so sure that few now could accuse John Ormond of being anything other than himself – a verbally fastidious poet who often revised his work obsessively. Randal Jenkins informs us, in *Poetry Wales*, that Ormond's (relatively recent poem) 'Salmon' took four and a half years to complete and went through about thirty drafts and three hundred or so work sheets. Of course there is a danger in revising too much – a too long search for the right word, the continual rubbing out of this phrase and replacing it by that, may turn off the original current of feeling that startled a first draft of a poem into rough existence.

After Dylan Thomas's death in late 1953 John Ormond's 'career' as a poet seemed to have come to a final full stop. He joined the BBC in Wales and proceeded to make a successful reputation for himself as a gifted documentary film director. In 1964, however, he began to write again – yet he did not at once allow himself to think that he may be, primarily, a professional poet rather than a BBC television director who happened to write verse in his spare time. Perhaps the publication of a selection of his poems, *Requiem and Celebration*, in 1969, by the small Welsh publisher, Christopher Davies, and the resultant attention given to his work by fellow Anglo-Welsh writers (plus important encouragement from the Welsh Arts Council) helped him to feel more secure in his primary vocation.

Leslie Norris, for instance, reviewing *Requiem and Celebration* in *Poetry Wales* remarked how, after his derivative beginnings, 'His imagery had grown infinitely more detailed, clear and relevant. He is at his best when he deals with other men and women.' To be sure, John Ormond has a very genuine gift as a portraitist. This is evident not only in his poems but in his television films on Vernon Watkins, Dylan Thomas, Alun Lewis, and R. S. Thomas, and can even be found, unexpectedly, in essays about painting. (John Ormond had a deep, lifelong interest in painting and when young wanted to become a painter rather than a poet.) Thus, in an essay on Ceri Richards, the painter, who was also born in Dunvant, Ormond indulged in some childhood reminiscences:

> One of my vivid recollections of Tom Richards (Ceri Richards's father) is of his occupying a corner in the Big Seat in Ebenezer. The preacher would open the Welsh Bible to his text: *Yn y dechreuad yr oedd y Gair.* Oh, Tom Richards would say, clearly very surprised. Then with a clatter of bindings falling off and a whispering of rice-paper, for there were two Bibles in the pulpit and both were used: *In the Beginning was the Word.* I *see*, Tom Richards would add, as though the whole meaning of everything that ever was now struck him, the actual syllables of Gospel, for that matter, never before that second having been uttered. He would draw his left hand (half his thumb, half his index-finger, and the top joint of his middle finger missing from an accident in the works) slowly across his brow, clearing his mind for the next revelation . . .

This perceptive and economical kind of humorous observation about Welsh character is evident in a number of his poems. Always, John Ormond communicated a rare warmth of feeling towards those whom he portrayed. Evidently liking people, he not only tolerated their odder behaviour but actively savoured and celebrated their eccentricities, their exaggerations. In telling us, in his poems, about the old cathedral builders, about the religious fanatic Johnny Randall, about the cemetery attendant Froga who 'had the eyes of a dying seal in a bankrupt circus', or about John Owen, market gardener and organist (that Benthamite of music), Ormond, in a curious way, is giving us more than amusing portrayals: he is writing a kind of love poetry. He is saying in a very open manner to his dusty kinsfolk, 'I love you'. Or, at least, 'I loved you.'

> Early and lately dead, each one
> Of you haunts me. Continue
> To tenant the air where I walk in the sun
> Beyond the shadow of yew.
> I speak these words to you, my kin
> And friends, in requiem and celebration.

In a review of *Requiem and Celebration* John Heath-Stubbs hinted that Ormond in writing about such characters as Johnny Randall 'moved, as it were, from the world of Dylan Thomas to that of R. S. Thomas.' I doubt if this is true. Johnny Randall, John Owen, and others, could have lived at ease in Dylan Thomas's *Under Milk Wood*. They could do so, I hasten to add, not so much because one writer has influenced another but rather because the characters that both poets portray share the same culture and tradition. Similarly, John Ormond's 'Froga' is a relation of Dylan Thomas's 'Hunchback in the Park' rather than a literary derivation; and like Dylan Thomas, and unlike R. S. Thomas, John Ormond owns a nice bawdy humour. The 'switchback lady' in 'Design for a Tomb', like Polly Garter in *Under Milk Wood*, knew the joy and voluptuousness of saying, 'Yes, yes, yes.'

> Dwell in this stone who once was tenant of flesh.
> Alas, lady, the phantasmagoria is over,
> Your smile must come to terms with dark for ever.
>
> Carved emblems, puff-cheeked cherubs and full vines,
> Buoy up your white memorial in the chapel
> Weightlessly over you who welcomed a little weight.
>
> Lie unprotesting who often lay in the dark,
> Once trembling switchback lady keep your stillness
> Lest marble crack, ornate devices tumble.

To Englishmen, the characters Ormond draws may seem rather histrionic, even operatic. The fact is, in Wales, the stage Welshman sometimes walks less on the boards of the theatre than on the ground of the not so green valleys where he holds forth with sublime and comic portentousness and sings expressively in a real choir. It is interesting to see Ormond, in a more recent poem, 'Paraphrase for Edwin Arlington Robinson', which he included in his second volume *Definition of a Waterfall* (O.U.P., 1973), portraying a non-Welsh personality. Perhaps it is significant that John Ormond chose to focus on this New England poet – a poet, incidentally, that Dylan Thomas greatly admired. Evidently Ormond, deaf in one ear, could feel a special sympathy for the partially deaf

Arlington Robinson who, in blank verse and dramatic monologue, also drew pert psychological portraits of local characters. Ormond's poem addressed to Arlington Robinson is more than a sympathetic portrayal of the American poet's life, it is a salute, 'each man sawing at his own bleak tune.'

> Sometimes you imagined you detected clues
> To a code, but it was only the singing wires
>
> Of the death of the aural, the eighth nerve
> Shrinking from lack of blood. That fenced you
>
> High on a dangerous peak of vertigo, giddy
> But unfalling. You said you mourned a 'lost
>
> Imperial music'. What you were emperor of
> Was a domain you did not recognize
>
> As worth the name: a kingdom of aspirers
> Without wings, a thin parish of prophets
>
> Without words – except for baffled Amen,
> A scraggy choir without a common hymn,
>
> But no man without music in the throng
> And each man sawing at his own bleak tune.

John Ormond does not only give us portraits. It has been said that his is 'the poetry of quest and dissatisfaction'. That is to say the quest for revelation. But Ormond, as can be seen from his poetry, is a secular man and one, apparently, not committed to any life-view, philosophical or political. As Randal Jenkins points out, 'he finds no consolatory answers to the eternal riddle'. However, in his search for such answers he asks the old questions of Who? and Why? and returns to his beginnings to read all the postcards from the past where 'nothing makes sense except the final X'. His enquiry leads him back to his own childhood village and its occupants, to his grandparents, to his mother when young, to his own birth:

> Upstairs in this stone house,
> Up the twelve crooked stairs
> My mother climbed to bear me.
> At eleven o'clock on a Spring night
> I fell from her dark into candlelight,
> Came to my own flesh as the string was cut
> And lay alone on the bloody sheet.

His questing search for 'a glimpse of holy law' leads him beyond 'the home patch', beyond a merely personal past. His historical imagination latches on to objects that have sent their signals forward over the chasm of centuries: ruined farmhouses, ancient monuments, fossils, artefacts of a distant Celtic culture whose shadows are barbarously anonymous and mysterious. His scrutiny of and speculation about the past leads him – despite the paradox of an elegiac tone – to a kind of affirmation. Life survives tenaciously as a flowering weed whatever the adversity, or to put it another way, 'it was the barley's world. Some monuments move,' and again there does appear to be a designed continuity in all things, 'a found world without end'.

One metaphor Ormond has taken to illustrate this is the river that, like a good marriage, is forever changing and is forever the same. Even the wild aberration of the rapids leading to a waterfall is but a temporary if beautiful diversion – the inconstancy of waters separated by rocks is soon reconciled and in that reconciliation there is a quality of joy, an imprisoned freedom:

> From ledge to pool breakneck across rocks
> Wild calm, calm chaos skein their paradox
>
> So that excited poise is fiercely dressed
> In a long instant's flow of rest,
>
> So that this bridegroom and his bride in white
> Parting together headlong reunite

Among her trailing braids. The inconstancy
Is reconciled to fall, falls and falls free.

In 'Salmon', incidentally, John Ormond addresses the Greek Heraclitus as the 'Weeping Philosopher' presumably because of his pessimism in teaching that 'You cannot step twice into the same river.' On the other hand, Heraclitus, though seeing the universe as a state of ceaseless change and flow, also taught 'the way up and the way down is one and the same' and 'in the circumference of a circle the beginning and the end are common'.

To some it may seem that John Ormond's backward look, his journey back full of instinct like the salmon, is but an existential search for roots. In any case, if his quest for revelation leads him to dwell on births and exits he is no original in that. But the poems he now writes as a result of such preoccupations – even those that fail, even those that are too abstract or too long for their weight – are all his own. Dylan Thomas has been dead these many years and readers need no longer be dazzled by his fixed star. Other figures can now be seen on the Welsh scene and one of the most interesting and rewarding of these is undoubtedly John Ormond.

Introductions

D. H. LAWRENCE

There are critics who believe that a poem should be examined without reference to the biography of the poet who wrote it. There are others who feel that a certain knowledge about the poet's life, while not making the poem any better, can add a dimension which allows the reader to be involved in it more immediately and personally. In some cases, gossip about a poet's life and death has become so public that it is virtually impossible for most readers to separate the poetry from their knowledge of a life that has been written about and mythologised.

D. H. Lawrence himself broadcast his biography – only thinly disguised – in novels, in plays, and in his poems. He was born the son of a miner in a mother-dominated family in Nottinghamshire. He, being the bright boy of the family, studied to become a teacher, went to Nottingham University College, and after a spell as a schoolmaster gave up this job to live as a full-time writer. 'If you don't like your work,' Lawrence advised, 'don't do it.'

When he was nineteen D. H. Lawrence began writing poems, and he continued to do so all his life. 'I remember perfectly the Sunday afternoon when I perpetrated my first two pieces: "To Guelder-Roses" and "To Campions",' he confessed, 'in springtime, of course, and, as I say, in my twentieth year. Any young lady might have written them and been pleased with them, as I was pleased with them. But it was after that, when I was twenty, that my real

---

D. H. Lawrence essay in *Modern Poets in Focus No. 3* (Corgi Books, Transworld, 1971). Other introductions for *Modern Poetry in Focus No. 5* (Corgi Books, Transworld, 1973)

demon would now and then get hold of me and shake more real poems out of me, making me uneasy. I never "liked" my real poems as I like "To Guelder-Roses".'

However, D. H. Lawrence's 'real demon' as he extravagantly put it, only shook real poems out of him with any frequency after he ceased to be over-concerned with metrical exactitude and rhyme – which was really not Lawrence's natural style at all. To write poetry unclothed of such devices, to write naked poetry, is no easy thing – for 'free' poetry of this kind has got its own disciplines – its cadences, for instance, have to match precisely the theme and the feeling and the stance of the poem as surely as when regular metre is being used. Lawrence learnt, of course, a great deal from Walt Whitman not only in his use of repetition, in King James's Bible parallelisms, and in other matters of technique, but also in subject matter:

> I believe a leaf of grass is no less than the journey-work of the
>   stars,
> And the pismire is equally perfect, and a grain of sand, and the
>   egg of the wren,
> And the tree-toad is a chef d'œuvre for the highest,
> And the running blackberry would adorn the parlors of heaven,
> And the narrowest hinge in my hand puts to scorn all machinery,
> And the cow crunching with depress'd head surpasses any statue,
> And a mouse is miracle enough to stagger sextillions of infidels. . .
>
> I think I could turn and live with animals, they're so placid and
>   self-contain'd,
> I stand and look at them long and long.
>
> They do not sweat and whine about their condition,
> They do not lie awake in the dark and weep for their sins,
> They do not make me sick discussing their duty to God,
> Not one is dissatisfied, not one is demented with the mania of
>   owning things,
> Not one kneels to another, nor to his kind that lived thousands
>   of years ago,
> Not one is respectable or unhappy over the whole earth . . .

These lines are by Whitman (and others of his could be as easily quoted). But how Lawrentian they now sound to us, in tone and in attitude. Lawrence's central fundamental attitude – and it informs so much of his work – was that he was overwhelmingly aware of the antagonism between the demands of man's instincts and the restrictions of our civilised codes. In some ways he was writing the literary equivalent to Freud's 'Civilisation and its Discontents' which appeared, by the way, in 1930, the very year that Lawrence died of TB at the age of 45. Or, as the poet James Reeves has remarked: 'He (Lawrence) had begun to diagnose the malady of civilised, urban society . . . He came to distrust mind as the agency by which civilisation had torn men from their roots in bodily well-being and the awareness of physical life . . .'.

Throughout his writing life D. H. Lawrence tried to put himself in touch with the elemental origins of his own being. He recognised . . .

> That my known self will never be more than a little clearing in
> the forest.
> That gods, strange gods, come forth from the forest into the
> clearing of my known self, and then go back.
> That I must have the courage to let them come and go.
> That I will never let mankind put anything over me, but that I
> will always try to recognize and submit to the gods in me
> and the gods in other men and women.

Lawrence was very much a man in search of his soul, a tormented, physically sick man whose explorations were not only inwards but outwards too, in that, geographically, they took him to Europe, to Australia and to New Mexico. Evidence of his interior and exterior journeyings remains like conspicuous fingermarks on most of his poems.

Moreover, he himself was happy that his personal life, its broadest outlines anyway, was known to the readers of his poetry. As he wrote in 1928, 'It seems to me that no poetry, not even the best, should be judged as if it existed in the absolute, in the vacuum of the absolute. Even the best poetry, when it is at all personal, needs the penumbra of its own time and place and circumstance to make it full and whole. If we knew a little more of Shakespeare's self and circumstances how much more complete the Sonnets would be to us . . .'.

D. H. Lawrence's poetry, as has been indicated, hardly needs the footnotes of ancillary biographical material. In 'After the Opera' and in the later poem, 'How Beastly the Bourgeois is' we encounter his lively, sardonic humour, and his working-class background is displayed like a badge:

> . . . among the wreck of the theatre crowd
> I stand and smile.
> They take tragedy so becomingly;
> Which pleases me.
>
> But when I meet the weary eyes
> The reddened, aching eyes of the bar-man with thin arms,
> I am glad to go back to where I came from.

His rasping dislike of the middle classes is characteristically the engine force of his more satirical inspiration:

> How beastly the bourgeois is
> especially the male of the species –
> Presentable, eminently presentable –
> shall I make you a present of him?

Again it would be possible in 'She Said As Well To Me' to gain an inkling, perhaps more than an inkling, of his sexual preoccupations; and in a number of the poems included here to experience his articulated, vivid awareness of the mystery, and indeed divinity, of non-human life and otherness. Or, as Aldous Huxley once wrote: 'He was always intensely aware of the mystery of the world, and mystery was always to him a *numen*, divine. Lawrence could never forget, as most of us almost continuously forget, the dark presence of the otherness that lies beyond the boundaries of man's conscious mind. This special sensibility was accompanied by a prodigious power of rendering the immediately experienced otherness in terms of literary art.'

By 'in terms of literary art' Huxley was probably thinking of the novel form. Certainly most people continue to think of Lawrence as primarily a novelist. Yet, whatever the significance of his prose, and despite his linguistic indiscretions in his poems, despite his frequent lack of concision, Lawrence is surely one of the major poets of the twentieth century. If, like Whitman, he takes the long route then it is often through this route, through divagations, through repetitions, that D. H. Lawrence's poetry works and resounds – as in 'Man and Bat' which is a remarkable *tour de force.* True, sometimes the route has been just that little bit too long, the divagations too frequent, the repetitions too many. Any competent editor could have said, 'There, Lawrence. There and there. Take it out.' And would it have been an impertinence? For example, I would have liked to have taken his poem, 'Fish' – too long to include here – and edited it, abridged it. But I do not dare.

The poem 'Fish', incidentally, with its physicality of images such as 'water wetly on fire on the grates of your gills' or 'the gold and green pure lacquer mucus comes off in my hand' will surely remind readers of a contemporary poet – Ted Hughes. It is possible that Ted Hughes's animal poems would hardly have been written without Lawrence's example – indeed the whole sequence of Ted Hughes's 'Crow' seems to me implicit in 'Fish' and in 'Humming Bird' (included in this selection), though both Lawrence and Hughes may well have called upon Pacific Coast creation myths. It hardly needs saying that many other living poets, apart from Ted Hughes, owe a very large debt indeed to D. H. Lawrence – as much as he owed in his turn to Walt Whitman.

His inconsistencies, his longwindedness, his technical carelessness, hardly matter finally. Every poet deserves to be judged by his best work, and when Lawrence is at his best there is no separation between what is being said and how it is being said: there is no word that is superfluous. On such occasions Lawrence's poems give themselves generously to us as we read and re-read them over the years.

EZRA POUND

'Keats was nothing if not a man of ideas,' asserted Lionel Trilling in an essay called 'The Poet as Hero'. Torn out of context that quotation seems absurd. We think of poets as men who primarily present us with ordered imaginative experiences rather than ideas, though of course all experiences defined, encapsulate ideas. If we accept that ideas in themselves can change us, can direct us into a different life-style, how much more powerfully can ordered imaginative experiences, by which I mean literature, affect us, and through us, change society at large?

It is this argument that serious writers can be 'unacknowledged legislators', with its connotations that such writers are potential heroes, or, for that matter, potential villains, that worries many critics, educators, and plain readers when they consider the reactionary ideas held by so many of the great writers of the modern movement.

One of the undisputed leaders of the modern movement is the American poet, Ezra Pound, whose reactionary attitudes, his fascism, his economic theories, and anti-Semitism, have made uneasy even his most ardent admirers. Pound, however, thought of himself as a crusader and reformer intent on building a better world. Of course, one man's better world is another man's hell. No doubt Hitler, too, in his own subjective sense, was intent on being the architect of a better world. We all have different ideas of what is true and good and beautiful.

Whether we are disturbed that Ezra Pound held such vicious views and that these views coloured his writings depends largely on whether we believe that literature, and poetry in particular, is in the great world important. Ironically, poets hardly ever consider themselves, in England anyway, as heroic sages. They usually depreciate the activist value of their writings, however much their work is infused by moral concerns. 'Poetry', W. H. Auden has written, 'makes nothing happen' and he goes on to say that it survives only 'in the valley of its saying where executives would never tamper.' Stephen Spender, too, once asked despairingly, 'What can we do in a world at war that matters?' Even Keats recognised that he merely belonged to a tribe of dreaming things:

What canst thou do, or all thy tribe
To the great world? Thou art a dreaming thing.

This attitude of the poets themselves about their own ineffectiveness as social reformers dominates, despite the generally accepted prestigious status of the poet which leads him to be invited to grace politically inspired platforms, to be cajoled into signing petitions, letters to *The Times*, and even to march on this or that foreign embassy.

Yet the poet as he is writing, in the actual making of a poem, is rarely concerned with moral values and forgets that literature is apprehended by others as having a moral centre. He is partly surprised when he is taken seriously by many who have never read him and who expect him, because of his trade, to make occasional public moral gestures. Not so with Ezra Pound. He had a continual sense of his own importance as poet, critic, editor, educator, and crusader, from the time of his early days in London, when he first became famous in 1909, because of a slim volume of poems, to that of his later disgrace in Washington in 1946, where, because of his broadcasts from Mussolini's wartime Italy, he was accused of being a traitor to the United States.

His grandiose conception of himself had led him to believe finally that, 'if he had been allowed to send his messages to the Axis which he wished to send, prior to 1940, there would have been no Axis even'. In other words, that if given a free hand by those who were engaged in stultifying him, he could have prevented the war! So magnified were his grandiose ideas that the jury at his trial brought in a verdict of 'unsound mind'.

Yet, as early as 1934, James Joyce – one of the many great artists that Pound had selflessly helped – thought Ezra Pound to be mad. And even in the London of 1909 there must have been some who, on meeting Pound dressed in 'trousers made of green billiard cloth, a pink coat, a blue shirt, a tie hand-painted by a Japanese friend, an immense sombrero, a flaming beard cut to a point, and a single large blue earring', wondered about his mental health – especially as his behaviour also could be equally bizarre.

One of his biographers, Charles Norman, tells us a nice story of

Pound at a literary supper in the London of that time. 'During the supper,' we are told, 'Yeats, always a good monologuer, held forth at length on his new way of bringing music and poetry together, and possibly Ezra Pound . . . may have felt he was not getting a fair share of the fun. So, in order to pass the time, perhaps, and seeing the supper table dressed with tulips, he presently took one of the flowers and proceeded to munch it. As Yeats, absorbed in his monologue, did not observe this strange behaviour, and the rest of us were too well-bred to take any notice, Ezra, having found the tulip to his taste, did likewise with a second flower.'

It is comforting, perhaps, for those of us who admire Ezra Pound's poetry to see his fascism and anti-Semitism as signs of insanity; to write off the vicious racism of so many of Pound's famous friends, Wyndham Lewis, Gaudier-Brzeska, A. R. Orage (some would add T. S. Eliot), as only the derangements of volatile artistic minds. It is the consoling thought of all humanists that evil is ultimately only a mental sickness, and, therefore open, one day anyway, to remedy.

But Pound's early poetry, his pre-Canto poetry, hardly presents problems to those of us who abhor what has been called by Peter Viereck, with some justification, his 'fascist diabolism'. For Pound eschewed any hectoring tone in his earlier poetry. He was in no way didactic. In an early letter to William Carlos Williams he put forward his principles of poetic practice: '1. To paint the thing as I see it. 2. Beauty. 3. Freedom from didacticism. 4. It is only good manners if you repeat a few other men to at least do it better or more briefly.' Pound in his poetry, in any case, spoke so often through a mask (or *persona*), using a borrowed voice from medieval Provence, ancient China, or wherever. So there is no question of turning the pages to uncover moral insensitivity in most of his pre-Canto work whether the poems are sanely humorous as in 'The Lake Isle' (where he alludes to Yeats's utopian Innisfree yearnings) or whether the poems are tender and delicate as in his Chinese re-creations; or full of gusto as in the 'Sestina: Altaforte'. Surely one would have to be a moral prig to object to that crazy paean of praise for war – borrowed from the Provençal of Bertrand de Born – which concludes:

And let the music of the swords make them crimson!
Hell grant soon we hear again the swords clash!
Hell blot black for alway the thought, 'Peace'.

F. S. Flint recalled Pound screaming out that technically brilliant poem, 'The Bloody Sestina' as it has been named. 'How the table shook and the decanters and cutlery vibrated in resonance with his voice,' Flint reminisced. The poem works so well in English because Pound in his 'translations' was hardly impeded by a scholarly conscience! His scrupulosity was directed rather towards the quality of the lines in English – the original sources being merely triggers. Of the genesis of the 'Sestina: Altaforte' Ezra Pound has written, 'I had had de Born in my mind. I had found him untranslatable. Then it occurred to me that I might present him in this manner. I wanted the curious involution and recurrence of the Sestina. I knew more or less of the arrangement. I wrote the first strophe and then went to the British Museum to make sure of the right order of the permutations . . . I did the rest of the poem at a sitting. Technically it is one of my best, though a poem on such a theme could never be very important.'

Pound's gusto, his musical delicacy, his linguistic tact, his wry humour, his sheer ability to write poems that can only be described as 'beautiful' in the old-fashioned sense, must surely, with regard to the pre-Canto phase of his career anyway, disarm even the most hostile liberal reader. This is not strictly true, of course. Someone like George Orwell once wrote of Pound, 'He *may* be a good writer – I personally have always regarded him as an entirely spurious writer – but the opinions that he has tried to disseminate in his works are evil.' But as I have said, Pound did not try to disseminate fascist propaganda in his earliest poems nor in those two long poems, 'Homage to Sextus Propertius' (1917) and the admirable 'Hugh Selwyn Mauberley' (1920) that preceded the Cantos. The poetry that Ezra Pound wrote in his twenties, in fact, acts as a perfect bridge from the nineteenth to the twentieth century. For Pound had one foot with Browning, and even the Pre-Raphaelites, and the other with those writers we consider modern, who are of our time. Pound, indeed, influenced, by the example of his own poetry and by his sensible and forceful critical views about poetry, not only his contemporaries, T. S. Eliot and William Carlos Williams among them, but also most working poets of a younger generation both sides of the Atlantic. Every young poet can still learn much about verse writing from the incisive instructions he proclaimed as long ago as 1913.

> Pay no attention to the criticism of men who have never themselves written a notable work. Consider the discrepancies beween the actual writing of the Greek poets and dramatists, and the theories of the Graeco-Roman grammarians, concocted to explain their metres.
>
> Use no superfluous word, no adjective which does not reveal something.
>
> Don't use such an expression as 'dim lands *of peace*'. It dulls the image. It mixes an abstraction, 'peace', with the concrete 'lands'. It comes from the writer's not realizing that the natural object is always the *adequate* symbol.
>
> Go in fear of abstractions. Do not retell in mediocre verse what has already been done in good prose. Don't think any intelligent person is going to be deceived when you try to shirk all the difficulties of the unspeakably difficult art of good prose by chopping your composition into line lengths.
>
> What the expert is tired of today the public will be tired of tomorrow.

The sequence Pound calls the Cantos, epic in intent, a sort of poetic philosophy of history, is another matter. Orwell, here, is probably right. Judged as a whole the Cantos are spurious. In 1924, Pound, then 38 years of age, and planning to live in Italy, had already begun the Cantos. Ten years later he declared that he was giving up literature for economics. Needless to say he did not give up literature – the writing of the Cantos was to remain his central occupation thereafter. However, his obsession with economics did flaw the continuing sequence known as the Cantos. Pound, unfortunately, forgot his earlier dictum about 'freedom from didacticism'.

Babette Deutsch has written of the Cantos, 'I do not think . . .

the finest lyricists have equalled Pound's gift for evolving particulars of breath-taking delicacy and lustre.' That observation is true for a small number of the Cantos as well as for sustained passages in many others. There are times when their jewelled elegance of diction can compete with . . . well, to be mischievous with, say, Ecclesiastes. Consider:

> Pull down thy vanity, it is not man
> Made courage, or made order, or made grace.
> Pull down thy vanity, I say pull down.
> Leave of the green world what can be thy place
> In scaled invention or true artistry,
> Pull down thy vanity
> Paquin pull down!
> The green casque has outdone your elegance.

Alas, too often, though, the Cantos are flawed by his self-indulgence in quoting at length extracts of letters or old official documents, by his privacy of reference, and by his occasional psychotic incoherence. One further accusation can be levelled against the Cantos: they are, *in toto*, simply boring except perhaps to those academics who enjoy discovering those recondite sources of information not easily available to the general reader. In short, though the Cantos may be – are – open to moral stricture they primarily fail, with notable exceptions, as poems. As for the 'political' ideas in them, these hardly seem to me to be defensible. Some may think them to be innocuous or just cranky. Yet others will side with Orwell when he says they are 'evil'.

That Jewish poet, Heine, once said playfully: 'Mine is a most peaceable disposition. My wishes are: a humble cottage with a thatched roof, but a good bed, good food, the freshest milk and butter, flowers before my window, and a few fine trees before my door; and if God wants to make my happiness complete He will grant me the joy of seeing some six or seven of my enemies hanging from those trees. Before their death I shall, moved in my heart, forgive them all the wrong they did me in my lifetime. One must, it is true, forgive one's enemies – but not before they have been hanged.'

However, the case of Ezra Pound, the man, who so recently died in Venice, is in any event closed. But his poetry – at least some of it, including a small number of the Cantos – will endure as long as the poetry of our century is read and enjoyed.

THOM GUNN

Thom Gunn has written a poem called 'Black Jackets' which is about those American working class youths who hunt together in packs and whose equivalents, in England, have been referred to as Hell's Angels. In Gunn's poem, the shoulders of one of the gang have been tattooed on one side with the gang's name, The Knights; on the other with the slogan, Born to Lose. Thom Gunn's own background differed radically from that of The Knights. He was born in Gravesend, Kent, in 1929, the son of a successful middle-class Fleet Street editor. Thom Gunn went to a 'good' school, University College School in London, before continuing his privileged education at Trinity College, Cambridge. If a slogan were to be tattooed on Thom Gunn's shoulder some would have thought Born to Succeed would have been apposite.

At Cambridge his career was particularly successful. He edited an anthology of undergraduate verse, he became President of the University English Club, he took a first in both parts of the English tripos and he had his first book of poems, *Fighting Terms*, accepted by the small but then fashionable Fantasy Press, based in Oxford. Moreover, this book when published elicited good reviews and led Robert Conquest to include him, as the youngest contributor, in his crusading, so-called anti-romantic anthology, *New Lines*. This much discussed anthology was instrumental in consolidating Thom Gunn's earlier success.

When, in 1957, Faber published his second volume, *The Sense of Movement*, it won the coveted Somerset Maugham Award and there were critics who named him as 'perhaps the most considerable poet of his generation'. It seemed a most auspicious beginning to a literary career. By now, Thom Gunn had settled in the USA and was teaching English at Stanford University, California.

It so happened that I was one reviewer of Thom Gunn's first

book. I must admit to being less generous than my colleagues. I did say savingly, perhaps patronisingly, that *Fighting Terms* 'makes interesting reading and is full of first promise'; but I was also young enough to resent the undergraduate posing of male vigour evident in the book. Nor did I feel at ease with the display of sexual immaturity that seemed to be the subject (not always intentionally) of a number of the poems. Importantly, also, the diction seemed to me often awkward and sometimes so clumsy that I wanted to laugh out loud.

These reservations still seem to me to be valid. What I failed to note, though, were certain positive virtues in Thom Gunn's work. Perhaps I should be more specific, referring to one or two poems in *Fighting Terms*. For instance, the first poem in the book, 'Carnal Knowledge', which I thought to be one of the better pieces (it had the virtue of honesty I supposed – 'Even in bed I pose' – the poem begins) was limited, I believed, not by cleverness but by a display of cleverness. The poem asked to be admired rather than to be experienced. Besides, there were lines in it that were particularly flawed in terms of the whole poem. (Mr Gunn tried to mend some of these lines when *Fighting Terms* was reissued by Faber in 1962.) What I missed, though, was the genuine feeling that enlivened the poem. The pain of a failed sexual relationship was obscured by the clever façade of the poem's movement. It is this kind of feeling which makes this poem now, for me, work despite its shortcomings.

Or consider the second poem in *Fighting Terms*. 'Here Come The Saints' is brief enough to quote in its entirety:

> Here come the saints: so near, so innocent
> They gravely cross the field of moonlit snow;
> We villagers gape humbly at the show.
> No act or gesture can suggest intent.
> They only wait until the first cock crow
> Batters our ears, and with abrupt and violent
> Motions into the terrible dark wood they go.

I considered those eight lines depended too heavily on the rather worn, romantic diction of 'the field of moonlit snow' and 'the terrible dark wood'. At odds with this poetic diction was the dreadfully prosaic line, 'No act or gesture can suggest intent.' That, I thought, was a most awkward way of putting it and was partly dictated by the poet wishing 'intent' to chime with 'innocent' and 'violent'. Hardly a good enough reason. And, besides, what is the poem about? Who are these saints? Has the cock crow anything to do with the betrayal of Jesus? If so, is that a Middle Eastern moonlight? And Middle Eastern snow! No, this must be a dream scene. Or the poem is suggested by a painting perhaps? And does it matter, finally, what it is all about when the poem is so flawed technically?

Or so I thought then. Now I am attracted to the visual mystery of the poem. Maybe it persists in my mind because of its riddle element? Perhaps, too, the clash between poetic and prose diction does not hurt the poem. Probably the poem would be less satisfactory if the diction had been consistent: if it had been romantically poetic all the way through, or prosaic and clumsy all the way through. The style, it seems, is in the error. This is true for a number of poems by Thom Gunn. He has written poems flawed either by clumsiness of expression, by failure of taste, or by, in the earliest work, a moral ambiguity.

There are those who, with the publication of further books by Thom Gunn – *My Sad Captains* (1961), *Positives* (1966), *Touch* (1967), and *Moly* (1971) – have, because of such flaws, seriously qualified their earlier praise. Thus Edward Lucie-Smith: 'The proportion of really good poems has been failing book by book.' And John Fuller, when reassessing *Fighting Terms*, objected to Thom Gunn's subsequent lack of definition and clarity of meaning in the poems included in *The Sense of Movement* and *My Sad Captains*. This fuzzing of expression John Fuller attributed to the growth of abstract philosophising in his work. Fuller also took exception, as others have done, to the moral ambiguity in Gunn's poems. (Gunn does praise heroes who are hoodlums; he is fascinated by violence, even sadism. On the other hand, a shocking poem like 'Innocence' which is about a young Nazi watching a Russian partisan being burned alive is surely a highly moral one).

'The poet', complained John Fuller, 'does not seem to be plainly enough saying what he wants to say. One would not even mind a body of verse which went beyond this rather conscious imagery of brutality or promiscuity into some plainly immoral creed. Morality would become irrelevant with more integrity. With individual exceptions, of course, it came to appear that Gunn was losing some central power of blending matter and manner. His Donnean candour and involvement became dissipated by evasiveness, irrelevancies, and a frequently pedantic tone. One supposes that this development is closely connected with the growth of philosophising in his poetry.'

There is no denying that Gunn has ignored the relatively modern critical incitement to be concerned with particulars rather than generalities, to focus on the concrete rather than the abstract, to present the image rather than the idea, to dwell on things rather than ideas. Indeed, it is evident that the source of inspiration of many poems in *The Sense of Movement*, and in later books, is to be found in the themes of existential philosophy: in the existential imperatives of casting off masks in the search for self; in the assumptions of being and dread; in absurdity and commitment; in the need to choose consciously when there is no individual reality except through energy in action, through deeds, and perhaps 'to dare a future from the taken routes'.

Thom Gunn, in an interview with Ian Hamilton in 1964, remarked, 'There has been a peculiar kind of superstition that has come up this century about abstraction. I certainly don't want to be like Robert Bly, who is writing purely in terms of particulars, and I don't want to be an Imagist which is something rather close . . . of course there is the other attack, an abstract language as such. I don't see why you can't use abstract language, if you do it well.'

'On the Move' is one poem where Thom Gunn does do it well. The poem celebrates energy in movement and hints at themes touched on by existentialist writers. It works despite the occasional dull thunder of approximate words, abstract ideas, and language. For attention is also given to the concrete, to the particulars of those motor cyclists who seem to have something in common with the outriders of Death in Cocteau's film *Orphée*.

On motorcycles, up the road, they come:
Small, black, as flies hanging in heat, the Boys,
Until the distance throws them forth, their hum
Bulges to thunder held by calf and thigh.
In goggles, donned impersonality,
In gleaming jackets trophied with the dust,
They strap in doubt – by hiding it, robust –
And almost hear a meaning in their noise.

The brilliant concreteness of this portrayal holds long enough to carry the abstractions that are more dominant as the poem proceeds. Yet it is interesting to compare 'On the Move' with a later poem of Gunn's (from *Moly*) called 'From the Wave' which also celebrates energy, pure athletic energy, with an almost religious intensity – doing so without philosophising, without bringing footnotes of commentary into the body of the poem.

'From the Wave' is one poem by Gunn that is entirely unflawed. Unlike 'On the Move' the style is not in the error. The error, by the way, is not always one of abstraction or clumsiness of language. It can even be one of fact. For instance, in 'In Santa Maria del Popolo' Gunn speaks of a painting by 'Caravaggio, of the Roman School'. Caravaggio was the prototype of the later Bohemian painter-hero and he, indeed, killed a man in a brawl. He was not, however, himself the victim of violence. He was not strangled as Thom Gunn states 'For money, by one such picked off the streets', but died of a fever at Porto Ercole on his way back from exile to Rome. What holds our attention in this poem finally is not this factual mistake but the marvellous concision of some of the lines including the poem's ending:

– For the large gesture of solitary man,
Resisting, by embracing, nothingness.

Perhaps the most astonishing error in Thom Gunn's verse is when he chooses an unsuitable rhythmic base for the content he is presenting. Thus in 'Epitaph for Anton Schmidt' (Gunn is much concerned with non-conforming heroes) he uses a rhythm – and some rhymes – more propitious for comic verse. Try to read these verses through for sound not sense:

I know he had unusual eyes
Whose power no orders might determine
Not to mistake the men he saw
As others did, for gods or vermin.

For five months, till his execution
Aware that action has its dangers,
He helped the Jews to get away
– Another race at that, and strangers.

This error of aural taste is so damaging it almost kills off the poem. Yet not quite. And that is the whole point about any critical assessment of Thom Gunn's work. Many of the poems survive victoriously despite the critic raising up his hands in horror as he says, 'Mr Gunn, you just can't do that!' Fortunately Thom Gunn can and does.

In any case other Gunn poems are unqualified successes without flaw or loss of definition. His latest volume, *Moly*, for instance, contains at least half a dozen such. To his credit he has not been put off course by gunning reviewers. Naturally there are differences in the cast of the poems in his latest book compared with his earliest. His attitudes have become more positive, more endearing. He sees in unsophisticated human (and animal) conduct attributes that no longer are only instinctive with violence but with the contraries of violence – with trust and with self-preserving concern. Even cats when they wrestle and feel each other's claws know how to break off before either of them is hurt:

And then they wrestle: parry, lock of paws,
    Blind hug of close defence,
    Tail-thump, and smothered mew.
    If either, though, feel claws,
  She abruptly rises, knowing well
How to stalk off in wise indifference.

Nor does Gunn now, in his maturity, seem to be posing, striking attitudes. His poetry has become clearly honest. Yet it is the same exploratory voice the reader hears. Whether writing regularly patterned poems or free verse it is always Thom Gunn himself speaking. It is an individual voice that, even in its earliest days, no literary influence could wholly disguise. It is a hesitant voice, often illuminating, sometimes provocative, always worth listening to.

FLEUR ADCOCK

Literary journalists yoke together the names of different poets so that they can make generalisations about their work. Sometimes poets are placed in one bracket because they appear to have similar stylistic aims or own similar political opinions or because they are all domiciled in the same geographical area of the world. There are other less legitimate categories. How illuminating, for instance, is the classification Women Poets? Yet it is one occasionally used – sometimes, of course, in jest. Thus Kingsley Amis:

> We men have got love well weighed up; our stuff
> Can get by without it.
> Women don't seem to think that's good enough;
> They write about it,
>
> And the awful way their poems lay them open
> Just doesn't strike them.
> Women are really much nicer than men:
> No wonder we like them.

In recent years, younger women poets such as the late Sylvia Plath, Anne Sexton, and in a more circumspect way, the New Zealand poet Fleur Adcock, have used a confessional mode persistently. The poems do, I suppose, 'lay them open' but such an exhibition is a deliberate one. Besides, this confessional manner is not restricted to women writers alone – notable male poets, too, have dropped their masks to tell us their bare-faced truths. Still, when C. K. Stead, another New Zealand poet, wrote about Fleur Adcock a year or two ago, he pronounced, 'Fleur Adcock's poems suggest not only a woman's sensibility and preoccupations but a woman's voice – as distinctly as handwriting can suggest the female hand.'

No one is foolish enough to deny that there is such a thing as a feminine sensibility or that a woman's preoccupations may well have a different bias from a man's. Alas, C. K. Stead continued, 'Fleur Adcock seems gifted with that slightly detached female intelligence that can marshal even the most wayward feelings and make vital sense and shape of them.' This is not convincing. Why should an intelligence be 'female' when it can organise verbally the most wayward of feelings? Do not good male poets do exactly that?

Even Fleur Adcock herself, faintheartedly it is true, wonders whether her traditional tastes and conservative practices in verse writing have something to do, along with other considerations, with the fact that she is a woman. Thus she writes in *Recent Poetry in New Zealand*, edited by Charles Doyle,

> I admire poetry which can wear a formal dress lightly and naturally (I think here of some of the work of Yeats, Graves and Auden, who, like the best of the Elizabethan and seventeenth-century poets, have written in strict verse-forms with no loss of grace, passion or precision.) I find understatement generally more telling than rhetorical exaggeration; and, without turning my face away from G. M. Hopkins or E. E. Cummings I feel that for most purposes our language is flexible enough to permit a variety of satisfying effects without the distortion of normal grammar and syntax. These rather conservative tastes may be explained as resulting from a classical education, from early influences in reading, or merely from temperament. It occurs to me at this point that a certain submissiveness in my approach to writing may be attributed to the fact that I am a woman . . .

Fleur Adcock was born in Papakura, New Zealand in 1934. She was already precociously publishing poems in New Zealand publications when, at eighteen, she married her compatriot, the poet Alistair Campbell. At that time Campbell was already well known in New Zealand. His first book of poems, *Mine Eyes Dazzle*, had gone through three editions and as a New Zealand critic remarked, 'Allowing for differences in size of population that fact suggests a comparison between Campbell and John Betjeman in terms of popular success.' Though, in New Zealand, Alistair Campbell was relatively 'famous', and was nine years older than Fleur Adcock when they married, his own work does not seem to have overtly influenced his young wife's work. On the contrary, her own cool tone may well, at a later date, have touched some of his writing. Certainly, in 'Spring in Porirua' he writes feelingly and economically in a personal, lucid way reminiscent of Fleur Adcock at her best:

> Sane as the sun I sit in the dayroom,
> Thinking of that lovely man, my father,
> Who died young of grief. The attendants come
> And lead us out into the sun. Father,
> Do you forgive me? Without any sound
> The pear trees drop their petals to the ground.

Six years, a first class honours degree in Classics (Victoria University of Wellington), and two children later, at twenty-four years of age, Fleur Adcock was divorced. And in 1963 she left New Zealand for London where she has settled and published verse that has attracted the attention of an increasing number of discerning readers.

One of her better known poems is called 'Miss Hamilton in London' and is a portrayal of a lady involved in the trivia of everyday routine living: she goes shopping, visits a museum, writes a letter, washes her hair, and does not appear to 'lack human contacts' – but finally, at night, awake in the darkness, desperately lonely, she lies pierced 'by thirty black spears'. Characteristically, the poet presents deadpan, coolly, the circumstances of Miss Hamilton's day and does not raise her voice when she remarks on Miss Hamilton's unenviable night. Stylistically, all Fleur Adcock's poems own a kind of reticence even though the subject matter be frank and may move from prosaic ordinariness to sudden horror. It is as if a speaker on the radio, say, reported a routine street scene but did not change his tone of voice when some unspeakable scandal and outrage suddenly occurred. So while Fleur Adcock's poems frequently hint at terror and unease, at the desperation of loneliness, or at impending tragedy, they never quite 'go over the top'. If the smile starts to become a grimace, if the speaking voice should begin to sob, then the author seems to say, 'Right . . . Cut!' And the lights go out or the curtains come down. Sometimes the poem ends just when the drama begins.

Fleur Adcock's portraits, though cool, are generally compassionate – and, indeed, the people that seem to capture her interest most are those who appear either a little detached from the crowd or frankly alienated. She is drawn to that lonely spinster, Miss Hamilton, or dwells with mild affection on a 'wearisome' Indian student who has visited the library in London where Adcock works. Or she relates with amused precision the crankiness of a gentleman much possessed by mysticism, occult physics, alchemy, and the Qabalah.

The oddness of people, their feelings of disconnection – the separateness between people, between man and woman, or between adult and child comprise some of her main themes. For example, in her poem 'Country Station', a child plays in isolation from her mother for long hours. 'Five trains have swooshed through' and the mother is still busy in the nearby telephone booth. The drama of this situation is only pointed at in a throwaway phrase, 'She isn't crying any more' – a reference to the mother telephoning. This parenthetical remark typifies the way Fleur Adcock understates the emotion inherent in a narrative. Moreover, we do not feel that Fleur Adcock has invented the situation so much as remembered it. This quality of apparent autobiographical actuality is another feature common to many of her poems.

Fleur Adcock's first book of poems, *The Eye of the Hurricane*, was published in New Zealand just before she left for London. The best of the poems in that volume were then included in her second book, *Tigers*, in 1967. What is notable about all the poems in *Tigers* is their thematic originality rather than their verbal enterprise. Fleur Adcock's poems, unlike Sylvia Plath's, do not depend primarily on linguistic energy to gain their effect. That is one reason why Fleur

Adcock is not very quotable: her successes depend less on individual lines than on the total poem, its lucidity, its layers of meaning, and its apt organisation. In its own way, a poem such as 'Advice to a Discarded Lover' is organised as skilfully as any fine, neat, seventeenth-century conceit. And what a nice cold anger informs it.

In *Tigers*, particularly in those poems about adult love relationships and intimacies, Fleur Adcock often has her claws out; and this same anger is only somewhat diluted in her most recent volume, *High Tide in the Garden* (1971). As a New Zealand critic, James Bertram, has remarked, 'It is Fleur Adcock's special distinction – writing with unusual candour as wife, lover, or mother-to-child, to avoid any trace of cosiness or sentimentality: in her poetry she is always alert, feline, and formidably possessed.' Mr Bertram could have added that there is a tenderness evident, too, especially in her poems about children; and not infrequently a touch of humour flavours the edginess of her most anxious poems.

This is especially true of the poems that seem to have been suggested by Fleur Adcock's night dreams, from what Herrick once called 'the civil wilderness of sleep'. The humour of absurdity defuses the explosive terror of her dream fantasies – the alarm clock does not terrify if, surrealistically, it is playing Schubert. Indeed, Fleur Adcock can be quite jocular about her own hauntings:

> At last I think I have woken up.
> I lift my head from the pillow, rejoicing
> The alarm-clock is playing Schubert:
> I am still asleep. This is too much.

'We are near waking when we dream we are dreaming,' Novalis once said. Some other Fleur Adcock dream-poems seem to rise from deeper levels of unconsciousness. In these, though absurdity abounds, the effects are not humorous. The underlying sense of unease and hysteria is not therefore nullified. Such is her dream fantasy, 'A Surprise in the Peninsula', about which C. K. Stead wrote accurately in the New Zealand literary periodical, *Landfall*, 'A balance is maintained on a fine line between terror and the absurd: hysteria is just out of the picture, giving it a sharpened point.' 'A Surprise in the Peninsula' is charged with the kind of atmosphere we find in a certain genre of novels. Conrad's *Heart of Darkness* comes to mind.

Over the last year, since *High Tide in the Garden*, Fleur Adcock has published very few poems. One new one, however, is included here, 'The Bullaun', and it evidently followed a visit to troubled Northern Ireland. It most successfully weds an autobiographical narrative to a larger public concern. It concludes:

> heading dutifully through the damp golf-course
> to Lough Neagh, I thought about the rock,
> wanting it. Not for my own salvation;
> hardly at all for me: for sick Belfast,
> for the gunmen and the slogan-writers,
> for the poor crazy girl I met in the station,
> for Kevin and Declan, who would soon mistrust
> all camera-carrying strangers. But of course
> the thing's already theirs: a monument,
> A functionless, archaic, pitted stone
> And a few mouthfuls of black rainwater.

It is as good a poem, it seems to me, as any Fleur Adcock has written. In some way, also, it is a peculiarly feminine poem, a product of a sympathetic, feminine sensibility. Perhaps there is something in the classification Women Poets after all.

Poetry and Poverty Revisited

1

Sometimes, during those immediate post-war evenings, I would cast my medical textbooks aside and quit my digs in London's Swiss Cottage to meet a girl or search for company in the chattering cafés of the nearby Finchley Road. That winter of 1946 I would pass the dolorous ruins of bombed buildings where darkness loitered and walk under the occasional functioning lamppost to the lit enticements of the Cosmo or the Cordial or the Winter Garden. Adventures, conversational or otherwise, beckoned.

Many refugees, most of them Jews from Germany and Austria, had come to live in the area. So much so that sometimes the conductors on No. 13 and No. 2 buses approaching Swiss Cottage would shout out with venom, 'Next stop, Tel Aviv.' Big joke.

The refugees brought with them the habits of a continental café life. Not a few were writers such as the poet Erich Fried, or the novelist Elias Canetti. There were musicians, too, like Hans Keller and members of the Amadeus Quartet; theatre people, like the director Peter Zadek and the actress Renee Goddard.

Soon British writers and artists frequented these Swiss Cottage cafés – among them the budding novelists, Peter Vansittart and Bernice Rubens, art critic David Sylvester, sculptor Bill Turnbull. Congenial company then for a young man such as myself who fancied himself as a poet, having had, in September 1946, a book of poems accepted by Hutchinson.

That book, which is so defective that I would now gladly burn

---

From *Aquarius* (1998). Tribute to John Heath-Stubbs on his 80th birthday all copies, did not appear until December 1948. Not long before its publication you could have discovered me, still neglecting my medical studies, in one or other of those Swiss Cottage cafés, discussing with art student Godfrey Rubens and red-haired Molly Owen the possibility of publishing a poetry magazine. We had no cash to pay a printer but Godfrey and Molly felt confident that they could steal paper and surreptitiously arrange for it to be roneoed and stitched at the firm where Molly worked. It would be called *Poetry and Poverty* – not only because we were broke but also we decided that in each successive issue a contributor would be invited to comment on the poverty of current literature.

'I'll design the magazine,' promised Godfrey, 'and you know poets who will contribute.'

A number of the younger British poets occasionally visited Swiss Cottage, among them Emanuel Litvinoff and John Heath-Stubbs. Litvinoff's poem 'To T. S. Eliot', which was to have later reverberations and consequences, appeared in the first issue of *Poetry and Poverty*, as did a now forgotten poem by John Heath-Stubbs called 'Meditation on a Name'.

Some months ago I happened to be speaking to John Heath-Stubbs on the telephone and I reminded him of that early poem of his which he has never re-published in book form. He could not remember it with any precision and invited me to read it out to him. I began:

> Take my name for instance, 'John, J,O,H,N, – Johannan,
> The light of God, the Light of Baal – Hannibal
> Dragging those poor bloody elephants on a route-march
> Over the Alps. The Baptist, the Beloved Disciple,
> And the worst king that ever sat on the throne of England.
> Jonah's Johanna Jan Ian
> Sean Ivan Jo Jun; Don Giovanni,
> The spectre haunted by sex, tinkering a mandolin
> To unreluctant windows. John Donne John Webster
> John Keats, John Bull John o'Groats John Nameless
> John Anderson my jo; and Saint John Goldenmouth,
> Unpopular with an Empress, writing the last prayer at Matins.

John, a commonplace John, honest John, John Stubbs,
John Stubbs scarves waving his hat and God Save the Queen
After the knife's quick agony and the searing iron.
Oh how irresponsible – my godfather and godmothers
Created this for me, out of water and a breath,
To cause what trouble at the Day of Judgment,
And go trundling round the universe and the spaces between
the stars.

After my telephone recital, John Heath-Stubbs said, 'Mmmm, I think I didn't put it in my *Collected Poems* because I thought it too egocentric' – a remark I found particularly interesting since his autobiography refuses to commence with the required 'I' and end with the expected 'Me'. Not that John Heath-Stubbs always hides behind veils of clandestine anonymity. Consider, for instance, his memorable 'Epitaph' which begins:

Mr Heath-Stubbs as you must understand
Came of a gentleman's family out of Staffordshire
Of as good blood as any in England
But he was wall-eyed and his legs too spare.

His elbows and finger-joints could bend more ways than one
And in frosty weather would creak audibly
As to delight his friends he would give demonstration
Which he might have done in public for a small fee.

Or his heartfelt love poem, 'Address not Known' which concludes:

The sun will not haver in its course for the lack of you,
Nor the flowers fail in colour, nor the bird stint in its song.
Only the heart that wanted somehow to have opened up
Finds the frost in the day's air, and the nights which appear
too long.

Though John Heath-Stubbs's 'Meditation on a Name' is not among his best work I still think it amusing enough and I recall how

I preferred it to another accompanying poem he sent me which I felt was bedeviled by a too florid, romantic grandeur of diction. I have usually favoured those poems of his which, in touching the colloquial, can reveal his considerable wit rather than the poems on stilts, loud with literature. In a very early poem written during the war, Heath-Stubbs had already recognised his own tendency to dwell on subject matter too removed from the real world. Addressing an ancestor he confesses:

> I need your courage for my different problems –
> To make words take their places, nor neglect
> The impingement on the world, which justifies
> The reverie in the garden, and the dream . . .

And did R. S. Thomas, I wonder, remember John Heath-Stubbs's 'Meditation on a Name' when he delivered a paper (in Welsh) at the National Eisteddfod of 1976? 'Our ancestors', said R. S. Thomas, 'tended religiously to avoid giving pagan names to their children for fear they might exert evil influence upon them. As a result our nation was overloaded with names like John and Mary. It puts a strain on one's belief in the immortality of the individual to cast an eye over the old church registers and see the number of John Jones and Mary Roberts "who have passed over the face of Wales like the shadow of a cloud."'

> 'Oh how irresponsible – my godfather and godmothers
> Created this for me, out of water and a breath
> to cause what trouble at the Day of Judgment . . .'

I don't think it is generally known that John Heath-Stubbs was lucky enough to have two Welsh grandmothers!

2

Amazingly Desmond MacCarthy reviewed that first issue of *Poetry and Poverty* in the *Sunday Times*. It was a warm, generous notice. Indeed, we were encouraged by the general response, but we had no resources to enable us to carry on. Molly Owen disappeared from sight, had left her firm, had left London. The other girl habitués of the Swiss Cottage cafés had no enthusiasm for typing out copy and stealing paper, however intimate we were with them. Besides I had to take my final medical examinations and become a responsible doctor.

One evening, though, soon after I had qualified and had married Joan Mercer, we visited the Cosmo and were collared by a young South African who demanded, 'Where's the second number of *Poetry and Poverty*?' We were happy to meet an admirer but utterly surprised when he offered to finance it for at least a couple of issues. 'Get it decently printed,' he commanded.

Because of my own commitments I could not immediately take advantage of his patronage. As a result, the second issue of *Poetry and Poverty* did not appear until 1952. Among the poems was one of Lawrence Durrell's best, 'Clouds of Glory' and some brilliant translations of Jacques Prévert by Paul Dehn. Peter Viereck wrote about the Ezra Pound Bollingen Prize controversy and Emanuel Litvinoff wrote the *Notes on the Poverty* (Literary) No.2. Meanwhile, two books I admired had come my way: *The Man Outside*, the prose works of the young German poet Wolfgang Borchert, who died in 1947 at the age of twenty-six, and *Nones* by W. H. Auden. I persuaded Michael Hamburger to review *The Man Outside* and John Heath-Stubbs to pen the notice of *Nones*.

John Heath-Stubbs wrote of Auden:

> Are some of those qualities which so charmed his readers in the nineteen-thirties abated in his later work? And, if so, is his religious re-orientation or his Americanization to be held responsible? The answer to these questions is, I think, 'Yes, partly.' The wit and the colloquial ease are still there, but the particular Audenesque combination of *Angst* and *Weltschmerz* has given place to a rather uneasy resignation to the limitations of the human condition. And the Audenesque mythology – Boy Scouts, Long Legged Scissor men, and the like has been replaced by such images as the rather classical baroque furies, 'with clear and dreadful brow.' But what have been lost, I think, were essentially adolescent and romantic qualities . . .

Those adolescent and romantic qualities were also being lost in the work of John Heath-Stubbs himself, or, at least, maturely modified. The poems he was writing in 1952 were later to be published in *A Charm Against the Toothache*, a volume I later reviewed in *Poetry and Poverty* in which I claimed that it was Heath-Stubbs's best book to date and that 'the earlier romantic grandeur of diction is now studded with contemporary slang and modern object references . . . his concessions in relaxing the high tone of his diction allow John Heath-Stubbs to display a humour and humanism that his earlier style forbade and this engagement with the street rather than the study make his poems applicable to others . . . His poetry, in my view had progressed into the second phase of neo-romanticism.'

By 1952 a violent reaction to neo-romanticism was in full swing. Another generation of young poets, my own generation, began to claim attention. All of these were graduates of Oxford or Cambridge, most of them having recently accepted academic posts in one or another university. Robert Conquest later was to corral them into a group known as The Movement. They were, ostensibly, anti-romantic. Kingsley Amis attacked Dylan Thomas and outlined the programme of The Movement poets succinctly in a poem he called 'Against Romanticism':

> Let us make at least visions that we need:
> Let mine be pallid, so that it cannot
> Force a single glance, form a single word . . .
> And at its other end a temperate zone:
> Woods devoid of beasts, roads that please the foot.

Those in sympathy with Kingsley Amis's views felt not only antagonistic to the work of Dylan Thomas, then the most popular poet in the English-speaking world, but to the New Apocalypse writers of the 1940s inspired by Henry Treece and J. F. Hendry who recognised the importance of myth, preferred eternal rather than contemporary subject matter and a hortatory mode of expression. The mood of these 1940s poets was exhibited in the publication by Herbert Read of the Routledge Series of poets, among whom could be numbered Sidney Keyes, Emanuel Litvinoff, John Heath-Stubbs and J. F. Hendry himself.

Though, in truth I, as editor of *Poetry and Poverty*, personally deplored the worst traits of many of the neo-romantic poets, their formlessness, their fear of writing about the quotidian, their floridity, their wilful obscurity due to a too private vision, I did not welcome replacing the fashion of neo-romanticism with a calibre of pallid poems so temperate they would read, at best, as a form of exquisite reportage. I had witnessed how Dylan Thomas's work had developed from the incoherence of much of the verse in his first book, published in 1934, to the communicable richness of poems like 'Fern Hill' and 'Poem in October', 'The Hunchback in the Park' and the villanelle 'Do Not Go Gentle Into That Good Night'. I believed then, as I do now, that Thomas's progression from that obscurity to a necessary degree of rationality, resulted, not altogether consciously, from his famous exposure to audiences, and to their expectancy, when giving his poetry readings.

In any event, I wrote in the editorial of *Poetry and Poverty* 4, in 1952,

> It is not then, in this over-compensated reaction to Neo-Romanticism that the poetry of the fifties has hope of importance or readability, but rather, I believe, in the modification and development of the romantic vision of the poets of the last decade. Nobody wants to save the corpse of *The New Apocalypse* . . . rather the time has come for poetry to move into a new and second phase of Neo-Romanticism. What should be discarded are its faults alone: there is no need to throw the whole apparatus of Romantic expression overboard, particularly as the present alternative mode of writing appears to be so trivial and precious.

Poetry and Poverty lost its African financial backer early. Our patron suddenly joined the Communist Party and decided that he could have nothing further to do with what he called 'bourgeois formalism'. However, the subscription list was growing and the actress Margaret Rawlings, unsolicited, sent me enough money to print one issue. I should record here, too, the generosity of Edith

Sitwell, who put a fiver into the kitty, again unsolicited, though I had in *Poetry and Poverty* No. 1 remarked that I had been 'nauseated by her narcissistic and pretentious comments upon her own work' when she had been allowed to broadcast on the Third Programme.

Poetry and Poverty continued for seven issues before finally concluding with the anti-Movement anthology *Mavericks*, which I co-edited with Howard Sergeant. John Heath-Stubbs was very much featured in the magazine. In No. 1 his poem 'Meditation on a Name' appeared; in No. 3, 'The Hundred and Thirty-Seventh Psalm Paraphrased'; in No. 7, 'Mors Poetarum' – all poems in which John Heath-Stubbs exhibited his wit, scholarship and technical virtuosity. In No. 2, he himself reviewed Auden; in No. 5, an anthology *Images of Tomorrow* which he had edited was noticed, as was his own *A Charm Against the Toothache* in No. 7. He would have appeared in *Mavericks* also, but in order to match the relative youthfulness of The Movement anthology *New Lines*, Howard Sergeant and I set the birth deadline of our contributors at 1920. John Heath-Stubbs was born in 1918, as readers of this magazine are all aware.

One reason I agreed to co-edit *Mavericks*, apart from a quarrel about linguistic style, was because I disliked the insular attitude of some of the *New Lines* contributors, their parochialism, their consciously contrived philistinism, their posture of being tough, cynical and sardonic. They rarely chanced themes that transcended barriers of custom and nationality. Much could be said in favour of linguistic tact and decorum but those who championed Movement verse did not appear to value 'feeling' in poetry or any ambitious excitements beyond discipline. They saw poetry as a modest art. Donald Davie, a poet with a genuine winter talent, in asking himself the question, 'how can I dare to feel?' wrote:

> Alas, alas, who's injured by my love?
> And recent history answers: Half Japan!
> Not love but hate? Well both are versions of
> The 'feeling' that you dare me to. Be dumb!
> Appear conceived only to make it scan!
> How dare we now be anything but numb?

A neutral tone was welcomed in the 1950s. Besides, many of the contributors to *New Lines* were truly gifted, not least Philip Larkin who, in his poetry, far from negated the plangent tones of feeling. Conquest's anthology proved to be a great critical success and the fashion of Movement-like verse thrived for the rest of the decade.

I recall a conversation I had with John Heath-Stubbs in Soho during the later Fifties. (Was it at the Mandrake Club in Meard Street?) We were discussing the popularity of *New Lines* and how so many of the plain, uninspiring and unaspiring poems that appeared in journals such as the *New Statesman* and *Spectator* were influenced and hampered by the Movement's critical strictures. John Heath-Stubbs commented somewhat ruefully, 'It'll be a long time before the brand of poetry we write will become fashionable.' I'm still waiting, John.

The Ass and the Green Thing

In February 1946, when I was a 22-year-old wide-eyed, poetry-writing medical student walking the groaning wards of Westminster Hospital in London, I would hesitate sometimes at the bed of a white-faced patient convalescing from major surgery. We had intermittent conversations about Sartre, Camus and Existentialism. And yes, he would quote Kierkegaard: 'Terror, perdition, annihilation dwell next door to every man.' We also discussed the Slow Rate of Demobilisation, the Character of Aneurin Bevan, the Rarity of Post-War Bananas. One afternoon I confessed to him that I wrote poetry and, at once, he advised me to send my verse to Hutchinson.

'They're on the look-out for new young poets,' he told me.

Apparently my patient had vague connections with the publishing world and was privy to all kinds of secrets. He assured me that Hutchinson wished to cash in on the wartime boom in poetry sales. In those austere days of powdered egg, spam, and paper shortage, books of poems had been bought and read avidly by lonely, far-away-from-home Servicemen and women. Hutchinson, incompetent as ever, had missed out on such sales and now, compounding their commercial error, did not realise that the wartime boom was soon to be superseded by a peace-time plop.

Over the previous two years I had written more than thirty poems. I had called one 'The Yellow Bird'. Perhaps that could be the title of my neophyte volume? Alun Lewis's younger sister, Mair, reminded me, though, how Alun had taken his title *Ha! Ha! among the Trumpets* from the Book of Job. I remember how I re-read Job, seeking out a

---

From *How Poets Work*, ed. Tony Curtis (Seren, 1996)

different title, and soon I came across the ass that 'searcheth after every green thing.' *After Every Green Thing*. Would any critic spot the source of my self-deprecating title? But first, of course, Hutchinson had to accept my manuscript, which I posted off, wishing it the best of luck as I pushed the big envelope into the red pillar box.

Months of silence. Then, in June 1946, I was invited to visit Hutchinson's editorial offices to meet a certain Mrs Webb. I combed my hair, rode a bus and sat in an outer waiting room until summoned. Mrs Webb explained to me that they were in a quandary. My book had been sent out to two readers. One declared it to be utter bosh, the other that it was of 'exceptional quality'. I liked that – *exceptional quality*! Mrs Webb, a Solomon if ever there was one, now pronounced that she would send my manuscript to a third reader. 'It will depend on that report,' she said, dismissing me. In September 1946, I received a letter from Hutchinson accepting *After Every Green Thing*. It was more than two years before the book was actually published – for, meanwhile, Hutchinson had slowly come to realise that verse was no longer a commercial enterprise. And when, finally, it did reach the bookshops I continued to be deluded: I still thought the book exceptional quality. Several years passed before I realised that most of it was bosh. Only then did I recall Aesop's fly, sitting on the axle of a chariot, that cried out, 'What a dust I do make!'

Recently, because I was putting together a *Selected Poems* for Penguin Books, I took down *After Every Green Thing* from my bookshelf to see if I could choose at least one or two early poems for the Penguin selection. The majority were too flawed. Being untutored, reading Medicine, not English, unaware of literary criticism, mixing with students who owned no knowledge or theories about the craft of poetry, I had made elementary mistakes. Some of these I might have avoided had someone pointed me towards the Don'ts of Ezra Pound. Politically evil that American poet might have been but he had climbed Parnassus and come down with a tablet of stone on which the Muse had writ some vital commandments for the apprentice poets, such as 'Go in fear of abstractions'.*

*For 'Don'ts' of Ezra Pound, see page 169.

I, the youthful author of *After Every Green Thing* did not go in fear of abstraction. Worse, the controlled explosion of a poem was too often triggered by a poetic idea rather than a true or imagined experience.

I fear, too, that I frequently babbled poetic expressions – not 'dove-grey hills' exactly, but a too liberal use of overworked poetic words: 'stars', 'wounds', 'golden', 'dazzling', 'brilliant' etc. To write a poem is rather like inviting guests to a banquet. Only the guests are words. The banquet is only a success if the right guests come, if the host places the correct guests next to each other. It is no use placing 'blue' next to 'sky' – they have talked too much to each other; like 'lonely' and 'heart' they have nothing more to say. It is a risk to ask 'wound' and 'blood' to the feast because they are tired guests; they have been overworked these last years. They are liable to fall asleep before the meal is through.

As for mopping up someone else's decorative vocabulary I had caught totally the inflated tone of the then fashionable neo-romantic poets whose work could be found pervasively in the poetry magazines then available and which I compulsively read: *Poetry Quarterly*, *Poetry London*, *Outposts*. Rhetoric was the order of the day. Of course there were gifted poets in the 1940s, not least those who had been killed in the war – Keith Douglas, Alun Lewis, Sidney Keyes. And Dylan Thomas, above all, managed to make a genuine and thrilling poetry out of his rhetorical energy. But there were many other poets, the vast majority in fact, who, in the pages of such magazines as *Poetry Quarterly* merely offered 'poems' that owned an ornamental emptiness and were crippled mortally by a florid profuseness of language.

Middleton Murry once remarked how rhetoric was the opposite of crystallisation, how 'instead of defining and making concrete your thought, by the aid of your sensuous perception you give way to a mere verbal exaggeration of your feeling or your thought. Instead of trying to make your expression more precise and true, you falsify it for the sake of a vague impressiveness . . . You try to replace quality by quantity and forget that all quantities raised to an infinite power are the same. By pounding on the keys with a hammer you merely break the strings.' The 'You' Middleton

Murry was addressing could have been the 'Me' of *After Every Green Thing*.

Sometimes I caught more than the organ vatic tones of those *Poetry Quarterly* rhetoricians. Nor did I escape the influence of the master neo-romantic himself – Dylan Thomas. Thus a phallic and soma poem of mine, 'The Marriage' begins:

> Once no morning could make quiet his spires
> his chapels and chimneys blasphemed the golden day;
> when choirs of wounds arose from the sunken bed
> arose the hairy hand of Esau which slept in his face
> and the book of children shut in his head.

And concludes:

> For the bird of his guilt no longer aspires
> to leave the cages of the golden day;
> her mouth is his wine and her breasts are his bread
> and wings are tied by chains to a yesterday.
> Now she dies in his eyes with the mortal dead.

Imprecision of language, words chosen more for sound than sense and, if all that was not enough of elementary error, here I was doing what Pound had imperiously said Don't do – mixing, as in 'bird of his guilt', an abstraction (guilt) with a concrete object (bird). Many other poems in *After Every Green Thing* were scarred in this way. Now, turning over its pages, I seek and I find 'delicious domes of possibility', 'ark of loving', 'panic of a blank page', 'private desert of insanity', 'slippers of darkness', 'white pain of the moon', 'pharoah of summer', 'mountains of dark', 'security of armchairs', 'a monastery of tears'. How easy it is to make up such expressions. Anybody half-literate can construct them. Some may appear more arresting than others and major poets might on occasions present one such (for instance, Wordsworth's 'Fields of Sleep') but, generally, as a poetic strategy, it is too easy an option and to write good poetry one must be committed to difficulty.

Sometimes, as an apprentice poet, in trying to avoid clichés and seeking a reaction of surprise, I forgot that the best word in context, like the best image, the best stanza, had not only to be surprising but appropriate. For example, I wrote in one poem, 'They with thoughts like gods in their muscles.' Surprising yes, a cliché no, but since thoughts are never like gods in muscles the expression is inappropriate, almost absurd. Images devised only to startle lose their small effervescence on a second reading to become utterly flat – boring as an anecdote told over and over. Thus a surrealistic mode of poetry, depending on strange conjunctions, on odd gestures of surprise – rather like somebody coming out from behind a curtain and shouting 'Boo' – is bound ultimately to fail. Such poetry worships the Arbitrary, that false idol. Poetry, to be authentic, must allow the reader an *illusion* of inevitability, however decorative its logic.

So many flawed poems then in that first youthful book of mine. It would have been useful if somebody with a greater literary sophistication than I possessed had listed these and other faults and, in so doing, speeded up my rather prolonged apprenticeship. On the other hand, I would not wish to suggest that a tutorless apprenticeship had no advantages or proved to be entirely barren. After all, the two most original poets of the 1940s, Dylan Thomas and George Barker, did not even go to University. Being a medical student allowed me entrance, painful entrance, to experiences that would have been missed had I merely read sweet English at Oxford or Cambridge. Besides, though over the years my poetry has become more conversationally pitched, more linguistically economical and, I hope, more authentic, appropriate, I find occasions, when the poem itself, in its development, *insists* on a singing tone. Then a neo-romantic mode reasserts itself – the Dionysian material, however, now partly tamed and shaped by Apollonian decorum. Indeed, soon after *After Every Green Thing* was published I wrote an Epithalamion of which I am still proud:

> Singing, today I married my white girl
> beautiful in a barley field.
> Green on thy finger a grass blade curled,
> so with this ring I thee wed, I thee wed,

and send our love to the loveless world
of all the living and all the dead.

Now, no more than vulnerable human,
we, more than one, less than two,
are nearly ourselves in a barley field –
and only love is the rent that's due
though the bailiffs of time return anew
to all the living but not the dead.

Shipwrecked, the sun sinks down harbours
of a sky, unloads its liquid cargoes
of marigolds, and I and my white girl
lie still in the barley – who else wishes
to speak, what more can be said
by all the living against all the dead?

Come then all you wedding guests:
green ghost of trees, gold of barley,
you blackbird priests in the field,
you wind that shakes the pansy head
fluttering on a stalk like a butterfly;
come the living and come the dead.

Listen flowers, birds, winds, worlds,
tell all today that I married
more than a white girl in the barley –
for today I took to my human bed
flower and bird and wind and world,
and all the living and all the dead.

I had begun to write poetry when I was a sixth form schoolboy living in a politically conscious household – one of my brothers, Leo, would become a Labour Member of Parliament. Like him, I hoped to change the world! For it seemed to me then, briefly at least, that a sacred indignation could touch one into a spontaneous eloquence. I thought, along with Wilfred Owen, that the poetry was in the pity and that the poetry did not matter. Thus the first 'raw' poems I wrote, those antecedent to the much more private artefacts in *After Every Green Thing*, had a missionary intention. I sympathised with George Herbert who, on his deathbed, had suggested his poems, *The Temple*, should only be published if they would do good. Herbert was not concerned whether his poetry would give pleasure or not, and as such he was a typically committed poet, albeit in his case not politically but religiously committed. His poetry, he felt, was only valuable if it were effective as God's propaganda. His intention was to bring despairing human beings nearer to God.

A year or two passed before I became aware how much committed fervour could be accompanied by humourless intolerance. I read Henry Vaughan's seventeenth-century hectoring introduction to *Silex Scintillans* with mounting irritation. 'That this kingdom,' thundered Vaughan,

> hath abounded with those ingenious persons, which in the late notion are termed Wits is too well known; many of them having cast away all their fair portion of time in no better employments than a deliberate search, or excogitation, of idle words, and a most vain, insatiable, desire to be reputed poets . . . And well it were for them, if those willingly studied and wilfully published vanities could defile no spirits but their own; but the case is far worse. These vipers survive their parents and for many ages after (like epidemic diseases) infect whole generations, corrupting always and unhallowing the best-gifted souls and the most capable vessels . . .

Despite my political concern, anger, about – as I put it – 'slums and cripples in a world of colours' – I felt sympathy for the brotherhood and sisterhood of Vaughan's vipers. I began to understand that missionary public poetry was of no greater significance than any other kind of poetry. No more, no less. British poets, particularly in our modern times, usually depreciate the activist value of their writings, however much their work is infused with moral concerns. They find it difficult to believe that literature, and poetry in particular, is important in the 'great world' other than allowing readers perdurable pleasure. Stephen Spender asked despairingly, 'What can we do in a world at war that matters?' and Auden asserted 'Poetry makes nothing happen', recognising that he merely belonged to a tribe of dreaming things.

What canst thou do, or all thy tribe
To the great world? Thou art a dreaming thing.

So wrote Keats looking in the mirror. On the other hand, poets of our time, those who have lived in totalitarian societies, have found that to be a dreaming thing can be lethal. Consider the unenviable fate of so many European poets, some of whom hardly wrote public poetry at all. Mayakovsky committing suicide, Mandelstam jumping through a window of a Soviet hospital, García Lorca murdered, Hernandez dying of TB in one of Franco's dark dungeons, Paul Celan and Primo Levi enduringly wounded though surviving Nazi concentration camps, Brecht and Milosz and Brodsky exiled – and so on.

It would appear that totalitarian governments believe poetry to be a subversive weapon whatever poets themselves might think. Poems politically coloured may not have the immediacy of certain TV images but some may set off detonations into the future. For if we accept that ideas in themselves can change us, can direct us into a different lifestyle, how much more powerfully can ordered imaginative experiences, by which I mean poems, affect us, influence us and through us change society at large?

But I am arguing with myself! I merely wish to signify how my poetry moved from platform verse towards work that did not strive to change the world. Indeed, many of the poems in *After Every Green Thing* were too private. Jung, in an essay 'Psychology and Literature' remarked that 'the personal aspect is a limitation – and even a sin – in the realm of art. When a form of art is primarily personal it deserves to be treated as if it were a neurosis.' If Jung had substituted the word 'private' for 'personal' then I would be able to agree with him. Paradoxically, the private with its tendency to become hermetic – as, for example, in the work of John Ashbery in the USA or of Medbh McGuckian in Northern Ireland – is perceived by the reader to be impersonal without any feeling in it; or at best, the feeling is muffled.

Of course, a poet with a missionary intention, a platform poet attempting to address a large audience, may feel his vocation to be worthwhile, one that is socially purposeful. Others, primarily writing with no audience in mind, avoiding hermeticism, committed only to making the best poem they can with the gift they have, may, in certain desolate moody moments, wonder whether their occupation and preoccupation with language in a society that thinks in Prose, is simply a self-indulgence, even a symptom of a neurotic personality. Sometimes, I confess, I have in my maturity asked myself this question. I find solace in two lines from a poem I wrote called 'Funland':

Love, read this, though it has little meaning
for by reading this you give me meaning.

4

Abse's 1984

Gerald Isaaman, the editor of a highly respected local newspaper in London, the *Hampstead and Highgate Express,* affectionately known as the *Ham and High*, is a great admirer of George Orwell. In December 1983, recalling Orwell's lively column for *Tribune* entitled 'As I Please', he decided that during 1984 he would like a similar series to grace the pages of the *Ham and High.*

George Orwell, alas, was not available. So he cast around for other writers, shortlisting a number of these, no doubt alphabetically, for soon he telephoned me. I could not mimic Orwell. I could only write my own kind of prose. Gerald Isaaman did not seem to mind and I agreed to offer him a fortnightly autobiographical column for one year only. He was to call my non-Orwellian 'As I Please' *Abse's 1984.* He proved to be an ideal editor. He only very occasionally made suggestions and never changed my copy.

*

I am not alone in believing my local park, Golders Hill Park, with its peacocks, llamas and emus etc., to be one of the most pleasant in London. Yet the park remains relatively unknown. One who enjoyed it earlier this century was W. H. Hudson (1841–1922). He often strolled this way with such a literary Hampstead friend as Ernest Rhys, the editor of the Everyman Library.

Yesterday afternoon the park spread out cold and moody and empty. I walked up its green slopes past the stark black trees towards

---

The Hampstead and Highgate Express (1984)

the abandoned bandstand and the little pond near the walled flower garden. Arriving at that pond I read the red board with its white painted admonition: DANGER, THIN ICE. And standing, asleep, one-legged on the ice, their heads beneath wings, stood the four flamingoes that I had come to visit.

Each winter I observe this odd, dream-like scene enacted. On each occasion, W. H. Hudson's description of a flamingo killing in Patagonia comes to mind. He wrote how he, carrying a gun and accompanied by his dog, encountered a small flock of flamingoes in a lagoon. He wrote, 'I crept up to the rushes in a fever of excitement; not that flamingoes are not common in this district, but because I had noticed that one of the birds before me was the largest and loveliest flamingo I had ever set eyes on . . . I think my hand trembled a great deal; nevertheless the bird dropped when I fired.'

How dare Hudson have killed such a benign creature? If he had not admired it, that flamingo would have lived out its blameless natural life. Nowadays, each winter, I turn angrily from the frozen pond to look for the phantom of W. H. Hudson. Yesterday afternoon I surely heard, in the distance, his ghost screech thin with grief. Else it was the startled cry of a peacock.

★

I took the record off – a Beethoven piano sonata – and I sat in the armchair thinking of nothing in particular. I did not even notice the silence after music. I sat there contentedly until the door opened. 'What's the matter?' she asked. I did not reply. 'You're depressed,' she said. I did not contradict her though I wanted to smile at her presumption.

I should have told her that my face misleadingly assumes, in repose, a melancholy aspect. Instead I stared at her without expression.

At once she spoke with such sympathy, such sweetness, such softness, that gradually I began to feel sorrowful. 'What have you got to be so sad about?' she asked. 'You're lucky. You've got so many things going for you. You should thank God . . .' I interrupted her. I felt that I should have a reason or two for my face, in repose, registering that fake despondency.

'It's 1984,' I remarked, implying that Old Age, like the Post Office, was just around the corner. 'And the leaders of all the nations are so reactionary, near the night borders of insanity as a matter of fact, that it's frightening. Why, if one of those psychopaths punched the button . . .'

She ceased frowning. She wanted to cheer me up, I could see that. She picked up the record I had not put away – the Beethoven sonata. 'This is so beautiful,' she said. 'Listen to this. It will raise your spirits.'

I sat there hearing Brendel playing again and soon I was restored, felt contented as before. Then I noticed, half way through the *largo e mesto*, how sad and serious her face had become.

★

A confession. On weekday afternoons, if I do not engage myself in dutiful or honourable activities such as working, or at least serious reading, then I experience a sense of unease. The ghost in the mirror points his finger at me. I used to suffer those same feelings on the occasions when, as a wayward medical student, I deliberately missed a lecture or a ward round, to spend instead a guilty afternoon at the Swiss Cottage Odeon.

By Wednesday lunchtime, though, I yearned for a wicked game of chess. So I telephoned my friend, the pipe-smoking LSE philosopher, John Watkins, who lives in Erskine Hill, Hampstead Garden Suburb.

'OK,' Professor Watkins agreed, 'if you come over here.'

The sky was high and February blue, the sun low, the light peculiarly bright and liquid as if reflected from cutlery. I walked down Finchley Road to turn up Hoop Lane, conscious that it was a lovely day. I felt curiously cheerful. Then, as I approached the railings of the cemetery, I observed in front of me the first black hearse with its flower-covered coffin, parked opposite the Crematorium gate.

Behind the hearse, another stationary, black limousine waited by the kerb. Three people sat bolt upright in the back, unsmiling, motionless, not talking to each other. They owned the melancholy faces of sleepers, except their eyes were open, their mouths shut. I walked on towards the roundabout.

Then came, silent as a conspiracy, a second funeral cortège. First the long car with the fresh coffin, followed by another shining, black automobile, chauffeur-driven. And in the back seat, again, three mourners sat upright, neither looking to the right nor to the left. They had similar despondent faces. I looked over my shoulder and saw behind me the parked, mourning car with its first three occupants and suddenly a possible line for a poem came into my head: 'Some talk in their sleep, very few sing.'

Some talk in their sleep, very few sing. I thought about that and a few more matching lines occurred to me so that as I walked on I struggled to get the sound of the meaning right. The funerals had set me ticking – as Sylvia Plath said in a different context – 'set me ticking like a fat gold watch'. Why not? The theme of Death is to Poetry what Mistaken Identity is to Comedy Drama.

But then those nascent lines in my head became derailed, as if I had been button-holed by a man from Porlock. For on the other side of the roundabout a third hearse with coffin approached. From poetic trance I was jolted into the ordinary, beautiful, common air of a particular Wednesday afternoon and was astonished.

For it was as if, from diverse corners of London, funeral cars were converging to this focal point in Golders Green and each hearse, in its turn, with its chauffeur of Death, had to wait, had to idle the minutes away, rather like an aeroplane circling and circling, not given clearance to land at some crowded airport.

However, behind the third, so-controlled cortège came, at last, another car – one not so sleek, one as a matter of fact battered, shabby, and driven neither by a ceremonial chauffeur, nor carrying three exhausted occupants in the back. The driver was young and the window next to him wound down so that, out of it, came the raucous noise of Radio One. The young driver had evidently turned the knob of his radio on to half past six because the volume of this so-called music was startlingly loud, spectacularly loud.

I was not offended. I welcomed this pollution of silence. For that blaring noise celebrated, there and then, informality, youth, vivid life. For some reason I could not understand, as I progressed into

Hampstead Garden suburb, I felt confident that that afternoon I was going to win my game of chess.

★

On my way home I read the newspaper placard: TITO GOBBI DIES IN ROME. Immediately I thought of my Uncle Joe – my favourite among the many brothers of my mother. Joe had told me how, one evening while on holiday in Italy, he had wandered into the hotel bar. In no time at all he found himself in conversation with an Italian gentleman.

'No, no, I was born in Bassano del Grappo in the Veneto region,' said the stranger. 'But I like this part of Italy.'

'I was born in Ystalyfera in South Wales,' offered my gregarious uncle.

Soon they were exchanging views about politics, about the relative qualities of Rome and London, about Napoleon Bonaparte, icthyology, the internal combustion engine, Shakespeare, celestial photography and one or two other ordinary conversational topics.

After another drink my uncle, curious about his new-found friend, remarked, 'I'm a doctor, you know. I have a practice in Hampstead Garden suburb in London. What, sir, do you do for a living?'

The Italian replied, smiling, 'I'm Tito Gobbi.' My uncle extended his hand. 'My name is Joe Shepherd. But, as I said, what do you do for a living?'

'I'm Tito Gobbi,' Tito Gobbi repeated, his smile retreating. My uncle decided that the stranger's English was, after all, somewhat deficient. 'Signor Gobbi,' my uncle now deliberated very slowly and clearly, enunciating each word so that he could be understood, 'What . . . do . . . you . . . do . . . for . . . a . . . living?'

Joe Shepherd went on to tell me how the fellow unaccountably bolted for the exit.

My uncle, a first-class general physician, a most capable diagnostician, could identify patients' diseases with precision. But he wasn't so hot at identifying the names of the patients themselves.

There was that time when we were in a theatre foyer and James

Mason hovered nearby. Because Mr Mason looked familiar to my uncle he assumed the film star was a patient of his.

'Feeling better?' he asked James Mason.

The actor stopped in his tracks. 'Thank you,' he said. My uncle nodded. 'You look better since you've had the treatment,' he added. James Mason looked over his shoulder rather wildly, I thought, as he ascended the staircase.

★

One of my two daughters, Susanna, has been travelling around the world with a friend since last August. Letters arrive from strange places – Thailand, India, Japan. She seems to be enjoying her adventure and will surely be enriched by it, but selfishly I'm beginning to miss her. There simply aren't enough people around this house for me to tell off or to ask, 'Who's the Best Driver in the World?'

So I wish Susanna, now that April is coming, would have some Home Thoughts from Abroad. How can I induce enough nostalgia in her to make a return journey imperative and soon? I shall send her a postcard naming names. I shall speak of the daffodils in Golders Hill Park; the fair at Hampstead Heath; the unexpected bit of canal at Camden Lock; the elegance of Kenwood; the delightful curve downhill of Fitzjohn's Avenue; the cherry blossom that will soon arrive on the trees of Golders Green like so many bits of the *Financial Times.*

How can she resist the power of nostalgia? Peter Vansittart told me a story I can never forget. It concerned a Chinese general who once – defending a city beseiged by the Mongols and with no food left, no hope remaining – climbed on to the battlements of the city one moonlit night.

The Mongols were all encamped around. The general could see them from the high walls. There was silence; there were the sleepers in the tents; there were the stars flung high above, and the general played on his pipe, played the most lonely, the most desolate melodies of the Steppes.

Soon after dawn, the enemy, now all utterly homesick, departed.

Remembering this I too play on my pipe for my daughter: Spaniard's Inn, Jack Straw's Castle, The Flask, The Everyman, The Screen on the Hill, Louis' Teashop, the Whitestone Pond and the donkeys, the *Ham and High.*

★

Another new, non-steroid, anti-inflammatory drug has been withdrawn as a result of the Committee on the Safety of Medicines turning their thumbs down. Three others over the last two years have met a similar fate.

This family of drugs is taken by hundreds of thousands of people in Britain. They have been prescribed widely, in the main for arthritic pains of all varieties. One of them, Osmosin, as a matter of fact, was prescribed for my father-in-law by a hospital doctor in Lancashire.

Fortunately he suffered no ill effects. Others, less luckily, have experienced adverse reactions – some of them dire. There have been medical disasters such as gastro-intestinal perforations and blood dyscrasias. There have been mortalities.

Who is to blame? The greedy pharmaceutical companies or the gullible incautious, prescribing doctors? Both. There's no question that sometimes certain pharmaceutical firms, even in those advertisements they place in such prestigious periodicals as the *British Medical Journal*, make excessive claims for their drugs and print in the smallest type available the serious possible side-effects of these same drugs. Doctors read their advertisements and are influenced by them.

The *Lancet*, another journal which I read regularly with interest, quite justly has castigated doctors for often 'ignoring the hazards of a particular drug'. They further accuse doctors of being 'incapable of making a reasoned judgement' concerning the risks and benefits of this or that medicament.

The *Lancet* is right. Doctors have not the pharmacological expertise to make such judgements and that is why they so often have to accept the information doled out to them by so-called reputable drug companies.

Of course, many new drugs are wonderfully effective but not every physician remembers Alexander Pope's advice, 'Be not the first by whom the new are tried, Nor yet the last to lay the old aside.'

Doctors have always done harm as well as good. My favourite story of one who caused medical mayhem is told by the American doctor, Lewis Thomas, in his autobiography, *The Youngest Science.* He relates how a certain old-time physician, during the early years of this century, became extremely successful in New York, noted for his skill in making early diagnoses – especially of typhoid fever which was then a common disease in New York.

This great diagnostician, wrote Lewis Thomas, placed particular reliance on examining the tongue. 'He believed that he could detect significant differences by palpating that organ. The ward rounds conducted by this man were, essentially, tongue rounds; each patient would stick out his tongue while the eminence took it between thumb and forefinger, feeling its texture and irregularities, then moving from bed to bed, diagnosing typhoid in its earliest stages over and over again, and turning out a week or so later to have been right, to everyone's amazement.'

What we then learn from Lewis Thomas is that the old-time great diagnostician was, in fact, a typhoid carrier!

★

I went for a morning walk on the beach at Ogmore-by-Sea. The post-Easter blue skies still persisted and sunlight threw down its mercury-backed mirror dazzle on the sea. The beach was empty. I looked towards the barely-outlined coast of Somerset across the Bristol Channel and walked on, half-listening to the erratic rhythm of the sea.

Then, ahead of me, I saw a man, alone, sitting on the pebbles, his trousers tucked into his socks. Nearby lay a white stick. The man looked out, seemingly towards Somerset but, of course, he was blind. And I, walking on sand, and hence silently, suddenly felt myself to be a voyeur, watching him watch nothing.

I noticed how he was feeling the pebbles around him one by one.

He picked them up, weighed them, felt, perhaps, the sun's faint warmth in them before replacing them, each one deliberately. He looked my way and seemed to smile so that I wondered, what parable is this? From behind a rock a woman now appeared, obviously his companion, and I strolled on listening once more to the sea and to the sorrowing of some seagulls.

★

Mr Keating telephoned to ask if he could visit me. 'I'm doing a thesis,' he explained. What a sensible fellow, I thought, to undertake a thesis on my work. I warmed to him at once. I would help him. However, I soon gathered that he wanted to interview me only because he had begun writing a thesis on Stevie Smith!

'I would be obliged,' he said, 'if you would give me your impressions of her as a person. I know you shared a platform with Stevie Smith on various occasions. I once heard you both at the Theatre Royal in Stratford East.'

He had heard us both, I pondered, and wanted to write a thesis on Stevie. I cooled towards the fellow in an instant. I claimed, truthfully, little acquaintance with Stevie Smith, but Mr Keating was insistent. Reluctantly I agreed to see him.

I would tell him about another telephone call I had once received that led to my one and only altercation with Stevie Smith. It was from David Carver, the then Secretary of PEN, who wanted my opinion about the current standing of Robin Skelton's reputation, who, visiting London from Canada, had offered to give a poetry reading for PEN. David Carver had, in any case, it seemed, intended to sponsor a PEN reading some time at the Porchester Hall and was, indeed, on the look-out for an important poet reader.

'Would Skelton attract a large enough audience?' asked Mr Carver. 'Do you think it would be better if I asked someone like Stevie Smith instead?'

'Why not both of them?' I suggested.

I knew that Stevie would draw an audience. During the last few years she had become popular partly because of the Poetry and Jazz readings arranged by Jeremy Robson. Stevie was considerably older than the other poets who shared that platform with her. She was almost 70 and looked like a very thin great-aunt about to say 'Don't'. Perhaps the audience had expected, from her appearance, to hear dull hymns to Flowers, Elves and Bees. At first they viewed her with suspicion but soon she was reciting:

> I was much too far out all my life
> And not waving but drowning.

Or surprisingly, she would sing her lines excruciatingly, daringly, off-key. The audience warmed to her, cheered her audacity.

Later David Carver telephoned to say that Stevie wanted to read solo. She had declared that she never read with anyone else!

'Nonsense,' I said. 'I'll persuade her if you like.'

Most poets prefer not to read in tandem but usually agree to do so if pressed. And if Robin Skelton wanted to read, well, why not?

My telephone call to Stevie was a disaster. She was harsh, regally adamant. She did not sound like the Stevie Smith I knew. She seemed to be invaded by some alien personality, one I had never met and I put down the telephone, upset, defeated. So Stevie Smith read at the Porchester Hall, solo. I did not attend her reading.

Some months later I met her at a party and, happily, we became 'friends' again. That was the last time I saw Stevie for, soon after, she became ill, suffering from a brain tumour. In retrospect, I wonder whether her apparent personality change, her uncharacteristic response to my telephone call, was an early sign of her lesion. Probably not. In any case, I can hardly imagine how such a surmise can help Mr Keating one way or another.

★

The man at the bar took the pipe out of his mouth and said to Vernon Scannell, 'Since you're a poet you should know where this comes from.' Then he proudly recited, 'Loveliest of trees . . .' Vernon interrupted him with, 'Housman'. The man narrowed his eyes. 'Look,' he said, 'if you can tell me who wrote this I'll buy you a pint.' He recited more Housman and Vernon Scannell replied,

'A. E. Housman' The pint glass was soon emptied. 'I'll buy you another one,' said the pipe-smoking gentleman reciter of poetry, 'if you guess who the author is this time.'

He intoned more lines of verse and yet again Vernon Scannell interrupted him with a triumphant, 'Housman.' The quiz continued, the prize always being a pint. However, the man who wanted to recite poetry and confound Vernon Scannell knew only the work of Housman. He kept on reciting his favourite poet and as Vernon called out Housman, each time less clearly, pints were bought for all. Just before closing time, though, I don't think Vernon heard what lines were being recited, yet clever as Dick, he mumbled, 'Housman.' And the man was amazed at Vernon's extraordinary erudition.

It always surprises me how many people, given half a chance, will with evident pleasure recite the verses they know off by heart. My own mother, after a couple of wine gums, could be persuaded, drear of tone and wild of eye, to recite 'Hiawatha'– the whole of it. Once my mother got going she was hard to stop. 'O the famine and the fever!' she would howl. 'O the wailing of the children!'

There used to be an annual Festival of Spoken Poetry. It went on successfully for some thirty years until 1959. The winner that last year was a beautiful young lady named Betty Mulcahy. Not long ago I happened to hear Ms Mulcahy read out loud, at a concert, a poem by Vernon Scannell. The poem, a striking one, was called 'Taken in Adultery'. The Master of Ceremonies who introduced the reading did so without punctuation. Breathlessly he said, 'Betty Mulcahy, taken in adultery by Vernon Scannell.' That made a few people raise their eyebrows.

★

The patient had the same name as me: Abse. He was a Lebanese Christian. 'Is Abse a common name in the Middle East?' I asked. Unsmiling, he nodded and told me he had encountered the name in Egypt and Syria as well as in the Lebanon. 'It's an old name,' he said. 'Have you heard of the poet, Abse?' Taken aback, I hesitated. 'The great poet, Abse,' he added. This is my day, I thought, but he continued, 'The great poet, Abse, who lived in the sixth century, at the time of the prophet.'

I swallowed. I looked at him suspiciously. But it was quite evident that he did not know that I too scribbled away, scribble, scribble, scribble. 'The great poet, Antara el Abse,' Mr Abse said. 'I'm not a literary man but Antara is famous among Arabs. He was a robber-prince and was half black.'

Later I learned from reading an essay by Bernard Lewis in an old *Encounter* that the blacks had been persecuted in the Moslem sixth-century world. No wonder Antara wrote:

> Half of me comes from the family of Abse,
> The other half I defend with my sword.

I like that. I wouldn't mind sticking those two lines at the top of my notepaper. Indeed, the more I hear of this Antara el Abse the more I'm willing to claim him as a long-lost ancestor.

Once, it seems, a crowd shrank before a huge wild bull. One man cried to Antara, 'Only Antara can deal with that bull.' Antara el Abse nodded in seeming agreement, then answered, 'Ye-es, but does that bull know I'm Antara?'

★

My companions discussed Goethe's dying words, 'Mehr licht.' One of them wondered whether Goethe, in pronouncing his 'More light' was merely requesting greater illumination in order that he might see more clearly the beautiful face of the woman at his bedside. Another, more religiously inclined, suggested that he was trying to tell those in attendance something about the nature of heaven whose gates he was at. After all, there is a legend that in the world to come the light of the moon shall be as the light of the sun and the light of the sun shall be sevenfold.

Why do Last Words interest us at all? Why do they seem more important than say, the utterances of a man or woman on the occasion of a 40th birthday? Do we assume that only at the end of life can a lifetime's vision be summarised in one pithy sentence, be whispered, like a secret, to the near and dear ones at the bedside? Or do we believe that a man faced with death will reveal himself as never before, not wishing in that solemn hour to deceive anyone?

More likely our curiosity springs from the childish belief that a man or woman at Death's portals is well placed to tell us something of the terrain from which no traveller returns and for which we are, alas, all eventually bound. We who are tourists not yet set out, listen fearfully to a tourist who has almost awesomely arrived.

The fact is, though, that those recorded words of the dying are almost always falsified or just simply manufactured. Goethe, for instance, did not actually whisper, 'Mehr licht.' Instead, he softly requested, 'Open the second shutter so that more light can come in.' But how much more memorable is the fictive, ambiguous, 'More light.' If Goethe had lived to record his own dying words they would doubtless have been more memorable still!

Spike Milligan once asked me if I knew Gladstone's Dying Words. I shook my head. Putting on a Spike Milligan funny voice Spike Milligan uttered, 'I feel better now.' Perhaps Gladstone did actually expire with those words. For surely the more banal the saying the more likely it is to be true. I do not believe Beethoven's spooky and striking, 'I shall hear in heaven.' I do believe King George V's 'How is the Empire?'

★

Research scientists imbued with a relentless spirit of enquiry are a rum lot, admirable though many of them may be. Think of those doctors such as John Hunter who audaciously experimented on themselves for the sake of suffering humankind.

Many watching the over-dramatised TV biography of Sigmund Freud will be reminded of his over-enthusiastic use of cocaine. What a bloodier meal the BBC drama department could have made of another cocaine story: that of the German surgeon August Bier and his assistant Hildenbrandt who, together, initiated the practice of spinal anaesthesia.

It was in the summer of 1898 that Bier suggested to his assistant that they inject cocaine into the spinal fluid before an operation rather than administer a general anaesthetic. First, though, they needed to discover whether this procedure would be effective, would delete the pain of major surgery. It was no use experimenting on animals. The creatures could not give the necessary subjective evidence, could not talk. So they injected cocaine into their own cerebro-spinal fluids before recording their sensations to pain-stimuli with teutonic thoroughness.

For instance, the injection having been given to Hildenbrandt, Bier made an incision in the skin of his assistant's leg, making blood flow. Hildenbrandt blithely remarked that he merely felt the mild pressure of the scalpel. Minutes later Bier grasped a long thick needle and plunged it through the muscles of Hildenbrandt's thigh until it grated against the bone. 'I'm feeling nothing,' Hildenbrandt exclaimed delightedly.

Bier lit a cigar and I can imagine how, momentarily, the two men stared at each other before Bier brought down his lit cigar to the skin. His assistant smelt his own flesh burning out but experienced no pain. August Bier picked up a heavy hammer. 'Go ahead,' said Hildenbrandt – in German, of course.

We have our own intrepid scientists in Britain, now, experimenting on themselves. One such is Professor Brindley who works in the Department of Physiology at the Institute of Psychiatry in South East London. With colleagues he has been conducting experiments that could lead to an organic treatment of impotence. He has reported in the *Lancet* that he has injected substances that caused erections lasting two to five hours. Some patients suffered them longer – sorry about that pun – up to forty hours. Such priapism of course is no joking matter. It is a condition terribly distressful as Professor Brindley could testify, for on experimenting on himself, as well as on other volunteers, he, too, suffered a sustained priapism.

Priapism outside the laboratory is far from common but it can be a most painful side-effect of certain modern drugs. So great credit to the professor because he has now probably discovered an effective therapy for it. For after taking the drug metaraminol he was able to report, 'The smallest dose (0.4 mg) caused conspicuous shrinkage of the penis lasting one and a half hours. During this time it was difficult but not impossible to obtain a psychogenic or reflex erection.'

I shake my head in astonishment. I know that one should be solemn about advances in the treatment of impotence or priapism but I cannot help but smile to myself as I picture the professor sitting in his laboratory, ruler in one hand, stop watch in the other, looking down and excitedly shouting, 'Eureka! Eureka!'

★

Every other Thursday morning I sit down at my desk to write the next instalment of my 1984 Diary. After cleaning my teeth, after picking up the letters from the hall-mat, after eating my buttered toast, drinking my two cups of tea (milk with one sugar, since I know you are all agog to know), after indulging in enormously commonplace activities that any Cabinet Minister would immediately transcribe into his diaries for posterity, I reach my desk and the blank page on which I will write *Abse's 1984.*

At this moment, since unvarnished truth in diaries must be told, my mind is full of other writers' journals. For before going to bed last night (I sleep on the right-hand side of a double bed) I watched on TV an admirably produced, adapted and well-acted film feature of Boswell's *London Diary*, unboundedly open in its communication; and not ten minutes ago while reading *The Times* over breakfast (and mumbling yet again, Why don't we take the *Guardian*?) I alighted on a book review of *The Castle Diaries* by Woodrow Wyatt of bow-tie fame.

Apparently, these diaries, even abridged, contain half a million words. Wyatt suggests that should a research student in some distant future pick his way through the unabridged version lodged in one or another University Library, then the student should promptly be certified as insane. In kinder mood, Woodrow Wyatt adds that 'there are some nuggets to be extracted' and with blithe pincers he pulls them out one by one for our delectation. Barbara Castle's hatred of Callaghan – 'Frankly I believe Jim Callaghan is capable of anything'; Harold Wilson's drinking habits – 'I think he had been taking comfort in his brandy again'; Roy Jenkins's ataraxic presence

– 'My private tête-à-tête with Roy took place one lunch at No 11. Why do I feel constrained at these intimate talks?' Nuggets, every one of them, Mr Wyatt assures us.

Perhaps they are. I remember the *Crossman Diaries, Volume III.* Wonderful nuggets there: 'I had a horrible office lunch of particularly disgusting sandwiches'; '. . . at 2 a.m. my stomach evacuated totally . . .'; 'I lunched at the Ritz with Peregrine Worsthorne'; and pure gold this – 'before Cabinet I had a frantic message that Tony Crosland wanted to lunch with me. I took him to lunch. (I don't know why he doesn't take me, perhaps because he doesn't have a club.) So off we went to the Athenaeum where I gave him grouse and claret.'

Politicians such as Crossman and Castle believe that their red-hot diary insertions will one day be of historical value. 'Back to a late reception at Lancaster House for the Commonwealth Prime Ministers' Conference. George Brown was rolling round (sic) distressingly sozzled.' (Castle); 'I went off to put up plaques at a couple of health centres and then I drove to Coventry to address the annual dinner of The College of Midwives with Doris Butterworth, Jolly Jack's wife, who is their President, in the chair.' (Crossman).

Why do so many people, other than politicians, keep diaries? I suspect that the majority of them are unsure of their identities and perhaps feel themselves, too often, to be half-dead like convicts in a prison. Diary-keeping, then, can be a therapeutic exercise, a prescription to prove to themselves that they are alive. Like the imperative diary pages of a prisoner their words proclaim, 'I am here, I am alive, I thought this, I did that.'

So meaningful can diary-keeping be that its author's life may be changed by it. It can become a dangerous activity. Even Boswell realised that he might have sought out certain adventures in order that he could claim them for his diary. Those who succumb to such temptations are rather like those tourists with busy cameras who only visit Venice, say, in order to return with snapshots of themselves standing amongst the pigeons of St Mark's Square or in front of the Doge's Palace. They may not have enjoyed the pleasurable offerings of Venice but, by damn, they have wonderful souvenirs in their albums.

Diary-keeping, though, can work as a moral force. It has been asserted that by the act of confessing their sins Catholics are not only allowed consolation but the very prospect of confession is an effective prophylactic. It is embarrassing for them to whisper to the priest yet again that, on Monday, they coveted their neighbour's wife, on Tuesday they masturbated, and that, on Wednesday, they committed adultery. In the same way the diarist may not wish to confess to his diary one more act of meanness and of spite and so behaves himself instead. Velleities do not become desires and desires do not become overt acts because of the power of the word on a page.

It is not comfortable, though, to be with one who obsessionally keeps a diary. Lately I was in Lancashire with the Welsh poet, Gillian Clarke. I was telling her about a cartoon I had seen concerning Reagan and Mondale. The cartoon showed Reagan with his Cabinet – Reagan was asleep. It also showed Mondale with his Cabinet – the Cabinet were asleep. 'It was that Republican Bob Hope who remarked that Mondale had had a charisma by-pass operation,' I added. Gillian laughed and said, 'I'll put that in my diary.' When I told her later about an incident involving a common friend of ours she said, 'Oh yes, I'll definitely put that in my diary tonight.' Because Gillian seemed to keep her midnight diary with such implacable regularity I began to feel bugged. I found myself thereafter being cautious about what I said, what I did.

Some writers, of course, bug themselves. The Goncourt brothers recorded how Victor Hugo 'always has a note book in his pocket and if, in conversation with you, he happens to express the tiniest thought, to put forward the smallest idea, he promptly turns away from you, takes out his note book and writes down what he has just said.' Thanks to the Goncourts, practised buggers, Hugo, the self-bugger, was bugged.

If I kept a diary with the conscientious ardour of Gillian Clarke or Virginia Woolf, say, who kept diaries between 1915–1941, thirty volumes of them, I think I would feel guilty. In a diary a writer is talking to himself: in other forms of prose, even autobiography, the writer is speaking to others. And it is a writer's job, is it not, to address others, however few these may seem to be? Virginia Woolf felt guilty when she devoted herself to her diary rather as I would if, instead of working, I slouched off in scowling truancy, on rainy weekday afternoons, to the Odeon. Virginia Woolf scolded herself for 'the lawless exercise' of writing diaries, for not addressing herself to the much more difficult task of shaping a novel.

Yet, of course, most diaries presuppose another reader. For instance, when André Gide confesses in his journals to using a chamber pot one night, why does he add firmly that this is not his usual habit? Gide knows perfectly well what his nocturnal micturating habits are, so whom is he addressing? I believe firmly that the diarist is one who likes to have secrets but he hopes that one day, maybe tomorrow, maybe centuries hence, those secrets will be whispered to others – the more the better.

Moreover, when his diaries are finally published – I was here, I was a great fellow – he is not so open to the wrath of his critics as novelists, poets, and autobiographers are. Diaries pretend to be spontaneous effusions, to be defenceless, unpremeditated scribblings and as such are not only self-indulgent but beg the indulgence of reader and critic. As I do now.

Replies to an Enquiry

How long have you been working as a writer?

I began writing during my last year in school. I have published since then four books of poems, two novels, and have had several plays produced on the stage and radio. At present I am working on an autobiographical book to be called *A Poet in the Family*, and it may be that I will want to include, in one of the chapters I have in mind, whatever answers result from the questions that follow.

Basically are you a Jewish poet or an English poet?

Generally, I don't feel myself to be a poet at all. I finish some five or six poems a year. Only then, after a poem has been completed satisfactorily, for a few hours only do I feel myself to be a poet. Between times, for months, I am uncertain whether I shall ever write a poem again. I think Dylan Thomas once said something like, 'Art is an accident of craft.' But the craft doesn't exist separately from the 'art' of the poem. The whole activity, craft included, seems to me like an accident; so that afterwards I am not quite sure how it happened. Since the poem seems partly 'given' I am never sure whether another 'gift' will be offered again. Indeed, I look back at certain poems I've written with continued surprise. Often I find this or that poem to be much cleverer than I am; more lyrical than I could ever be; more sharp than the sharpness I think I contain; more tender than the tenderness I know; and these poems, when they work, use words with a skill that I can hardly believe myself to

---

Jewish Quarterly, Vol. 11, No. 40 (39) (Winter 1963–64)

own. I am not suggesting that the making of poems is purely a visceral activity, or that the poet is a dummy for the ventriloquist Muse, White Goddess, or some pristine Jungian divinity. Simply, poetry is written in the brain but the brain is bathed in blood.

Sometimes, I discover the poem, when I look at it later as an analytical observer, contains a Jewish note – this has happened more frequently in recent years; there are more 'Jewish' poems in my most recent volume, *Poems, Golders Green*, than in previous volumes. Still I don't think of myself, when I think of myself as a poet at all, as a Jewish poet or as an English poet, or for that matter as a Welsh poet, or a five foot eight and a half poet, or a younger, growing-older poet, or whatever.

But Jewish notes, as you put it, do enter your work?

Sometimes, yes; and often in an obscure or arcane way. Without conscious design on my part, I find myself working, for example, on a poem about the remnant of a tree that has been previously struck by lightning. In short, a misfit of a tree rather than say, a tall, straight, beautiful elm. Or I take as subject matter a shunter – you know those slow, slave-like engines you see on railway tracks – rather than an express train. That I choose one object rather than another, even if not consciously, seems to me to have something to do with the fact that I am a Jew living in the twentieth century; and therefore someone who must be aware of the situational predicament of the Jew in a special, close way. Not that I'm using the misfit tree or the shunter by way of allegory or symbol. I'm not: I intend to write only about a tree as tree, and shunter as shunter.

In any case, apart from poems of this kind, I have published poems which own a Jewish theme more explicitly. It doesn't often happen; though I've written more poems of this kind than I've ever published. Generally, they don't work as poems – and finally I'm committed not to any one single theme, but to poetry. So it is, sometimes, that one tells a lie in a poem for the sake of the poem, or advocates a viewpoint that one doesn't wholly accept. Oddly, you see, poetry is fiction.

Jewish Symbolism

Apart from poems, you've also published two novels and had several plays produced. Do Jewish themes enter this work of yours too?

I've written plays in which the protagonists are Jews. But then I've also tried to make characters that are Welsh. If I choose to write about a Jew or a Welshman it is simply because I happen to have more of an ear for their intonations, their dialogue, than I have for, say, a Methodist Serb living in Burnley. So one shouldn't make too much of that. But less obvious Jewish attitudes inhere in *apparently* non-Jewish things I write. A play like *House of Cowards* which perhaps you've seen on the stage or read in J. C. Trewin's *Plays of the Year*, may not on the face of it have anything to do with 'Jewishness.' Yet I believe it has, if only because it is concerned with the illusion of the Messiah as a future state of perfection. Moreover, even some of the devices in the play have Jewish terms of reference. Take the end of Act I. The main character in the play, old Bill Hicks, has received news which makes him very happy indeed. For a moment he recalls the health and vigour of his youth. He dances grotesquely with a spinster, Miss Chantry, who is lodging in the house, as his wife sings and beats an accompaniment. Let me read you the end of Act I:

MISS CHANTRY: Ooh, I'm out of breath.
MRS HICKS: Hurrah, hurrah.
HICKS (*stops dancing*): Hurrah.
MISS CHANTRY: (*sinking into a chair*): Oh, Mr Hicks, you *are* really. (*pause*)
HICKS: Funny, why I'm not out of breath at all. I'm like I used to be when I was young. I feel I could lift up 'undredweights. I feel strong. I can't tell you how I feel.
Threateningly, he now slowly goes over to Mrs Hicks who still has a glass in her hand.
'Ere, give me a kiss darling.
MRS HICKS (*Laughing uncomfortably*): Ha ha ha. Get away with you. Don't be soppy.

Hicks snatches the wine glass from her hand, and deliberately, carefully, places it on the floor. Then slowly he brings his heel down to crunch the glass to pieces.

MISS CHANTRY: Oooh!

MRS HICKS: Ha ha ha.

MR HICKS: Ha ha ha.

ALL TOGETHER: Ha ha ha, ha ha ha, ha ha ha, etc.

Curtain

Now all those who have been to a Jewish wedding will recognise the source of the glass-breaking on the floor. The '*Oooh*' of Miss Chantry is the '*Oooh*' of those matrons and spinsters who always exclaim involuntarily when this ritual is carried out in the synagogue. I wanted to portray old Mr Hicks's sudden feeling of virility – so, as a dramatic shortcut, and an emotionally loaded one, I used the defloration symbol which is unconsciously used in the Jewish marriage ceremony. But one chooses such devices because one is a Jew conversant, at least partially, with Jewish ritual. (I might add here, in parenthesis, that on the first night of *House of Cowards* during the first interval, one of the audience, accidentally, walked through one of those modern glass doors, shattering it!)

'The Age of the Victim'

Sometimes, thoughts on the Jewish predicament enter my writing almost uninvited. Or I use a situation, deliberately, to express through the mouths of the characters what I, as a Jew, discuss too much with myself. Take this piece of dialogue from *Ash on a Young Man's Sleeve*, my first novel. The time is war-time – in Wales. Doctor Aaronowich and his wife, along with their daughter-in-law, Ennis, and her baby, wait during an air raid in their Anderson shelter at the bottom of the garden:

'Are you comfortable, Sarah?' asked Dr Aaronowich.

'I'd rather be in the house,' she replied.

When the flares dropped, turning the darkness into a ghastly, green luminosity, old Mrs Aaronowich began to shake. 'I can't help it,' she said. 'I'm not afraid, but I can't help it.'

The Rev. Aaronowich sat quiet, thinking: this is the Age of the Victim. 'In the old days,' he started to say, 'the romantic hero was the martyr. All the heroes in tragedy, real or literary, were martyrs – martyrs because they knew why they were dying, and chose to die rather than surrender their faith. But for our world' – he nodded at the livid sky and the fires above the rooftops – 'the symbol is the victim. It is the quality of the victim to be unaware and to have no choice. Like the Jews of Europe who went into the gas chambers asking, 'why, why?' because they had disinherited themselves from their faith. The symbol of our Age is the trail that's gone off the rails, the mangled accident, the passengers flung across the tracks or drowning at sea whispering 'why? why?' And in war-time, it is the bombed, or those majorities in uniform who kill and are killed without ever understanding words like 'Democracy', 'Communism', 'Fascism'. Victims, not martyrs, those Jews of Europe, passengers, soldiers, civilians – because they did not choose, and do not understand why they are dying.'

'Jack is not a victim,' said Ennis. 'He and millions of others know why they are fighting.'

'We are all victims,' replied the old man. 'All of us. The Age of the Martyr is over: the Age of the Victim has begun. This is our world where heroes are victims, not martyrs. What a subject for tragedy. Who apart from Kafka will make a romantic hero of the victim?'

'What are you babbling about?' complained his wife. 'Look, you've woken the baby.'

The baby began to cry, and Ennis hummed, rocking the child gently.

I have read you short extracts which, I suppose, would seem to indicate that I am indeed a 'Jewish' writer. I hasten to add, though, that I could have easily, indeed more easily, read other extracts that have no Jewish content whatsoever.

The Gas Chambers of Another Decade . . .

What has been the impact on your work of the war-time destruction of the Jews in Europe?

I think my work would be even less Jewish than it is if that bestial event hadn't occurred. I mean Hitler has made me more of a Jew than Moses. Indeed, as the years have passed, as I take in more fully the unbearable reality of what has happened in Europe, as I read biographies of Hitler, Himmler, Goebbels, Goering, as I read the testimony of survivors, as I see films, as I come to know the documents of history, then gradually I feel myself to be more of a Jew than ever. It takes a long time to become aware that here, in England, one is a survivor also. The realisation of the destruction of the Jews, of one single event only – that two million Jews have been exterminated in Auschwitz alone, that thousands of children, there, were thrown on the pyre alive and not even gassed – changes, poisons subtly, one's attitude to other people. I am aware that ordinary, decent people one has met, with ordinary passive prejudices, could be, under other circumstances, the murderers of one's own children, or the executioners of adults whom one loves and reveres. This is not a paranoiac delusion, alas. As a doctor, I know that listening to say, Mr Robinson sitting opposite me, complaining of this or that minor symptom and ventilating strange anxieties, that I am hearing the muted voice of some potential Gestapo official. I have heard in the course of one week the heart beat of Eichmann, palpated the liver of Goering, seen the X-rays of Himmler, read the electroencephalogram of Hitler. Almost every Jewish father and mother, however much they disaffiliate themselves from Judaism or Jewry have, perhaps once a year, because of a remark uttered inadvertently, or because of a headline, looked across the table at their young children and wondered for half a second whether one day their beloved offspring might be forced to enter the gas chambers of another decade. Even the most optimistic Jew must admit the possibility to be there. This is something that many non-Jews can hardly credit.

Of course, it is difficult to sustain suspicious attitudes towards other people, now, here, in tolerant, liberal, mild, decent, democratic England. No doubt it would be sick to do so. It also might be sick not to do so. As a Jew, I was brought up to believe that man was essentially good. Didn't I, as a boy, say in my morning prayer: *My God, the soul which thou has given me is pure . . . ?* Karl Marx explained the evil in society in environmental terms. He wasn't a Jew and an optimist for nothing. But Sigmund Freud, another Jew, has given us back Original Sin not as a genetic or theological proposition, but clandestinely and more realistically in terms of our early and inevitable Oedipus complex. How can we be anything but (neurotically?) afraid of anti-Semitism, seeing what has happened in Europe? Why is it that every Jew over-reacts, however much he feels himself to be delivered from a ghetto mentality, when a Jewish figure like Peter Rachman features villainously in some contemporary scandal? The fact is, I don't believe any Jew in the Diaspora, however much he proclaims the contrary, is other than a Ghetto Jew, in the deepest sense – and this is, above all, because of the war-time destruction of the Jew in Europe. As for writing – well, a writer brings into his work more of himself than he realises. I don't know in concrete terms what the impact on my work is of the Jewish catastrophe. I am certain, though, that in devious ways it is there.

Common Myths and Needs

Is your Jewishness as a writer based also on Judaism as well as on the Jewish predicament?

As the years go by I become less and less interested in *Judaism*. I don't know whether I am religious or not; but I do not want to go to synagogue, or observe Jewish ritualistic customs, though some I recognise as being beautiful and poetic. (Others seem to me to be neither, and merely pathological). I can accept and assent to the fact that Judaism teaches there is a direct way between man and God. Judaism is intended to be a religion without Mediator, Sacrament, or Priests. But for me, and I know this lacks any humility, for *me* – obviously not for others – between man and God, or that particular experience that man has labelled God, is the synagogue and its schedules, the dull prayers of dead religious maniacs, symbols that have often lost their potency, and restrictive disciplines. For *me*, they are barriers not bridges.

Some people maintain that one is not Jewish unless one is a Jew in the strict and orthodox religious sense. But the Jews are bound to each other not only because of their religion and religious past; they are also bound together because of their immediate, secular history, their common heroes, their common enemies, their common contemporary predicament, their common myths and needs, their common concern for the State of Israel, by the common positive as well as negative aspects of 'otherness', and even because of their present liking for certain foods, trivial as that may seem. I believe if one reaches 'God', one does it through the enlargement of life and the pleasure of the senses: through the amazement of looking, and hearing, and tasting, and touching, and smelling; or through certain pleasureful activities – like making love when one is in love, or like singing and congenial working. And writing poetry, by the way, is a kind of singing and a kind of beautiful work that names things. And the naming of things, itself, ultimately – a country or a star, a flower or a baby – is a kind of worship.

An Interview with Dannie Abse at Princeton University

Dannie Abse was born on 22 September 1923, the youngest of four children of a lower-middle class Jewish family in Cardiff. After attending a state primary school, Abse went on to an Irish Catholic High School in Cardiff, where he was taught by the Christian Brothers. Then, with the strong influence of his eldest brother, Wilfred (a medical student at the time, and now an eminent psychiatrist), Abse decided upon a medical career. After one year at the University of Wales in Cardiff, he left for London and King's College. He completed his medical training at Westminster Hospital in 1950, but not before he had spent the previous year free-lancing, going to football games, and meeting and later marrying Joan Mercer. He then did a stint with the RAF, achieving the rank of squadron leader, afterwards joining the Central Medical Establishment in London as a diagnostic physician. This past academic year, Dannie Abse has been teaching fiction and poetry in Princeton's Creative Writing Program, and it is the first time he has taught. After this year, he will return to London with his wife and three children.

Abse says of his schooling 'It was only a technological education. I'm completely uneducated'. Apart from a standard introduction to Browning, Keats and Tennyson, as well as to 'those deadly dull' Catholic poets, Belloc and Chesterton, Abse never received formal instruction in literature. His interest in poetry was actually stirred, he told me, through his brother Leo's fervour for the Republicans in the Spanish Civil War. Leo (now an outstanding Member of

Anglo-Welsh Review, Vol. 25, No. 54 (Spring 1974)

Parliament) subscribed to *The Left Review*, a journal which ran poems as well as articles on the war; and when one of Leo's friends died in that war, Abse wrote a commemorative poem. He continued with poems with a political undertone, but he then 'started to read poetry, Auden, MacNeice, Spender, and became more and more interested in poetry and less in politics'. When he would return to Cardiff for the summer after studying m London, he would go to the library and read poetry where he 'started with A and read to Zed'. Thus, he describes his poetical education as having been 'completely on my own'.

In referring to his middle teens, Abse says 'I became more and more committed to the act of writing a poem, and that still remains my ambition: to write the next poem and the one after'. Actually, his literary ambition exceeds poetry, where alone his productivity has been impressive. He has written six volumes of verse (the years following all titles are their British publication dates): *After Every Green Thing* (1949), *Walking Under Water* (1952), *Tenants of the House* (1957), *Poems, Golders Green* (1962), *A Small Desperation* (1968), and *Funland and Other Poems* (1973). In addition, Abse has written three novels: the autobiographical *Ash on a Young Man's Sleeve* (1954), *Some Corner of an English Field* (1956), and *O. Jones, O. Jones* (1970); a straight autobiography: *A Poet in the Family* (published in 1974); three one-act plays: *The Eccentric* (1959), *Gone* (1964), and *The Joker* (1962); and three full-length plays: *House of Cowards* (1959), *In the Cage* (1964) and *The Dogs of Pavlov* (1969). In addition to these accomplishments, throughout his career he has written reviews, edited magazines and has served as a judge in the award of several prizes.

INTERVIEWER: You're rather prolific for a man with two careers.

ABSE: Well, I'm fifty years of age! But also I was lucky enough to have found a limited job, a diagnostic job in a chest clinic, which is ideal. It's an agreeable way to make a basic living, and I've found that over the years I've been able to see fewer patients and to write more. If I had to do more medicine I couldn't and wouldn't. From freelance writing I learned what a terrible life that is because you're always on an escalator and always have to do hack work. I much prefer to be a part-time doctor, which is a more honorable thing to do, I think, and more pleasant.

INTERVIEWER: Has it ever occurred to you to stop your medical practice for more than this one year, or to give it up altogether ?
ABSE: Not in exchange for doing literary journalism, and not to settle permanently in America to do the sorts of things I'm doing now. Or even to settle in America permanently full stop because it isn't home and I feel more at ease in England and Wales.

If someone offered me the same job as this one in the university in Cardiff, I think I'd be very tempted to do that. But there's not that kind of money and it's a different world. The only real alternatives in England are literary journalism, such as the BBC and book reviews for the Sunday papers, and I would rather do medicine than that.
INTERVIEWER: If I'm not being too impertinent, about how much of your living do you make from each of your careers?
ABSE: It's about fifty-fifty. But I don't earn that much as a doctor compared to other doctors. It varies from time to time, but of course it's not just from poetry or poetry readings. I've written plays and other things and so on. I do a certain amount of journalism. Money is a question that all writers talk about incessantly. I feel you must be a writer. [Laughs.]
INTERVIEWER: No, not yet. Let's talk about the way your medical career has entered your poetry. There are a few poems about medicine and research in your earlier poems, but not very many and they don't involve the speaker as a practitioner. An example is 'Letter to Alex Comfort'.
ABSE: Yes. Well, that shows that I had some medical education and contact. And most of the poems later on until the last eight years didn't have any medical undertones. Now there are poems like 'The Pathology of Colours' and 'The Smile Was' and 'In the Theatre' which are explicitly medical. I'm glad that at last I've been able to call upon my medical experience. What interests me is that for so long I wasn't able to do it. I had two lives, as it were. I think I didn't wish to be known as 'Doctor' Dannie Abse, but 'Poet' Dannie Abse, in this rather juvenile way. If somebody said at a party 'What do you do?' it was only gradually that I was able to answer 'I'm a doctor'; but earlier on something inside me wanted to scream 'I AM A WRITER!', that kind of juvenile thing. But I think I gradually

began to accept that part of my identity which was a doctor, especially after *Tenants of the House* was published and I began to have some small reputation in Britain.

I'm a Welshman, that touches my work. I'm a Jew, that comes into my work. I'm a married man, that comes into my work. But the fact that I was a doctor didn't come into my work. I think that one should write as a whole man, and if one is a doctor, that should come in. And as I've become more mature I've been able to accept myself as a doctor.

INTERVIEWER: Have you found that having a second career has helped you as a poet?

ABSE: I think you raise some important issues here. For instance, there was a poet killed during the war called Alun Lewis. He was a short-story writer and a poet, a rather good one, and somebody said to him, 'Alun, you think that war only exists that you should write about it'. He was appalled by that, being a Welshman, but in actual fact most writers do have this narcissistic attitude, immature attitude, that things exist so that they should write about them.

But anyway, I think I can honestly say that I'm delighted I've been a doctor. I'm delighted that I've been able to call upon my medicine and to write poems.

INTERVIEWER: Do you ever feel you've got to leave one for the other as a kind of refuge? Supposing you've been bogged down in your writing, do you feel it's necessary then for you to leave it for a while and just doctor?

ABSE: There are occasions when you've got a poem in your head but you've got to carry on seeing patients. But if you hear somebody relate his suffering, then, of course, you will forget all about the poem. Then at the end of it, if there's no poem, if it's gone, then that poem wasn't really worthwhile. If a poem is worthwhile it will make itself insistent and knock and knock until it's born properly.

So I'm not sure about this question of needing to get away. I think you can go about your normal activity and poems will sort of half form. And if they're insistent enough, they will make themselves felt on the page.

INTERVIEWER: You've mentioned to me that as a young writer

you used to produce upwards of twenty poems a month, but now that's tapered off.

ABSE: Yes. I write about six poems a year. If I write seven, it's a wonderful year. If I write five, then it's a bad year. [Laughs.] But in the Forties I was writing twenty poems a month. Most of them were quite bad, really, rather defective poems. If my *Selected Poems* were more representative of my earlier poetry, then I would have had to include many bad poems. But as I've got older, I know from previous workouts when a poem isn't going to be worthwhile following through. So I can give up the poem, refuse it before it's born, as it were.

INTERVIEWER: A comment has been made about you, that you have 'a healthy indifference to prevailing literary fashions'. Do you feel that's an apt comment?

ABSE: No, I don't. Not to my earlier poetry. I certainly wasn't indifferent. I was committed, I was arguing. The poetry I was writing, certainly in the Fifties, was unfashionable in that it was in opposition to the kind of poetry that the new Movement poets were writing. I certainly wasn't oblivious. I certainly cared, and I guess what happens with young poets is that the kind of criticism and views they have is a defence of their own work. That's why they haven't eclectic views but dynamic ones.

INTERVIEWER: This comment was made, though, just before *Funland* came out, I believe. Do you think it pertains to your work in the past decade?

ABSE: Well, I'm more interested in what *I* do. I'm interested in reading other people's poetry, but I'm more concerned with *my* next poem and the one after. I'm not watching the field as I used to.

INTERVIEWER: I'm going to quote you. 'With the Movement Poets one hardly ever gets the impression that the poem has seized the poet and that a struggle has ensued between the poem and the poet, between the nameless, amorphous, Dionysian material and the conscious, law-abiding, articulating craftsman'.

ABSE: That was in the introduction to *Mavericks* [an anthology of non-Movement poets Abse edited in 1957], and it's a pretentious way of saying that I believe all poetry should be written out of a personal predicament and should be necessary; that there is an unconscious aspect to poetry, that it's not all on the surface. It's not an essay turned into neat, civilised verse. When I hear that being quoted back at me I realise how inflated that language was. But of course, when one's young one feels defensive and tends to embroider, tries to obfuscate things with larger words. I would say the same thing today, if I had to, but more simply.

INTERVIEWER: Why don't you say it? Does your poetry come into being out of a struggle with the nameless and amorphous?

ABSE: I'm committed to the idea of difficulty, anyway; that poetry is a difficult thing to do. I don't know how to write a poem. If it were a totally conscious thing I would be able to write at will. I could be commissioned to write a poem. But I can't be commissioned. I don't know how a poem comes about. I suppose out of some dichotomy or conflict.

INTERVIEWER: Let's turn to some of your poems, because I think I've detected some of those dichotomies and conflicts. One theme that emerges out of your poetry is a certain suspicion over words, or sentiments even. 'After a Departure', for example. I also picked this up a bit in *Ash on a Young Man's Sleeve*.

ABSE: I think I'm suspicious in so far as the act of uttering is to change our experience, because whatever our experience is, in formulating it we omit or select, and therefore we transform it. I think the great mystics don't attempt to articulate their experience because in so doing they change their experience and they want that experience pure and remembered as it was. Whereas if you write an autobiography, you rub out your past, and in a sense it does what a photograph does, which tells a terrible lie. Every photograph we have buries us in a way, because when you think of the people you know, you remember their photographs, not their real faces, not as they really were. In a similar way, when you write an autobiography you are changing your past.

For instance, in *Ash On a Young Man's Sleeve*, I invented several things. I didn't invent the characters, but I invented certain things. And now, for instance, my mother says 'Do you remember when so and so happened?' and I realise it never actually happened, that I made it up. So not only do you change your own rememberings, you change other people's. In that sense I'm suspicious of words.

Just as Auden warns girls to be suspicious of any love poem addressed to them because the poet is too interested in making the best poem he can. That's not very different from what you said about *using* things for writing. How despicable the whole thing is in a sense, yet one needs to do it. I'm saying this, but I don't really believe it's a despicable act!

INTERVIEWER: I want to turn for a moment to your style. Occasionally your poems are about being a poet. One such poem is 'The Water Diviner', and another is 'A Note Left on the Mantelpiece'. In the latter there's a line that goes 'and still thought I/lacked inspiration, the uncommon touch, not/mere expertise'. And another that says 'a poet should have studied style, not form'.

ABSE: Yes. Well, of course, I was making puns there because it's about horse racing. That was a punning poem. But regarding style – style is something which is basically unconscious. One doesn't know one's own style, and if one does then there's something wrong. One looks in a mirror and sees no reflection. That's why one doesn't know what one's voice is.

On the other hand, I think after a certain number of years one can stand back from one's poetry and see how it has changed. If I look at my early poetry I can see that the style and content are different, on the whole, from my recent work. I think the poetry I wrote in the Fifties and before the Fifties was sometimes lyrical, sometimes dramatic, sometimes meditative, but only occasionally was it more colloquial. The earlier poetry had a basic hortatory tone, as Roland Mathias once put it.

INTERVIEWER: A what tone?

ABSE: Hortatory. Good word. A sort of bardic tone, a sort of ceremonial, singing tone. I didn't want to use the word 'rhetoric'.

When I look at a book of mine called *Tenants of the House*, I can see how it reflects my interests at the time. I was interested in French existentialism, Sartre and so on, and certain philosophical abstractions, which I later ceased to be interested in at all. But in that book was a poem called 'Looking at a Map', which I remember my wife digging out of my notebook. She saved it, really. She said, 'Why don't you use this poem? I like it'. And I said 'Well, it's rather trivial'. You see, I was really reaching for the stars then, the big stuff, the major stuff with a capital M. And then my attitudes changed, and, indeed, I've written many more poems like 'Looking at a Map' as time has passed. That is to say, I've tried for a more circumscribed vision. I've written about things that are common to all of us, common realities, as it were. I've written 'I start with the visible/and am startled by the visible'. And more and more I've been interested not in ideas but in things, more in concrete matters. So I've written poems about somebody transferring names in an old diary to a new diary, or looking at a television set, or leaving a note on the mantelpiece, things which appear more everyday and commonplace. I think one can make large statements out of small concerns. And I don't comment in my poems; that is, I try to leave the poem to make its own statement without adding to it. So, the style has changed and with it the content. It's not as simple as all that, because I did indicate earlier that I sometimes wrote more colloquial poems when I began, and I still, today, sometimes revert to a more hortatory tone.

INTERVIEWER: Surprise is a recurring element in your poetry, and what interests me is that you or your speaker experiences surprise at contact with other people, at communication and human warmth. 'The Moment', for example, where you're startled out of some void into which you've drifted; 'Car Journeys', where you see your son and are surprised at your warm reunion.

ABSE: Well I'm delighted that one retains, if I have, the capacity to be startled, because I think that a poet, ideally, should be a perpetual convalescent and therefore see all colours new and find everything remarkable and rinsed. But of course one doesn't feel like that all the time.

INTERVIEWER: But what surprised me here is that you are surprised at your ability to communicate and be receptive to others' communications.

ABSE: Well, I suppose my books in England sell rather well. My *Selected Poems* has gone into a third impression, so I know people are reading me. Nevertheless, I'm continually startled when somebody knows a poem of mine. I have the feeling that if I see somebody reading my book in a bus, I wonder 'How did he come to read that poem?' I think this is not a particularly unique experience, that most poets feel like this. They're startled that their poems make any resonance at all. Yet they would be very disappointed if they didn't.

Are we talking at cross-purposes?

INTERVIEWER: We're somewhat on the same line, except that I was directing this at your surprise, or sensation of something being a bit strange even when you're in contact with your loved ones.

ABSE: Everything is perplexing, everything is foreign. One is startled by the visible. Everything is mysterious, I suppose. I mean that's the basic thing.

INTERVIEWER: The effect of these poems is rather curious. On the one hand, you've even noted, you focus on the concrete, the commonplace. At the same time, that concreteness has an elusive quality to it. There is a sense of a something that cannot be wholly taken in, and so it seems that focusing in on reality leads one to focus in on a kind of gap. You are there and not there. There are voices behind voices, there are dualities and dichotomies which in their irreconcilability are strange. I wonder how these themes connect with your professional life, having two careers.

ABSE: I guess I don't feel too different from many other writers who feel a certain amount of alienation. For instance – I went to a Catholic school, I'm not a Catholic; I was a poet in a family, that's strange enough; I'm a Welsh Jew, that's odd; I lived in Cardiff which is a border town so it's Welsh and yet not as Welsh as Swansea or the valleys; I went to Westminster Hospital where most of the students had upper-class backgrounds and quite a number had been to Oxford or Cambridge, so that my interests were different from theirs in many ways; in the RAF I found I got on with other people well enough, but finally felt that my politics weren't those of the other officers in the mess; and so on and so forth. So that all my life I've felt both a part of the society in which I am and yet felt I was an onlooker. And, indeed, I think, like a lot of writers, I'm not only an onlooker but view myself onlooking. I see myself doing things.

Even here in Princeton: my predecessor in this office has left his marks, his books and pictures. I have not. I feel I'm a transient visitor, that I'm here and not here, that life in Princeton is real and pleasant enough, yet it's rather dream-like. I can't even remember my own telephone number, which worries me, but I suppose that's because I don't feel it's worth remembering. I do have a sense of being a visitor and that I will be moving on. I don't know if there's something to be written in this gap of not being here and not in England.

People have remarked on the dichotomies in my poetry, the contrasts in 'Odd' or 'Dualities', not that they are consciously worked up. But they do arise and people have pointed them out before. But I suspect the dualities are deeper than the contrast between my being a doctor and a writer. There are basic ambivalences and dualities, male and female, violence and passivity, flattery and aggression . . . I say flattery and aggression because I suddenly thought of a Yiddish poet by the name of Manger, and I can always remember him saying, just after I had my first book of poems published – he must have been about the age I am now and had been drinking vodka – and he suddenly said to me, 'Mr Abse, you're a very good poet'. And I said 'Thank you, Mr Manger'. And he said, 'You're a good-looking boy'. And then I said, 'Thank you, Mr Manger'. And then he hit me on the jaw, very hard, and he came at me shouting 'You killed all the Jews in Europe!'

This kind of ambivalence – it's very fascinating, and fascinating when it comes to working it out, not just unconsciously, but quite consciously in theatrical terms, in terms of character.

INTERVIEWER: You mentioned the word 'alienation', which I feel applies to your work in a sense, but not entirely. Even though your poems sense a kind of removal from what they focus upon, I still detect an overall affirmative note, if not in the same poems, then in others. For example, in 'The Grand View' you write 'no more to make a home out of despair'. What I don't feel connected with the sense of alienation in your poetry is an accompanying sense of despair. One might even call you rather happy.

ABSE: I'm almost as happy as possible, to quote Edward Thomas, who was a most melancholy man! Well, one contains multitudes, as Whitman said, so sometimes one despairs. Sometimes one feels celebratory. I'm a secular man, but I have had hints of the mystery, have had intimations that I suppose you could call religious, and out of these intimations came 'The Grand View'. Momentarily, I felt inspired by the not-merely-human. But not for long.

INTERVIEWER: Two poems come to mind which illustrate a point made about you, that you have spiritual intuitions. One is 'In the Theatre', which is explicitly about the soul, and 'Hunt the Thimble', which I thought was also about the soul.
ABSE: About the soul? I don't know if I mentioned this fact at my reading [in Princeton], but at the time *Selected Poems* was published a reviewer in the London *Times* said 'Hunt the Thimble' was a small masterpiece, with which I agree, of course. [Laughs.] But he also said it was a dialogue which took place inside a mortuary, which was something I didn't know. However, I find that interesting because, after all, if I had written a dialogue in a mortuary it might have turned out as 'Hunt the Thimble'. It is about things not palpable, about mysteries, about communication, about questions that cannot be answered. And, of course, very often these questions have a metaphysical tinge to them.
INTERVIEWER: Is that the way you see yourself as a religious poet. With a 'tinge of the metaphysical'?
ABSE: The trouble about it is that 'religion' is a word like 'love'. When you say 'religious' people I think, O God! They're so dreary, they have banners, they wear clothes with a certain cut, they've got . . .
INTERVIEWER: Scrubbed fecal . . .
ABSE: Scrubbed excremental visions, yes. You see, someone has said I'm an anti-religious poet. I suppose that's as meaningful as saying one's a religious poet. If one is aware, as most people are, of the mystery, and if one is startled, as, indeed, most people can be, and if that's being religious, then I'm religious!
INTERVIEWER: Some of your poems seem to hint at an afterlife, as in 'Epithalamion' where you hear voices, or 'Car Journeys' where an Asian child plays with a shadow. And yet spirits and spirituality exist for you as a kind of lack.
ABSE: God exists because he is absent. I'm a secular Jew. I've said before that Auschwitz and Hitler have made me more of a Jew than Moses has. On the other hand, one of the large central things in public life in my lifetime has been Auschwitz, and I can't forget it, ever. But I m not a *religious* Jew. That is not to say that one doesn't apprehend the mystery.

Earlier you suggested that I try to define that which is undefinable and I think that's probably right. However, I never saw any of those images you've mentioned as having anything to do with an afterlife. It's legitimate for other people to see it that way if they wish to.

INTERVIEWER: You've got many poems with death entering them, too. Aunt Alice's death is an occasion for humour, but other deaths aren't quite so funny.

ABSE: Well, sure. Death is a mystery, as life is. I don't know how much death comes into the poetry. I know it does, but I suppose it comes into a lot of people's poetry. It comes into all of literature. There would hardly be any literature without death. And sometimes I think, indeed, that literature, which should tell us how to live, too often tells us merely how to die.

I think, probably, while I was a medical student, I met death more quickly than I would have otherwise done, earlier than many other people. In latter years some of the poems about death revolve about the death of my father.

INTERVIEWER: 'Peachstone', for instance?

ABSE: 'Peachstone' really was about my father, yes. I didn't say it, but it is so. That was the most recent poem about his death. Nearer the time I wrote 'In Llandough Hospital' and 'After the Funeral', which for some reason I didn't put in my *Selected Poems*, as you probably don't know !

INTERVIEWER: Also in connection with this matter of death and religious intimations, occasionally you focus on illusions. The poem I'm thinking of is 'Miss Book World'.

ABSE: Before we go into that, I wonder if we could just state something about death. You see, I haven't any conscious attitude or *weltanschauung* now about death. I have no view, really. Death is zero plus zero. But while I was a medical student, or while I was writing *Tenants of the House*, I did have a view. For instance, at one time I would study a skull in the hope that I would be more conscious of the vividness of things by being aware that death is so proximate; that knowing this, one could then live life more fully and vividly. This was a youthful view and I suppose it was related to the kind of reading I was doing in Sartre and Camus. So I felt that if one was aware of death one would behave in a better way. Well, all that is, of course, a youthful fantasy.

INTERVIEWER: You say you have no view about death?

ABSE: Well, I have a view: I find it repugnant. What is, after all, so terrible is being bored: and we're going to be bored for all those millennia. [Laughs.]

INTERVIEWER: What I was going to say was that you're a rather undogmatic poet. Like an atheist, dogmas seem irrelevant to your poems' existences.

ABSE: You mean I don't go round, waking up every morning screaming, 'I am a Welsh Jew, five foot eight and a half, who has a structured view about death?'

INTERVIEWER: No, I mean that there is nothing, no prop or scaffolding between you and your, or your poems', experience. I'm thinking in terms of a poet like Wallace Stevens, poets who develop a kind of mythology out of their poetry.

ABSE: No, I distrust these mythologies, you see. When I read, say, Rilke's attitude or Yeats's attitudes, or all these people who have these marvellous, colourful *weltanschauungs*, they all seem faked. It's like definitions of poetry. They may sound nice but they're not valid. So I distrust all poets' rather marvellous comments, although I love to read them because of the excitement of words put together in a beautiful way.

INTERVIEWER: There is an introduction to your poems as they appear in an anthology [*Corgi Modern Poets* 3, ed. J. Robson] with which you might disagree, I think. It says, in referring to *A Small Desperation*, 'There is in it at times a new and tragic intensity, an obsession with death, and with the indefinable, nameless things which order our existence'. The word I think you'll disagree with is 'order'.

ABSE: I'm aware of the nameless things that *underline* our existence, but I don't know about *order*. I'm aware of the odour in a telephone booth. Perhaps when we touch things like odours, or mysteries, or departures, why one can't articulate them is that one is entering upon things which it's impossible to be articulate about. And this is why, of course, one can continue to write poems about them, because one can never totally define them. But as for order . . . I'm not quite sure what he means by that.

INTERVIEWER: Let's get back to 'Miss Book World', which seems to be about illusions, man's need for them, and your detachment from what you see as the illusions of our society.
ABSE: I'm sure I have illusions, I just don't know what they are. So I must be deluded about many things, but I don't know what. I've written a play, *House of Cowards*, about men's private and public illusions and their need for a messianic figure. What I know is how I've been deluded about how good I thought my own poetry was. When I wrote the second book I knew how bad the first one was, and when I wrote the third one, *Tenants of the House*, I knew how bad the second one was.
INTERVIEWER: This is close to the way I felt about your lack of dogmatism. Your poems confront experience one step at a time.
ABSE: Yes. And wiping out previous experience, which is even more worrying. We're wiping out our previous experience into namelessness.
INTERVIEWER: For example, 'A New Diary'.
ABSE: Yes. And there's what I said to you about photographs burying our resemblances. They bury us.
INTERVIEWER: You once mentioned to me that you hope your politics enter your poetry. One way in which I saw this happening was in connection with your Jewish background, as in a poem like 'No More Mozart'. As you pointed out earlier, the horrors of Nazi Germany are very much alive for you.
ABSE: I went to Germany very briefly and I wrote that poem there. I'd never been to Germany before and was only there for three or four days visiting a hospital. You know, I think it's impossible for a Jew to visit Germany and not find these old reverberations.
INTERVIEWER: How do you feel about the poem now?
ABSE: About the poem? It's not central to the book, I don't feel. It's in *Funland and Other Poems*. It has a certain intensity, I suppose. I like lines like 'The German streets tonight/are soaped in moonlight./The streets of Germany are clean/like the hands of Lady Macbeth'. I think I like that because it's succinct. The word 'soaped' is a terrible word, isn't it, because it does conjure up the image of people being turned into soap, and yet it's accurate because moonlight can have that sort of colour. I think those lines are good, as a matter of fact.

INTERVIEWER: I was just wondering whether you think it's quite fair any more to . . .
ABSE: To blame Germans, is that what you're saying? I'm a mass of prejudices, you know, especially about Germans my age and older. When I encounter them, say, in Britain or France, I still have this nagging feeling to ask, 'What were you doing in the war, Hans?' I don't feel the same way toward younger Germans. No, it's impossible to be suspicious of people continually once they've become individualised and you know them. But when they're just ciphers and just called Germans, then my prejudices remain intact. I said that very early on in a poem written just after the war: 'I, myself, don't like Germans, but prefer the unkempt/voyagers'.
INTERVIEWER: That was 'Letter to Alex Comfort'. I saw those Germans as scientists . . .
ABSE: They were, but they were also . . . You know, one was very conscious of 'The Germans'.
INTERVIEWER: Another poem, 'After the Release of Ezra Pound'. Do you feel unkind toward Pound?
ABSE: I don't feel unkind toward Ezra Pound's *poetry*. Some people seem to object to that poem. I once read it in Stratford East, a theatre in London, and was actually attacked afterwards by somebody who thought I was being . . . Well, he didn't listen enough to the poem, because I was praising the poetry but not the man. One can do that, although Robert Lowell has told me he likes the poem but that he doesn't think I should have written it. I don't agree about that.
INTERVIEWER: I want to get to 'Funland', but I'd like to turn to one more thing before we do. Occasionally sports provide the subject of your poems, and you told me that during your year away from your medical studies you were in regular attendance at football matches. Evidently, you're rather fond of sports.
ABSE: I used to play a lot of games, yes. I once broke my collarbone playing rugby. I still like playing games but I don't play football, of course, any more.
INTERVIEWER: Do you play physical games or board games?
ABSE: Any kind of game whatsoever.
INTERVIEWER: That's right, you asked me over for a game of chess. So you're competitive?

ABSE: Terribly competitive. You ask my family. I'm very fond of watching Cardiff City play football. Did I mention to you that I've subscribed to no magazine since I've been here, like *The Times Literary Supplement* or the *New Statesman*? But I've got the *South Wales Football Echo* being sent to me every week, much to my son's delight. As a matter of fact, it's addressed to my son, but, of course, I read it. It's a sort of juvenile attachment I have. But now I don't play cricket or squash or football. I've become just an onlooker.

But what I find interesting is that I can't get attached to a successful football team in London. I hark back to my interest in Cardiff City. They are in the second division and always struggling. I suppose it's because I have this syndrome of sympathy with the underdog. We were talking about the Germans before, and I was fascinated by the fact that when Cardiff City played some Russian team in Germany, when the Russian team started to win the Germans were shouting for the Russians like mad. They wanted the winning team to win. And I felt, my God! you know, the English always want the losing team to win.

INTERVIEWER: Let's turn to 'Funland'. I can see the experience of writing 'Funland' as somewhat draining.

ABSE: At the moment I feel somewhat drained, but I'm not sure how much of this is attributable to being in America, away from home, or whether it's due to the fact that I'd finished this autobiography just before I left, or to 'Funland' itself. I do feel the need to recharge somewhat.

INTERVIEWER: Was it the last poem you've written?

ABSE: No. I've written three others since then, but only one of them has been published. And then, 'Funland' itself was written over a period of some time. I wrote it first in its first six parts, then I wrote some other poems, and then I picked 'Funland' up again and enlarged it with its final three sections.

INTERVIEWER: Would you call it your most ambitious poem?

ABSE: Well, actually, I've written other ambitious poems which I've suppressed. They've been published but they're not in *Selected Poems* so you don't know them. It's certainly my longest poem and it's as ambitious as any other poem I've written. Probably the most ambitious. OK. The answer to that is yes. Scrub out everything else.

INTERVIEWER: Stylistically, is it as much a break with your recent development as it seems to be to me? Is it a new departure?
ABSE: Well, stylistically I would relate 'Funland' to those earlier poems. Some poems in *Tenants of the House*, and some even earlier, more defective poems, are like it. You see, the poems in *Tenants of the House* did use a symbolic infrastructure or a series of allegorical devices, something which I eschewed very consciously about halfway through *Poems, Golders Green*. But with 'Funland' I've returned to that, and in that sense it's not a new departure.
INTERVIEWER: I think at your reading here you named your debt to Eliot.
ABSE: I can't talk about 'Funland' without naming my debt to Eliot. It's *The Waste Land* gone mad, that's what 'Funland' is. But I should also mention my debt to Zbigniew Herbert, a Polish poet, and to other sources. I'm thinking of the life history of Wilhelm Reich. Then there is my life experience, which is even more important than literary sources.
INTERVIEWER: Have you been to mental hospitals?
ABSE: I've never been an inmate, but I've visited mental hospitals as a medical student. And in the early years of the war I visited my brother Wilfred who was working at Abergavenny Mental Hospital, the one where Rudolph Hess was taken.
INTERVIEWER: Yet it seemed to me that actual experiences of your own were less important to the writing of 'Funland' than they are to other poems of yours.
ABSE: I'm not sure about that. I'm a doctor, and I have had patients who have worried about whether their bowels are turning into glass. And then, on visiting a mental hospital, I have actually seen a man obsessionally swear before a wall 'Fuck shit cunt fuck shit cunt' and not be able to say anything else. There is something extraordinarily sad about poets who are supposed to communicate but who can only say 'Fu-er-uck'.
INTERVIEWER: I think in 'Funland' you are talking about the cruelty of society, not American or British, but society as an institution. And in saying that, you are saying something about human nature. Can you respond to that?
ABSE: I don't know if I can. I mean I don't know whether I want

to paraphrase 'Funland'. I'm quite willing to talk about its literary sources, which I've already done, and its experiential basis. But I think other people should draw their own conclusions. I'm sorry if that means I can't be very illuminating about the poem.

INTERVIEWER: If you feel you can't, I can respect that as much as if you could.

ABSE: Well you see, somebody like Ted Hughes, who is a friend of mine, does talk about *Crow*, and his conversation about it gets longer and longer. His prolegomenon on the platform gets longer and longer, and I can see him, perhaps, making a marvellous mythology, *post hoc*, about *Crow*. I don't want to do that to 'Funland'. I don't mean to criticise Ted Hughes. It's just that one man needs to do this and one man needs to do something other. I think if I started to think and talk about 'Funland' too much I would really be crippling my next poem.

INTERVIEWER: There's something I've got to say that I think you'll be able to respond to. Without making too much of it, I think I can call you an optimistic poet . . .

ABSE: No, other people have talked about this affirmative note, which I'm delighted about when it happens. But you were going to say that 'Funland' is extremely pessimistic. I think it's a pessimistic poem. But to say that a poem of mine is pessimistic is not to say that I am pessimistic. What I really mean is that one doesn't set out to write an optimistic poem or a pessimistic poem. One wishes only to relay some kind of view of reality. Afterwards you might say, 'Well, my God, that poem is more pessimistic than I thought', or 'That does strike an affirmative note'. It's more pleasant to strike an affirmative note. That's a rarer thing to do. It's easier to gather images of despair and more poets are doing it. Therefore, if one does the opposite by accident, one is delighted. I think it would be phony if you set out by saying 'I'm going to write an optimistic poem. I'm going to affirm'. That would be all too bright and would turn out false, I think.

INTERVIEWER: 'Funland' strikes me as a savage poem, and yet it has its lighter moments.

ABSE: Well, there's a line in there which says 'Sometimes even Funland can be beautiful'. I suppose you could concentrate on that line and see an affirmative note. But it was intended to be a savage poem, and it was intended to have humorous moments because I felt it would be more acceptable as a poem if it had humorous moments, and would make the savagery more true as a counterbalance. I think I said at my reading that I felt Eliot's *Waste Land* has become a museum piece. Without decrying the quality of Eliot's poem, I think the world has become more savage, and I think 'Funland' is more savage than this rather placid, though wonderful, depressed thing that Eliot gave us.

INTERVIEWER: Let's move on to another topic. It's been said that, because the focus of English poetry has shifted from Britain to America in this century, Americans are rather ignorant of the British scene. Who are the more prominent British poets? What I'm trying to do is to find a way to ask you if you are among them.

ABSE: Prominent? I can tell you what poets I like. Among them I would certainly put Ted Hughes, Philip Larkin, the earlier poetry of Donald Davie, Dennis Enright; younger poets such as Douglas Dunn, Stewart Conn, Seamus Heaney. All these poets are worth reading. And such poets as Vernon Scannell and David Wright are very good. Indeed, it's a scandal that these two aren't known in America. On the other hand, we in Britain don't know some fine American poets, like William Meredith, David Wagoner, Daniel Hoffman and Donald Justice.

INTERVIEWER: Is there anyone in Britain who has achieved the status of, say, Robert Lowell?

ABSE: You mean, perhaps someone who may win the Nobel Prize? You'd hardly give it to Robert Lowell? He's not a major poet. He's a minor poet, a very good minor poet who's been writing rather bad stuff lately and he's been writing it for some time. I hope, with any luck, he'll be writing very fine stuff again, but he's not now.

You've got some very good poets in America, but they're minor poets. There's no major poet in America at the moment. There's not even a Wallace Stevens or a William Carlos Williams. Elizabeth Bishop is as good as anybody writing in America, but one doesn't feel she's going to win the Nobel Prize.

Therefore, when you turn to Britain, you also see some very

good minor poets. You see Ted Hughes, Philip Larkin, David Wright, Charles Tomlinson. I'd like to include myself! There's no competition, we're all doing different things, but there's not much qualitative difference between us. There's been a great deal of publicity directed toward Robert Lowell in a way there hasn't been toward, say, Vernon Scannell or Iain Crichton Smith or John Ormond or John Heath-Stubbs or Thomas Blackburn or others of my generation, but that's an accident of place, time, geography, friends, all sorts of reasons.

INTERVIEWER: It's been said that over the past decade or so there has been a renaissance of interest in poetry in America, with more and more people writing more and more books. How does that compare with things in Britain?

ABSE: It's fine. You can see it in different ways. What's happening is that, as in America, there is a more democratic 'scene'. That is to say, different kinds of poetry are allowed to live side by side. In the Fifties, somebody was saying you could only write *this* kind of poetry. The critics were more autocratic and more homogeneous. There was more of an establishment view. Now there are all kinds of styles and modes. And though there's more bad poetry being written and published, more obviously bad poetry, it allows people to be themselves and risk more, I think. So it has its advantages and disadvantages. But on the whole, things are alive; certainly, British poetry is alive and well and living in Britain.

INTERVIEWER: I want to direct a little attention toward your fiction. You've written three novels. Would you say you regard yourself more as a poet than a novelist?

ABSE: I'm not a novelist. I don't think like one.

INTERVIEWER: Since you've come to Princeton have you been able to do any writing?

ABSE: No, I haven't. I've been here three months and I really haven't written anything.

INTERVIEWER: What would you attribute that to?

ABSE: I don't know. I have a sense of unreality here. I feel that this is very much a station on the way back to England, a very pleasant . . .

INTERVIEWER: A not-Not Adlestrop.

ABSE: Yes. But I like it here. I've enjoyed my teaching. It's rather like poetry readings, you like some more than others. Some classes have been better than others, but I don't know if the students would agree. However, I *sometimes* resent having to read student material when there's so much durable stuff I should read.
INTERVIEWER: When do you go back to London?
ABSE: In May. But I don't want to jump that far ahead. I'm enjoying myself here.

[The interviewer was Mark Boada]